Popular Music in Japan

Popular Music in Japan

Transformation Inspired by the West

Tōru Mitsui

BLOOMSBURY ACADEMIC
NEW YORK • LONDON • OXFORD • NEW DELHI • SYDNEY

Bloomsbury Academic
Bloomsbury Publishing Inc
1385 Broadway, New York, NY 10018, USA
50 Bedford Square, London, WC1B 3DP, UK
29 Earlsfort Terrace, Dublin 2, Ireland

BLOOMSBURY, BLOOMSBURY ACADEMIC and the Diana logo
are trademarks of Bloomsbury Publishing Plc

First published in the United States of America 2020
This paperback edition published in 2022

Copyright © Tōru Mitsui, 2020

Cover design: Louise Dugdale
Cover image: 1920s Nipponophone 78 rpm paper sleeve with
'Arabia-no Uta' ('Song of Araby') displayed through the cut-out.
Courtesy of Hideo Nagai, Yokohama, Japan.

All rights reserved. No part of this publication may be reproduced or transmitted in any form or by any means, electronic or mechanical, including photocopying, recording, or any information storage or retrieval system, without prior permission in writing from the publishers.

Bloomsbury Publishing Inc does not have any control over, or responsibility for, any third-party websites referred to or in this book. All internet addresses given in this book were correct at the time of going to press. The author and publisher regret any inconvenience caused if addresses have changed or sites have ceased to exist, but can accept no responsibility for any such changes.

Whilst every effort has been made to locate copyright holders the publishers would be grateful to hear from any person(s) not here acknowledged.

Library of Congress Cataloging-in-Publication Data
Names: Mitsui, Tōru, 1940- author.
Title: Popular music in Japan : transformation inspired by the West / Toru Mitsui.
Description: New York : Bloomsbury Academic, 2020. | Includes bibliographical references and index. | Summary: "An overview of popular music in Japan with a focus on the role of western influence"– Provided by publisher.
Identifiers: LCCN 2020003312 | ISBN 9781501363863 (hardback) | ISBN 9781501363887 (pdf) | ISBN 9781501363870 (ebook)
Subjects: LCSH: Popular music–Japan–History and criticism. | Music–Japan–Western influences.
Classification: LCC ML3501 .M54 2020 | DDC 781.63/1640952–dcundefined
LC record available at https://lccn.loc.gov/2020003312

ISBN:	HB:	978-1-5013-6386-3
	PB:	978-1-5013-9177-4
	ePDF:	978-1-5013-6388-7
	eBook:	978-1-5013-6387-0

Typeset by Integra Software Services Pvt. Ltd.

To find out more about our authors and books visit www.bloomsbury.com and sign up for our newsletters.

Contents

List of figures		vii
Preface		viii
Notes on names, spelling and translation		ix
A note on the cover image		x
	Transformation inspired by the West (1)	1
1	The French Revolution and the emergence of *enka*	13
	Transformation inspired by the West (2)	21
2	Songs in triple time sung in duple time	25
	Transformation inspired by the West (3)	43
3	"Sing Me a Song of Araby" and "My Blue Heaven": When the production of hit songs began in the late 1920s	47
	Transformation inspired by the West (4)	75
4	Far Western in the Far East: Japanese Country & Western	85
	Transformation inspired by the West (5)	105
5	Music and protest in the late 1960s: The rise of underground folk	109
	Transformation inspired by the West (6)	125
6	Japan in Japan: Looking for inexpensive potential stars from abroad	131
	Transformation inspired by the West (7)	145
7	Nurturing the Japanese version of an American tradition: Music from the South	149

	Transformation inspired by the West (8)	169
8	Domestic exoticism: A trend in the age of 'world music'	173
	Transformation inspired by the West (9)	185

References 191
Index 207

Figures

2.1	"Kago-no Tori" sung by Shun'yō Tottori and Kyōko Tatsumi	26
2.2	"Heart Song" sung by Shun'yō Tottori	28
2.3	"Kago-no Tori" sung by older people in Neagari	32
2.4	"Kago-no Tori" sung by Shōichi Ozawa	33
2.5	"Kago-no Tori" sung by Chieko Masaki	34
2.6	"Kago-no Tori" sung by Kazuo Yoshida and Mitsue Yoshida	35
2.7	"Manzai Shin Kago-no Tori" sung by Suteji Sunakawa	35
2.8	"Furusato" composed by Teiichi Okano	36
2.9	"Furusato" performed by a male harmonica player and sung by older women	37
2.10	"Minato" composed by Tarihiko Hatano	38
2.11	"Minato" arranged in duple time by author	39
2.12	"Minato" arranged in duple time by author beginning with an anacrusis	40
3.1	The first six bars of "Sing Me a Song of Araby" composed by Fred Fisher and arranged by Paul Van Loan	71
3.2	The first eight bars of "My Blue Heaven" composed by Walter Donaldson and arranged by Ferde Grofé	72
4.1	"Wagon Master" sung by Kazuya Kosaka	86
4.2	Riff in "Wagon Master"	86
6.1	Portraits of members of Japan by their fans, printed in the second issue of the fan club's magazine, *Japan* (June 1979)	138

Preface

In this book, I see popular music in Japan from an historical perspective with an emphasis on its transformation inspired by the West since the Meiji era, which began in the late 1860s.

What I regard, in this book, as popular music in Japan, with popular song as its mainstay, was preceded by *hayari-uta*. In a concise overview of 'Popular music before the Meiji period', Gerald Groemer says that 'From around the seventeenth century, when the term came into common parlance, most Japanese differentiated *hayari-uta* from songs that seemed more resistant to change. [...] Between the peasant's timeless ditty and the courtier's time-honoured chant lay *hayari-uta*: ephemeral strains and verses often identified with professions or sectors of society that the country bumpkin could not and the samurai would not fully know' (2008: 261). The Meiji era began right after Japanese people were, as often figuratively described, 'aroused from their 200-year sleep', which had remained undisturbed in the national isolationism. They opened their doors to Western countries, and *hayari-uta* began to be transformed, though the word continued to exist for the time being.

In discussing various phases and topics of popular music in Japan since the Meiji era, this book serves of its own accord as the first book ever published that covers those years – not only in English, but also in Japanese. Moreover, as the title suggests, this book examines popular music *in* Japan without confining it to Japanese popular songs or music per se.

The title article, 'Transformation inspired by the West', is in nine sections and weaves its way through the whole book, which consists of eight chapters. These chapters and the title article are a selection from my contributions to books and periodicals in overseas countries between 1983 and 2014. I have revised them for the compilation of this book and amended their titles so that they are more in line with the contents.

I thank the copyright holders for their permission to reuse the originals (the details of these are cited at the head of each relevant piece). At the same time, I also thank the members of Bloomsbury Academic's publishing board for unanimously approving the publication of this book – particularly Leah Babb-Rosenfeld and Amy Martin.

Notes on names, spelling and translation

Throughout this book, Japanese personal names are phonetically transcribed into the modern English alphabet and appear in the westernized style with given names followed by surnames. This order is the reverse of standard Japanese practice.

Titles of books, articles, songs, albums and films are also phonetically transcribed into the English alphabet in the generally received method, though well-known proper names such as Tokyo (*Tōkyō*) and Toshiba (*Tōshiba*) are left unchanged and so are spelt internationally without diacritics. English words such as jazz, folk and rock used in Japanese writings are spelt here as they are in the original English (the consonants -z and -k are pronounced in Japanese as -zu and -ku because consonants are invariably combined with a vowel; however, it is unnecessary to spell them phonetically here as jazu, fōku and rokku).

Titles are translated into English by the author and presented in parentheses; quotations from materials in the Japanese language have also been translated into English by the author.

A note on the cover image

The cover photo of this book shows an example of the square, soft paper sleeve (coloured or monochrome) used for many Nipponophone 78 rpm, ten-by-ten-inch shellac records released in 1920–8. Each disc was put in this sleeve with a circular cut-out in the centre, through which the label of the disc was displayed. Here, in this sleeve, 16855 is put in with the label of the B side, "Arabia-no Uta" (Song of Araby), being displayed through the cut-out. Side A of this disc is "Aozora" (Blue Heaven), which is also about three minutes long, and its label is displayed through the circular cut-out on the other side of this sleeve. (See Chapter 3.) By courtesy of Hideo Nagai in Yokohama.

Transformation inspired by the West (1)

This title article in nine sections, weaving its way through the whole book, is a much enlarged version of the main part of the introduction to *Made in Japan: Studies in Popular Music*, edited by Tōru Mitsui and published by Routledge, pp. 1–13 (© 2014 Taylor & Francis).

At the time when the Japanese were 'aroused from their 200-year sleep'

It is intriguing to find in *All the Year Round*, a British weekly literary magazine 'conducted by Charles Dickens' between 1859 and 1895, a reference to a teenage Japanese officer who was thrilled by the song "Pop Goes the Weasel". He was in Washington, DC, in 1860, several years after this well-known and much-loved nursery rhyme had crossed the Atlantic. The anonymous writer with musical literacy remarks:

> This air was regarded as the peculiar property of the youngest officer of the body, the third interpreter of the embassy, a lad seventeen years old, whose handsome and dignified appearance, winning manners, and affectionate disposition, made him an object of far greater interest than even the lofty envoys themselves. "Poppy goes the weasel" he always would have it, and seemed to think the extra syllable a capital invention of his own. ('Music among the Japanese' 1861: 150)

This very interesting article, 'Music among the Japanese', begins with an appeal: 'Let us render partial justice to our often misappreciated Oriental friends, in respect of a faculty which has uniformly, and rather unfairly, been denied them. "They have no musical perceptions", is the general verdict […]' (ibid.: 149). Hence, the writer wanted to test the 'musical capacities' of the Japanese and 'to discover, if possible, whether they were as utterly destitute of musical feeling as they had been pronounced to be', when 'the Japanese envoys and their seventy officers and attendants to the United States of America' visited Washington. No information about the envoys is given by the writer, but it can be evidenced historically that those people were the members of the mission dispatched by the Togugawa shogunate to exchange ratifications of the Japan–US Friendship and Trade Treaty. They arrived in Washington in mid-May 1860, a year before this article was published, and stayed there for three and a half weeks. The seventeen-year-old officer mentioned above, Onojirō Tateishi, was sociable and full of curiosity, and became so popular in the cities he visited with other envoy members that the news media reported on what he did almost every day, and referred to him as 'Tommy'. A photograph of him dressed up, complete with two swords, can be found at the Houghton Library in the Harvard Theatre Collection (see Mihara 2000 and Kanai 1979).

In the second half of the article, the writer describes his joy at hearing a 'pure Japanese melody'. One medical student 'beguiled himself by murmuring fragments of a new and unknown song' while 'poring over a pile of manuscripts', and other students 'presently joined in the chorus very excitedly, and worked it and themselves up with great energy'; 'These students, it seemed, were musical as well as medical, in a very high degree' ('Music among the Japanese' 1861: 151–2). The writer manages to have them sing the tune repeatedly so that he can write it down in staff notation, though it should be noted that the ending note of this tune is wrongly notated as the writer interprets the scale as minor. This observation is significant in itself as he asserts the song to be 'the first Japanese song ever publicly heard outside their own land'. However, this song and 'additional specimens of Japanese music' heard by the writer didn't apparently attract wider notice.

More interesting in retrospect is the first half of the article in which he describes how the mission members were enthralled by Western music:

> [T]hey were by no means slow to repeat such melodies as they could catch and remember from the street bands of Washington, or the pianofortes of Willard's Hotel, where they resided. There was not an under officer who had not his favourite tune; and as for the third class attendants, they were in perpetual league with those among their American acquaintance who would consent to instruct them in light and simple songs, words included as well as music. (Ibid.: 150)

Along with "Pop Goes the Weasel", the other song mentioned is "Kemo, kimo", which the Japanese officers sang 'whenever they could find listeners, and often, indeed, among themselves alone, with a delicious abandon that betokened the heartiest enjoyment to be imagined'. "Pop Goes the Weasel" was introduced to Japan decades later and was popular for a period of time.

A similar Japanese fascination with Western music had already been witnessed six years before, in 1854, on the front deck of one of the battleships led by Commodore Perry at Edo Bay (now Tokyo Bay). Before the signing of the trade treaty between the US and the shogunate, who avoided armed intervention, the Japanese invited the Americans to a feast, and the Americans invited some Japanese dignitaries to a feast on a ship. A minstrel show was performed after dinner by a troupe that consisted of the black-faced players of a tambourine, a triangle, a banjo, a flute, a bone castanet and three guitars. It was at the time when Stephen Foster's plantation songs were quite popular, and, actually, some of his songs, including "Massa's in the Cold Ground" and "Camptown Races", were performed there on the ship and at two other places. According to a note written at the occasion by an American crewman, the show performed on the front deck was well received by the Japanese, whose ascetic solemnity was soon dissipated: 'they fought hard to stifle the laugh that rose to their throats because they are not accustomed to laugh with the mouth wide open as we do' (Kasahara 2001: 111–12). Moreover, according to an observation made by a Japanese officer, one of Uraga's police officers was enticed to dance himself when some of the black-faced players danced in the show (ibid.: 111). Minstrel shows were also performed in Yokohama and Hakodate for Japanese officers, and two pictures painted by a Japanese artist are now in the possession of Kanagawa Historical Museum in Yokohama (one of which depicts the whole black-faced troupe in uniform performing together). Even in the United States it may be difficult to find a painted picture of a minstrel show from the 1850s.

However, Japanese music veritably sounded displeasing to Western ears in general, as documented by many remarks regarding the Japanese secular music performed by a number of Japanese acrobatic troupes, which were immensely popular in American and European theatres (Mihara 1998). The remarks are cited in periodicals published mostly in 1867 and 1868. For example, the *New York Times* commented thus on Japanese singing in late January 1868: 'The different acts were accompanied by what is called music [...] by three ladies and one man. This hideous noise grates terribly upon the ear, and sounds more like a pack of hounds in full cry, or a bevy of Thomas cats at midnight' (ibid.: 140). The *New York Clipper*, meanwhile, reported on an instrumental performance in March 1867: 'Their music is execrable – it is a mixture of broken China, Japan ware, etc., and is made on instruments resembling a banjo on the square [...] picked on with a broken stick; a fife, or something like it, [which] helps make up a horrible discord, and this is the sum total of their music.' These comments may remind some readers of the entry for 'music' in the 1891 one-volume encyclopaedia *Things Japanese*, written by Basil Chamberlain, a British Japanologist and a Wagnerian. It begins with: 'Music, if that beautiful word must be allowed to fall so low as to denote the strummings and squealings of Orientals, is supposed to have existed in Japan ever since mythological times' (Chamberlain [1891] 1971: 330).

The remarkable interest in Western music was prominent at the time when the Japanese people were 'aroused from their 200-year sleep' which had been undisturbed in the nursery of isolationism since 1639. The interest was clearly one-sided, as is often with an interest one has in anything, and this one-sidedness would soon begin characterizing Japanese popular music, which would be typified to one degree or another by the hybridization of Western and indigenous music. In its hybridization, this popular music can be compared to Japanese 'traditional' music, consisting of Japanese classical and vernacular music (the stylized forms of which have been preserved), and also to 'serious' music, which has fundamentally been dominated by Western classical music. Around the time when Rudyard Kipling chanted 'Oh, East is East, and West is West, and never the twain shall meet' in 'The Ballad of East and West' (1889), the twain was already meeting, notwithstanding this statement which has long generated its own momentum. The meeting, though one-sided, came about in Japan and in the form of popular music, and it has endured up to the present.

From this viewpoint, below is a survey of how popular music in Japan from the late 1860s to the early 2000s has undergone a sweeping transformation, which, in general, has been enjoyed domestically, rather than internationally.[1]

Gunka

Because of the visit of the intimidating American fleet to Japan in 1853, military music was more significant to the Japanese in general than music performed for a limited number of Japanese officers. Many Japanese were exposed to music performed on land by a drum and fife band as well as by a brass band. At the first visit in 1853, a drum and fife band performed on the Kurihama beach such tunes as "Yankee Doodle", "Hail Columbia" and "Star-Spangled Banner", and in 1854, a military band performed "Hail Columbia" in Yokohama. Even a funeral march was performed when a funeral service was held for a deceased soldier (Kasahara 2001: 88–94).

As early as 1855, the year after Commodore Perry's second visit, the shogunate formed a training institute for the navy in Nagasaki, dispatching about forty trainees. It was soon followed by other navy institutes in many parts of Japan. All the institutes were equipped with musical instruments in addition to weapons and military uniforms (for more about the Japanese military bands, see Nakamura 2003: 135–46). In the new era, the Meiji, civil activities were not the primary duties of the military bands, and a rush of orders to perform from all quarters compelled the Department of the Navy to promote the formation of civil brass bands in 1886. The first band formed in the next year was called Tokyo City Band, and they performed polkas, waltzes and marches at horse races, celebrations and garden parties. Before long, civil brass bands went on increasing not only in Tokyo, but in other major cities, resulting in a progressively marked difference in quality among the bands by around 1910. Moreover, the number of members often had to be reduced for financial reasons, with an emphasis upon melody instruments and percussions at the sacrifice of some harmony instruments. The small-scale bands – which usually consisted of a clarinet, a cornet, a trombone, a bass drum and a side drum – tended to cater for the general public without sharing much repertoire with military bands. They played military songs as well as civil songs without much harmony, which began to be called *jinta* (for more about *jinta*, see Horiuchi 1935).

It is arguably out of the propagation of military bands that "Miya-san" (Dear Prince) (also known as "Ton'yare-bushi" (Ton'yare Song)), the first widespread popular song in the new era, was born (*c.* 1868). It became popular just at the time of the Meiji Restoration, when the shogunate government was overthrown, and was said to have been sung by the soldiers of the anti-shogunate army on the side of the emperor (*mikado*) who marched to Edo (now Tokyo), the seat of the shogunate. As Keizō Horiuchi, an authority of *gunka*, who regarded it as the first *gunka* (martial song or military song), wrote in 1942: 'The tune is based on a Japanese folksong scale, but it is a very lively marching one with a rhythm unknown to folksongs, which might have been influenced by a fife and drum corps' (Horiuchi [1942] 1948: 38). This song was incorporated in Gilbert and Sullivan's misconception-ridden operetta *Mikado* in 1885, by adjusting it to a Western musical frame (for further details, see Mitsui and Matsumoto 2005).

In the same year, 1885, appeared "Battō-tai" (Corps with Drawn Swords) in minor scale, which had until then been unknown to the Japanese. It was composed by Charles Leroux, a French officer who had taken on the job of teaching the Imperial Military Band a year before. While soon being incorporated into popular songs, it was arranged along with another minor-scale composition of his, which he titled "Fou-sō-ka" (Fusō Song), as an instrumental piece for military marching (for the details of the appearance of "Battō-tai", see Horiuchi 1935: 59). It is even now played officially by the Self-Defence Army Band and police brass bands. In the following decade, newly composed *gunka* tended to become disengaged from traditional scales, typically represented by "Teki-wa Ikuman" (Enemy Amounting to Tens of Thousands). This song, acclaimed as a masterpiece of *gunka* by Horiuchi, used a pentatonic major scale (CDEGAC), reflecting the development of new songs composed for primary-school education by the new government, which were called *shōka*. It was written in 1891, three years before the beginning of the first Sino–Japanese War, the first international war in which Japan was involved.

Then, in 1900, shortly before the Russo–Japanese War began, the most famous Japanese piece of martial music, "Gunkan Kōshinkyoku" (Battleship March, more generally known as the "Gunkan March"), was composed by Tōkichi Setoguchi, a member of the Imperial Navy Band, to lyrics written three years earlier for another tune. This energizing march in major scale, with the tune lacking the seventh note, is still regularly performed by the Self-Defence Navy Band, although the bellicose lyrics are no longer sung. Out of all the songs produced during the Russo–Japanese War (1904–5), "Sen'yū" (Comrade in Arms) (1905) is noteworthy for the way it moved the public, in contrast to more high-spirited songs, with its sentimental lament over the death of a comrade on the battlefield in Manchuria. It is set to a plaintively swaying tune in the scale of EFABCE with the addition of the lower D in the closing phrase. This song was so popular that it remained on people's lips until the post-war period.

The Anglo–Japanese Alliance necessitated Japan entering the First World War, but its participation was limited and did not encourage the active production of *gunka*. Its sudden increase in the 1930s was linked with the two incidents leading up to the Second Sino–Japanese War. A decade had passed since the formation of the national radio network and the decision by record companies to popularize intentionally produced songs through recording had begun. In their first years, the recording industry and the press fell in line with the national policy of whipping up war sentiment. Soon after the Manchurian Incident in September 1931 (in which a section of Japanese-owned railroad was dynamited by Japanese forces to provide a pretext for invasion), the *Asahi*, a leading newspaper, worked with Nippon Victor to release "Manshū Kōshinkyoku" (Manchuarian March) in January 1932. The song, in the folksong scale, valiantly sung by Tamaki Tokuyama with the accompaniment of Victor Orchestra, was then linked up in March with *Manshū Kōshinkyoku*, a part-talkie film produced by Shōchiku. It obviously followed the success of "Shingun" (Marching) in 1929, which was used as the theme song of a silent film, *Shingun*, featuring Shōchiku stars.

Just when "Manshū Kōshinkyoku" began to be disseminated, the Shanghai Incident (a short war between the armies of Japan and China) occurred in February 1932. Late in that February, three soldiers who had killed themselves using their own bombs to smash the enemy's barbed-wire entanglements were hero-worshipped on the front pages of the press. It prompted the recording industry, the press and the film industry to seize upon this opportunity to compete with one another to cover the incident and gain a profit from doing so. The most successful release was "Bakudan San'yūshi" (Three Brave Bombers), a song in the scale of CDEGAC, composed and recorded by Toyama Military School Band with its chorus and released by Polydor in May 1932, in cooperation with two major newspapers in Tokyo and Osaka. The papers had initiated a contest to provide lyrics for the music, and the prize-winner was the famous poet, Hiroshi Yosano.

At the outbreak of the Second Sino–Japanese War in the summer of 1937, the same two newspapers, still savouring their success with the lyric-writing contest, launched another competition, this time for the lyrics of "Shingun-no Uta" (Marching Song), which was again composed by Toyama Military School Band in the invariable scale of ABCEFA. This song, the lyrics of which were chosen out of some 50,000 entries, was released by Nicchiku in October 1937 and proved quite popular. However, the song on its B side, "Roei-no Uta" (Encampment Song), touched the hearts of the public and was more enduring, as was the case with the old "Sen'yū", with its sentimental monologue by a soldier on the battlefield set to a melancholic tune in the scale of EFABCE with the addition of D in the closing phrase, though sung to a lively beat.

Around the time that "Shingun-no Uta" came out, the War Cabinet responded to the gravity of the war by establishing the Intelligence Division, whose first assigned task was to launch a contest for a song they titled "Aikoku Kōshinkyoku" (Patriotic March). Clearly, the contest was modelled on those initiated by the press, but this time the competiton required the creation of both the words and music. The lyrics were reportedly chosen from more than 57,000 entries, but were drastically revised by seven judges, including well-known poets, and set to a tune by Setoguchi, the composer of the immortal "Gunkan March", who won against nearly 10,000 entries. As the Intelligence Division declared in 1937 that the copyright of the song was in the public domain,[2] this heroic song was recorded by various recording companies and purportedly sold more than a million copies, and the government actively broadcast the song over the radio network. At the same time, it endorsed a short film *Aikoku Kōshinkyoku*, in which moving images of Mount Fuji, the Imperial Palace, cherry blossoms, a fleet, a mounted troop, a tank corps and so on are accompanied by a continuous singing of this song in unison.

Needless to say, the Intelligence Division took the initiative in encouraging the composition of more patriotic songs in parallel with the expansion of the war. Record companies released songs which were connected with one war after another, including "Mugi-to Heitai" (Wheats and Soldiers) (1938), which was acclaimed for its touches of humanity, and songs such as "Jūgo-dayori'" (Letter from the Home Front) (1938) and "Senjō-no Komori-uta" (Lullaby on the Battlefield) (1938). The most enduring song from the period was "Sen'yū-no Uta" (Song of Comrades) (1938), commonly known as "Dōki-no Sakura" (Cherry Blossoms in the Same Class), in which the narrator fondly likens himself and his comrade to blossoms flowering on the same tree, which was sung by the public long after the end of the Second World War.

Japan's entry into the Second World War in late 1941 further accelerated the active production of marching, patriotic and home-front songs. There also appeared a number of songs based on actual warfare, such as "Sora-no Shinpei" (Divine Soldier in the Sky) (1942), which marvels at a surprise attack by a parachute troop; "Sen'yū-no Ikotsu-o Idaite" (Embracing the Ashes of My Comrade) (1943), written by a sergeant in Singapore; and "Gōchin" (Sending Straight to the Bottom) (1944), a monologue by a crew member of a submarine on his daily life on the ship. However, the majority of *gunka* during Japan's participation in the Second World War were short-lived despite their proliferation during the conflict. (For the history of *gunka*, see Horiuchi 1969 and additionally Osada 1968.)

In the twenty-first century, the recorded *gunka* songs, and march-oriented ones at that, are heard in public only through the blaring loudspeakers set up in the armoured cars of right-wing organizations occasionally cruising around in large cities. In the meantime, older generations in Southeast Asian countries such as Indonesia, who grew up in the colonization period during which the Japanese government compelled them to learn Japanese, have kept singing representative *gunka* songs they had memorized.

Shōka

Conscious of Japan's relative underdevelopment in terms of industrialization and democratization, the new post-restoration government accelerated the westernization of Japan in all aspects, including the Ministry of Education officially assigning newly formed primary schools to incorporate Western melodies into songs to be learnt. Interestingly, this was at the time when there was no equivalent of the word 'music' in Japan. Thus, although *shōka* did not make its appearance as popular song, it did contribute largely to the formation of the new Japanese musicality. The first book of *shōka* for primary schools, published in 1882–4, included such Western tunes as a Spanish folksong known in Germany as "Alles neu macht der Mai" and an eighteenth-century tune used in England for the hymn "Greenville" and in the United States for a children's song "Go Tell Aunt Rhody". "Chō-chō" (Butterfly) was written to the former and "Miwataseba" (Looking Out Over) to the latter. Though simple, these songs are characterized by the Western tonality, particularly by the inclusion of the fourth note, which indicates a dominant chord, and in the latter's melody the presence of the sixth note suggests, along with the fourth note, a subdominant chord as well. Such tunes, including a Scottish folksong "The Bells of Scotland", a German folksong "Frühlings Ankunft", and an Irish melody "The Last Rose of Summer", are all definitely tonal, complete with three basic chords being implied, and pentatonic-major tunes such as Scottish folksongs "Auld Lang Syne" and "Comin' Through the Rye" were favoured more by the Japanese. Combined with new Japanese lyrics, these tunes (becoming increasingly well known to most Japanese) helped significantly to familiarize the Japanese, an insular nation in the Far East, with Western musical characteristics.

Around 1900, domestically composed *shōka* songs, reflecting Western influence, began to increase, and gradually became stylized with a pentatonic-major scale (CDEGAC), quadruple rhythm, a unit of four phrases and didactic lyrics, while there also appeared some domestic songs in triple time that had been unknown to the Japanese. (The songs discussed above and those published in subsequent years can be found in the books of *shōka* compiled with annotations by Kindaichi and Anzai 1977.)

Notes

1   However, it should be noted that, in about seventy years from the Meiji Restoration, 'Japan's international reference point and source of new cultural elements, which for many centuries had been China, was shifting

from China to the West', but that '[i]n the midst of this shift, a form of Chinese-derived music known as *minshingaku* played a significant role in Japanese musical culture and in the development of Japanese popular music' (Pope 2012; see also Pope 2014: 10–11).

2 This doesn't imply that the idea of copyright was known to Japanese people. In the mid-1930s, even lawyers were unfamiliar with copyright law in Japan (Mitsui 1994: 130).

(To be continued: see page 21 for (2).)

1

The French Revolution and the emergence of *enka*

This is a revised version of 'The French Revolution and the emergence of a new form of popular song in Japan', a paper presented in Paris on 17 July 1989, when the French Revolution bicentennial was celebrated at Colloque International/*1789–1989 Musique, Histoire, Démocratie* oraganisé par l'International Association for the Study of Popular Music et la revue Vibrations, Musique Médias Société. It was published in 1992, in *1789–1989 Musique, Histoire, Démocratie* by Editions de la Maison des Sciences de l'Homme, vol. 1, pp. 61–5.

"Song of Liberty"

If one has any basic knowledge of Japanese history, one may wonder if the French Revolution (1789–99) could really have had an influence on Japanese music, because the Tokugawa shogunate closed the country to foreigners for more than 200 years.

It was not until as late as 1858 that the shogunate and the Japanese people were aroused from their undisturbed isolation by the threatening boom of cannons as the American 'black ships' loomed off the coast of Uraga. The fleet was led by Commodore Perry, who came to demand that Japan open trade relations with America. In Perry's wake came missions from France and Britain. Along with the United States, these countries had recently become the capitalist powers of the world through modern revolutions.

However, when Rousseau's philosophy and the story of the Revolution came to Japan, albeit about eighty years later, they helped to nourish the *minken-undō* (the democratic rights movement) that produced many political songs. Let me first quote some verses, in my English translation, from a Japanese song composed a little more than 100 years ago. The title is "Jiyū-no Uta" (Song of Liberty) and its full text is in Soeda ([1933] 1982: 41–3).

In Heaven I'd be a demon of liberty, on Earth I would be a man of liberty
Liberty, liberty, oh, yes, liberty; the relationship between you and I
Is a promise that was naturally made; forever and ever till the end of the world
I'll keep the promise made until this world comes to an end
[...]
Caesar of Rome was assassinated, when he was ambitious to become the Emperor
By the hands of his bosom friend, in the midst of the assembly members
Saying, 'I would rather take his life, than hold our people in slavery'
[...]
Louis, King of France, used all his power to oppress liberty
But wrong would never overcome right
The anger of the people overflowed, like a flood and like a fire
With a force that could break rocks; the revered crown of gold
On the head of His Majesty, fell down on the guillotine
He had no one to blame but himself; his own oppression brought his ruin
It was so with the English revolution; yesterday's king was today's outlaw
The flag of liberty for the people, held in the hands of Oliver Cromwell
Fluttered so strongly as shake to the heavens, and caused the killing of Charles I
To establish freedom in Britain; the United States in the North America
Was established by the British people, but what motivated their immigration
Was to win their freedom in the New World
[...]
We, the people here in the Orient, though living in a different land
Have the similar hearts and minds; people are naturally born free

This song, written by Kutsuzan Komuro, was one of the songs 'young people were fond of singing' in the years when the democratic rights movement flourished: between 1881 and 1888 (ibid: 41).[1] The early 1880s, when this song appeared, was about fifteen years after the Meiji Restoration, which restored imperialism in Japan with a newly organized imperial government. The Restoration put an end to the long years of feudalism, depriving the former lords of the clans of their power and abolishing the class system of warriors, farmers, artisans and tradesmen. But the new government, which was formed by members of several of the clans that had succeeded in restoring the power of the Emperor, was an absolute monarchy; though, as it was groping for a secure basis of rule, not an entirely stable one. This absolute monarchy aroused opposition among the people, who had just recently learned such Western democratic thought as that of John Stuart Mill and Jean-Jacques Rousseau, and of democratization such as was established by the American Revolution and the French Revolution. It was these young Japanese who started what was called the democratic rights movement, demanding that the government should frame a constitution, inaugurate a national legislature and give suffrage to the people.

Democratic rights movement

The movement is said to have had its beginnings in 1874, when a political association called Risshisha was formed in Kōchi by several former warriors (*samurai*), who belonged to the Tosa clan. Risshisha, which asserted that 'the nation is the people', recruited new members from all over Japan, and three years later, in 1877, sent a long petition to the Emperor, demanding the establishment of a legislature. The petition was dismissed. In the following year, many more political associations were formed in the wake of Risshisha all over Japan, largely by such urban intellectuals as journalists, teachers and senior civil servants. It was some time before and during this period that there emerged a couple of songs that were made popular by members of Risshisha campaigning around the nation to gather support. One of the songs, "Minken Kazoe-uta" (Democratic Rights Counting Song), written by Edamori Ueki – which begins 'One, oh, one, all men are equal under the sun / And so they have equal rights' – asserts that sovereignty rests with the people, and refers to the United States as a nation that liberated itself from the tyranny of Britain. Another song that became popular at around the same time, "Yoshiya-bushi" (*Yoshiya* Song) (attributed to Michitarō Yasuoka), says 'Even in the oppressed land in the southern sea / There blows a gallant wind of liberty'. The 'land' in question is Kōchi Prefecture, located in the southern part of Japan.

The number of songs and their popularity increased as the democratic rights movement grew with petitions, appeals and protests for the establishment of a legislature and a constitution, among other demands. The song quoted at the beginning of this chapter – "Jiyū-no Uta" (Song of Liberty) – was one such song composed in this vigorous spirit, and the year in which it is believed to have been written marked one of the most important stages in the movement. On 18 March 1881, a daily newspaper called *Tōyō Jiyū Shinbun* (Oriental Liberty Journal) was first published. Its owner was Kinmochi Saionji (1849–1946), a descendant of a renowned aristocratic family, who was influenced by liberal thought during his stay in France; and its chief writer was Chōmin Nakae

(1847–1901). Nakae, who was thirty-three years old at the time, two years older than Saionji, also studied in France. Particularly impressed with the writings of Jean-Jacques Rousseau, he continued to study them after his return from France. The newspaper was characterized by the influence of French thought in its discussion of democratic rights, and the editorials by Nakae were judged to be the most lucid arguments ever put forward for democratic rights. He did not merely transplant Western thought but, after digesting it, tried to apply it carefully to the Japanese way of thinking. He partially translated Rousseau's *Du contract social, ou principes du droit politique* (1762) into classical Chinese, which was to the educated Japanese what Latin was to educated Europeans. What had been one of the seeds of the French Revolution, with its detailed examination of the idea of a republic, was published several years later and provided a strong ideological base for the democratic rights movement.[2] But the *Tōyō Jiyū Shinbun* did not last long because the government was offended by the fact that Saionji, an imperial aristocrat, was heading a pro-democratic rights paper, and he was secretly dismissed. The paper was forced to close six weeks after its birth.

Several months after the demise of this influential paper, the democratic rights movement finally succeeded at least in obtaining the government's promise of a national legislature in ten years' time. But that was the only concession the government made to the democratic rights movement's demands, and the government rejected both the plan for people's sovereignty in the manner of the French administration and that for constitutional sovereignty in the British manner. Government oppression became stricter after it had conceded the inauguration of a national legislature. The democratic rights movement continued to resist the government even more resolutely, to the extent that in the following year, 1882, Tomomi Iwakura, one of the leaders of the government remarked 'even the dawn of the French Revolution might not have been very different from this situation'. (For the birth of songs in the democratic rights movement, see Nishizawa 1990a: 1413–1496.)

Singing became a guerrilla tactic

The authorities tried hard to suppress the democratic rights movement by violently disrupting any public speech-making by its activists. Under this rigid governmental control, singing became a kind of a guerrilla tactic. Singing in the street was easier than making a speech because the singers could run away when threatened with arrest. The songs they sang took the place, as it were, of public speeches, and some historians say that this is the reason why the songs began to be called *enka*, or speech songs (*enzetsu* means public speaking), when they might more commonly have been called *sōshi-bushi* or *sōshi* songs (although further etymological research is needed here). The lyrics were more like rhyming speech – rap with a Japanese rhythm – than ordinary songs and were often sung to existing folk or popular tunes. It is unlikely that the singers ever received any musical training, and, according to some contemporary observations, the singing was quite ragged and harsh. The lyrics were written on folio papers and were sold to the audience after or during the performance, partly to earn the singer's daily bread. The money raised was also used to fund the campaigns of the democratic rights movement.

A song often cited from this time is "Dynamite-bushi" (Dynamite Song), known also as "Dynamite Don" (Dynamite Boom!), which was composed in 1885 by a member of the Liberal Party. As its title suggests, it is a high-spirited song, and begins as follows:

> With the Japanese spirit polished by a flood of tears
> Shed by the activists of the people's rights
> We'll strive for the good and welfare for the people
> If we cannot, there will be the boom of dynamite. (Soeda [1933] 1982: 38)

This song, characterized by the explosive refrain 'the boom of dynamite', was sung by young members at the Liberal Party's training centre in Tokyo and became very popular with the general public. In late 1887, two years after the song was written, the cabinet led by Prime Minister Hirobumi Itō was goaded by the strength of anti-government feeling into hurriedly passing a law by administrative fiat prohibiting any unsanctioned forming of an association or society, restricting open-air public meetings, censoring newspapers and granting itself the right to inspect the comings and goings of travellers.

Government suppression made the street singing of *enka* more like a guerrilla war. It was even incorporated into vaudeville plays by a sympathetic group led by the actor, Otojirō Kawakami. 'I would like to clean up the nation / With the water of liberty if it's possible / *Oppekepeppō-peppoppō*' was part of the song he was said to have first sung in 1891, and a series of songs he composed and sang were called '*oppeke* songs', after this comical nonsense refrain (Soeda [1933] 1982: 67–70). This catchy refrain was arguably not his invention, but he used it to good effect to popularize himself and his songs.

His plays incorporating the *oppeke* songs ruthlessly criticized and satirized the authorities to the extent that they were often disrupted or closed down by the police.

Enka made a comeback

Meanwhile, however, social conditions were changing with the eventual inauguration of the national legislature in 1890 and victory in the Sino–Japanese War in 1895, among other things, and *enka* gradually fell out of fashion. In 1901, Seinen Club, or the Youth Club, the leading group of *enka* singers in Tokyo formed around 1887, finally disbanded. It was at the time of the war between Japan and Russia, 1904–5, that *enka* made a comeback when "Rappa-bushi" (Bugle Song), first widely sung by Azenbō Soeda (1872–1940), became very popular. Soeda was attracted to the *enka* form as late as 1890 when he heard it sung in Yokohama by the young men in the democratic rights movement, and he started singing in the streets himself. He was eventually invited to join the Youth Club and could frequently be found singing in the streets of Tokyo. "Rappa-bushi" enjoyed huge popularity, beginning in 1905 (Soeda 1963: 110–11). Its tune (not composed by Azenbō) was commented on by a musicologist in 1910 as a Japanization of "Battō-tai" (Corps with Drawn Swords), a *gunka* composed by Charles Leroux in 1885, and 'particularly the addition of the non-sense refrain *tokototto* turned it to be a typical *hayari-uta*' (Moto-ori 1910: 9):

> I am quite a careless man; I was pleased to find a wallet in the road
> But when I got back home, it was simply a toad run over by a carriage
> *Tokotottoto* [...]
> I raised up my dying comrade-in-arms, and called his name with my mouth to
>   his ear
> He smiled at me with tears in his eyes, and gave three cheers in his heart.

The popular success of this song was due to its subject matter being wider than usual for *enka*, covering topical subjects, aspects of modern life and historical events. This change was suggested, according to Soeda's memoirs, when an experienced song-vendor commented that *enka* lyrics were too serious and stilted, and asked him to write something plainer and easier. He also used the form of this song for a later protest song called "Shakaitō Rappa-bushi" (Social Party Bugle Song), or "Heimin Rappa-bushi" (Common Man's Bugle

Song), which he wrote after his conversion to socialism under the influence of Toshihiko Sakai and after becoming one of the founding members of the Socialist Party in 1906. The last verse goes as follows:

> Our poor conductors and motormen, labouring for fifteen hours
> Every time the wheels grate, they scrape off their body and soul. (Soeda 1963: 117–18)

After the Russo–Japanese War, from the growing numbers of students in Tokyo emerged a new generation of *enka* singers who sang to support themselves through their studies. *Enka* came to be known as *shosei-bushi* (student songs) for some years. *Shosei-bushi* were devoted chiefly to satirizing and parodying current events, moving away from political criticism. For example, part of "High-collar-bushi" (Stylish Song) goes as follows:

> High-collar girls with gold-rimmed spectacles, are the students of the West End college
> Poems by Byron and Goethe in hand; they chant about something to do with Naturalism
> When rustle the rice plants of Waseda College, gently blows the breeze of love
>
> Tinkle, tinkle, ringing the bell, here comes a dandy on a bicycle
> Trying to show off his trick cycling, with both his hands off the handlebars
> Look out, don't go that way; look out, don't come this way
> Now you have fallen off, you see, I told you 'Be careful'. (Soeda 1963: 144–5)

More musical and more lyrical

In about 1907, Ryōgetsu Kaminaga used the violin to accompany his singing of *enka* for the first time. Since then, the sawing sound of the fiddle has come to typify the aural image of this old form of *enka*. Subsequently, during the Taishō era (1912–26), there emerged many professional *enka* singers. The melodies became more musical and the lyrics more lyrical, taking love as a theme. The anger and irony were forgotten, and the new concentration on sentimentality foreshadowed the direction in which the form would develop after the demise of the tradition of street-singing with the appearance of two new forms of media – radio and phonograph records – in the mid-1920s.

Enka was once an important vehicle for the dissemination of liberal ideas in a time of repression and resistance to progressive social change. The ideas of freedom and the sovereignty of the people, born in the heat of the French Revolution 200 years ago, were now the accepted wisdom of the democratic nations. But these freedoms were hard-won, and in Japan, as elsewhere, the medium of song was at once both their most potent weapon and their safest retreat from the forces that wished to eradicate them. (For a history of *enka*, see Nishizawa 1990a: 13–44.)

Notes

1. This remark, 'Young people were fond of singing', made in 1933, can be corroborated by the writing of Morihiko Fujisawa in 1914: 'After 1881 the demand for democratic rights was brimming with energy and students in high spirits aspired to be statemen, with "Jiyū-no Uta" (Song of Liberty) by Kutsuzan Komuro representing the people's will and with the song asserting "Even Washington and Napoleon were students at one time" becoming popular; the songs were soon followed by "Yacchoro-sandai-bushi" and "Dynamite-don"' (Fujisawa 1914: 295).
2. Nakae's partial translation of *Du contract social* into classical Chinese is available with full annotations and a translation into Japanese by Kenji Shimada in Kuwabara 1966: 177–246.

Transformation inspired by the West (2)

Enka

Some *shōka* and *gunka* tunes began to be adopted with modifications by *enka* singer-songwriters in the 1910s, when *enka* songs were often set to westernized tunes that were commonly in a pentatonic major or a new pentatonic minor (ABCEFA).

Enka is said to have emerged around 1883, when a group of men with a rough demeanour began to appear in the streets of Tokyo, shouting songs of social and political protest and selling brochures in which songs were printed. Those stalwart men, who were called *sōshi*, sympathized with the anti-despotic sentiments and activities of the democratic rights movement and critiqued society in general. The songs they sang were called *sōshi-bushi* (*sōshi* song) or *enka*, which is a combination of *en* (perform) and *ka* (song), indicating singing in public. Singing songs of protest in public was prohibited by the police authorities, but, nevertheless, it was easier for singers to gain a public audience.

The establishment of a parliament in 1890 and Japan's victory in the First Sino–Japanese War in 1895 led to the decline of *sōshi-bushi*, and the associated club, Seinen Club (the Youth Club) organized by Kiseki Hisada in 1888, was dissolved in 1902. However, *enka* re-emerged a decade later during the Russo–Japanese War (1904–5), chiefly due to the immense popularity of "Rappa-bushi" (Bugle Song), a song written by Azenbō Soeda. He also wrote many other well-known songs, including "Democracy-bushi" (Democracy Song) and "Nonki-bushi" (Carefree Song), which were passed down through the generations. "Rappa-bushi" presents a comical sketch of daily life by representing people's resentment and desperation satirically, self-deprecatingly and farcically. In doing so, it heralded a new age of *enka*, one in which the music disengaged itself from political critique and became topical, satirical and humorous. (For a history of *enka*, see Soeda 1963; Morimoto 1981 and Nishizawa 1990a: 13–44.)

This was also a time when an increasing number of students came to the metropolitan area and began singing on the street to earn money and pay their school expenses. As a result, *enka* also became known as *shosei-bushi* (student song), a name it kept for many years. (For more about *shosei-bushi*, see Hosokawa and Okada 1993.) During this period, *enka* songs were often set to westernized tunes and incorporated modified school songs, martial songs (*gunka*) and other current popular songs. They were commonly in the scale of CDEGAC or ABCEFA.

The process of borrowing from existing songs increased in the 1910s. Vernacular songs and popular songs were common sources, but after 1918 there was a growth in popular tunes composed in Western modes. Older tunes, too, were borrowed, such as "Marching Through Georgia" (1865), learned from an American missionary and combined with comical lyrics in 1919. In the mid-1910s, many singers who took up street-singing professionally began to introduce songs about man–woman relationships, particularly the painful aspects, and the violin was introduced to *enka* as an accompanying instrument played in unison with the voice around 1910 by Ryōgetsu Kaminaga; while the shouting delivery popular in early *enka* fell further into disuse.[1]

A despairing monologue song "Sendō Ko-uta" (Boatman's Ditty), which is also known as "Kare Susuki" (Withered Silver Grass), and a love-stricken dialogue song "Kago-no Tori" (Caged Bird) became enormously popular not only because of their lyrics but also their tunes, composed by Shinpei Nakayama in 1921 and Shun'yō Tottori in around 1923, respectively. Their scale (ABCEFA) appeared to touch the heartstrings of the Japanese. (For more on the music of *enka*, see Gondō 1988 and 2001.)

Tottori, an *enka* singer-songwriter, was a talented, self-taught musician who was innovative enough to incorporate contemporary jazz idioms into his arrangement of folksongs before dying at a young age in 1930. Nakayama was a graduate of the Tokyo College of Music and although not in the field of *enka*, he supplied a lot of songs to *enka* singers. He had already been made famous with "Katyūsha-no Uta" (Katyusha Song), which he composed in 1914 to the lyrics written by Gyofū Sōma as a song to be sung by a housemaid in the play *Fukkatsu* (Resurrection), based on Tolstoi's novel and written by Hōgetsu Shimamura. This song, about the pain of a lovesick parting, sung to a tune basically in the pentatonic major, nurtured in *shōka*, became very popular, particularly among students. Its epoch-making significance was stressed in the same year by the author of a history of *hayar-iuta* (meaning, literally, a fashionable ditty; a song that was widely accepted among the public) in its concluding pages (Fujisawa 1914: 360–4). It should also be noted that its popularity originated in the connection between theatre and phonograph recording. Following suit, "Sendō Ko-uta" and "Kago-no Tori" were very successfully adapted as silent films with the same names, coming after the success of their records in 1922 and 1924 respectively, as a synergy undertaken in the entertainment industry.

This new musical tendency developed in the Taishō era, which followed the Meiji era (1868–1912).[2] The Taishō era began in 1912, when the newly crowned Emperor Taishō succeeded the deceased Emperor Meiji, and lasted until 1926. There was a certain zeitgeist, which long afterwards became known as the Taishō Democracy. Approximately covering the Taishō era, the Taishō Democracy refers to a growing democratic and liberal tendency in Japanese politics, society and culture in general. It was fostered by, among other things, an easing of strained relations among Asian nations following the termination of the Russo–Japanese war in 1905, and also the awakening to political and civil liberty of the urban middle- and non-propertied class, which grew up in association with the rapid development of capitalism after the same war (Heibonsha 1985: 8, 1267). It was this era that produced the first commoner premier in Japan, Takashi Hara, who promoted Japanese–US cooperation in foreign transactions before he was assassinated in 1921, three years after assuming office.

Notes

1 *Enka* singers made recordings as early as 1912, but by the late 1920s, the life of the street singer was almost at an end, with the advent of a new age in which radio, records and films dominated the entertainment world, and

the significance of the form declined. However, the sole energetic survivor, Ichimatsu Ishida, who appeared in vaudeville houses, won an election to the House of Representatives in 1946 by singing *enka* songs of unyielding resistance, including "Jiji Ko-uta" (Topical Song), which was an updated version of "Nonki-bushi" (Carefree Song), originally composed by his mentor, Azenbō Soeda.

2. The genre called *naniwabushi* or *rōkyoku* that dominated Japanese popular amusements from around 1900 to the mid-1930s is not discussed here because it was not open to the Western influence. It is a stage entertainment that was established in the late 1860s as a form of story-reciting to a *shamisen* accompaniment. For details, see Masaoka (1968) and Minami et al. (1981).

(To be continued: see page 43 for (3).)

2

Songs in triple time sung in duple time

This is a revised version of Chapter 5 'Songs in Triple Time are Still Sung in Duple Time', in *Made in Japan: Studies in Popular Music* edited by Tōru Mitsui and published by Routledge, pp. 84–99 (© 2014 Taylor & Francis).

Songs in triple time, which didn't exist in Japan before, began to be composed in the late nineteenth century, although they had long been sung in duple time among the majority of Japanese, and even now the practice is common among many people.

Recordings of "Kago-no Tori" (Caged Bird) around 1924

What might be called a discovery was actually the result of research into the reason why "Kago-no Tori" (Caged Bird), an enormous hit in the mid-1920s, appeared to be sung irregularly in the fourth bar of its tune in the contemporary records. The tune is in AB form and consists of eight bars.

However, this song has long been favoured and recorded by numerous professional singers, and, indeed, all of them sang coherently in triple time, without one additional beat in the fourth bar, obviously owing to the accompaniment of an orchestra. An orchestral arrangement of the tune is naturally based on the music notation of the song, which is written in triple time.

The composer is Shun'yō Tottori (1900–32), a singer-songwriter who used to sing on the street at the time when (old) *enka* had ceased to be a voice of dissent but rather, with the accompaniment of a violin, appearing romantic. His musical literacy is reflected in his compositions and arrangements, some of which were even in the flavour of newly imported jazz, showing his innovatory talent. He recorded the song "Kago-no Tori", the lyrics of which were written by Kaoru Chino, with a female vocalist, Kyōko Tatsumi, who alternately responds to him in a long dialogue form. The record was among many others released in 1924, when the song became very fashionable. In addition to the records, more than a couple of motion pictures were produced with the same title, using the song as the theme song which was sung at theatres in the days of silent films.[1] The tune was sung in a typically rough voice when Tottori was twenty-four years old, sounding very similar to the voices of young American hillbilly singers in the same period (See Figure 2.1).

The Japanese pentatonic minor in which this song was written had begun to pull on the heartstrings of the Japanese, particularly since 1920 when "Sendō Kouta" (Boatman's Ditty) also became so popular that it was cinematized; in fact, Shun'yō Tottori's popularity was boosted by his recording of this song of despair. His singing of "Kago-no Tori" is supported by the piano accompaniment, which consistently underscores the triple time of this tune. When instrumental breaks are played, the piano is joined by the violin, verifying the recollection by an aged *enka* singer: 'It was just around the time when the accompaniment of the violin characterized the latest form of *enka*, which was formerly called *shosei-bushi* for a short period' (Kaminaga 1970: 40–1). The first syllable of this *enka* was spelt in a different Chinese character.[2]

This consistency of the triple time turns out to be exceptional when comparing it to other versions of this song recorded in the same year and some years afterwards. The version that was available in later years through its reissue in 1970 to those who were interested in the historical recordings of Japanese popular songs is "Kago-no Tori" sung by Yaeko Utagawa in 1924. It was one of 157 tracks in *Original-ban-niyoru Meiji-Taishō-Shōwa Ryūkōka-no Ayumi* (The history of Japanese popular songs in the Meiji, Taishō and Shōwa eras through original discs), a ten-album boxed set, released by Nippon Columbia,

Figure 2.1 "Kago-no Tori" sung by Shun'yō Tottori and Kyōko Tatsumi. Transcribed by author.

commemorating the sixtieth anniversary of its founding since it was called Nicchiku. The piano introduction to the singing plays the whole tune firmly in triple time, but the female singer lengthens the half-note in the fourth bar in phrase A (as shown in Figure 2.1) in the length of a half-note plus a quarter-note, and perplexingly, the piano also adds the fourth beat in this bar in accordance with her vocal elongation. After singing three verses, her narration is inserted to publicize the same-titled film in which she plays the leading role, before singing three more verses, with each verse being sung with the half-note in question being elongated and the irregularity being aided by the piano.

There were more than fifteen records of "Kago-no Tori" released around 1924, including those by Shun'yō Tottori, with Kyōko Tatsumi, and Yaeko Utagawa, an actress without musical literacy. Two of these fifteen records also show the fourth bar handled in the same way: one is recorded, presumably in 1924 or earlier in 1923, by a couple, Kazuo Yoshida and Mitsue Yoshida, who can easily be ascertained to be *enka* singers from their manner of delivery and the violin accompaniment. It can also be observed that they learnt the song by ear without having musical literacy, from the way they alter the original melody, particularly at the beginning. In this performance, the last note in the fourth bar is elongated in the similar way to Utagawa's singing, showing that the stress inevitably put on this half-note by the flow of the melody requires the note to be stretched. Furthermore, very intriguingly, it is followed by a brief instrumental, syncopated adornment played in pizzicato by the violin. The syncopation produced by playing the first note of this brief bar (assuming that the tune is transcribed) as an anacrusis at the end of the preceding bar is interesting in itself as an unexpected musical device carried out in Japan more than eighty years ago. This brief syncopated phrase in duple time is inserted each time the tune is repeated along with verses, and demonstrates that the performers feel uncomfortable in dealing with the last note in the fourth bar. The other version, also recorded by a couple, Ichiryū Ishida and Fumiko Ishida, was titled "Shin Kago-no Tori" (New Version of Caged Bird) and is generally similar to the Yoshida version. The performance on this record, which appeared to have been released in late 1924 or even later as the title implies, does not include the unique pizzicato phrase, but does lengthen the last half-note in the fourth bar, as well as resembling the Yoshida version in its vocalization and the scratching sound of the violin. Their tune is another variation of the original, denoting that they must have also learned the tune by ear.

Then, more remarkably, in the "Kago-no Tori" recorded eight years later, in 1932 (the year its composer Tottori died at the age of thirty-two), the vocalist sang the fourth bar in quadruple time with the backing of an orchestra that keeps step with her singing. This performance, which is converted from a pentatonic minor to a pentatonic major, is part of a two 78 rpm disc-set, consisting of four sides, titled *Enka-no Hensen* (Transition of *enka*): note the word *Enka* now appears with the first syllable spelt in a different character, reflecting the recollection by Kaminaga mentioned above. In this series of *enka* songs, following an explanatory narrative in female voice, the first couple of verses of each song are sung by Chieko Masaki, another female, with the accompaniment of a small-scale orchestra. The orchestra, which includes a *shamisen*, plays the introduction consisting of five bars with a different melody unmistakably in triple time, but Masaki's lengthening of the last note in the fourth bar is firmly supported by accentuating the metre of the bar in quadruple time.

These recordings show that the fourth bar in question is a defect in this triple-time composition. Let's take a look again at Figure 2.1. If the fourth bar begins with and consists of a half-note as in the fourth bar in the second phrase, the note is naturally stressed to fit in the triple-time bar. In this hypothetical arrangement, the beginning two eighth-notes in the fourth bar in the present composition could be moved to the preceding bar, where the two quarter-notes could accordingly be shortened to two eighth-notes. Tottori composed at least five more songs in triple time, of which three can be sung coherently in triple time, as the fourth bar in the 8-bar tune of "Heart Song" shows (see Figure 2.2). Two tunes, "Sutare-mono" (Down-and-out) and "Tsubaki-hime-no Uta" (Song of Princess Camellia), both consisting of sixteen bars, also look natural with the fourth bar of each phrase consisting of a stressed single note.[3]

Figure 2.2 "Heart Song" sung by Shun'yō Tottori. Transcribed by author.

Now the deficiency in the tune of "Kago-no Tori", which was composed presumably in 1923, is demonstrated above by contemporary recordings. However, a question remains regarding the seeming irregularity observed in the old recordings: the juxtaposition of three bars in triple time and one bar in quadruple time in the first phrase. It is generally accepted by those who study the music that triple time did not exist in traditional Japanese music, but could the juxtaposition be explained simply by the fact that the introduction of triple-time songs to Japan was still novel?

Duple-time singing at parties

I came up against a wall with this question and left it hanging for several years before discovering that the folk-culture museum in a village called Niizato in Iwate Prefecture, where Tottori was born, had begun collecting relevant materials, glorifying him as a great local figure in the late 1970s. Their response to my letter of inquiries, around 2005, regarding his other recordings of "Kago-no Tori", was negative, because the 1924 version previously discussed was the only "Kago-no Tori" disc by Tottori in their repositories. However, the museum kindly sent me a CD-R copy of an album, titled *Enka-no Roots: Machikado-no Uta – Tottori Shun'yō Collection* (The roots of *enka*: Street songs – Tottori Shun'yō collection), which was released by Nippon Columbia in 1979 as a 33 ⅓ rpm album. This album is based upon a series of radio-shows by Iwate Broadcasting Station, in which Shōichi Ozawa (1929–2012), a renowned actor and researcher of Japanese public entertainment, talked about Tottori and played his twenty-seven records released in the 1920s and 1930s, although not always in full.

My attention was first and foremost drawn to "Kago-no Tori", at the beginning of the album, sung by Ozawa himself in deference to this song on which Tottori's limited fame is dependent. He slowly sings all the original verses without restraint and almost unaccompanied. A female violinist, who was evidently trained in Western classical music, accompanies him in unison, but modestly without stressing the triple metre. Keeping time with my hands with the notation in mind (see Figure 2.1), I found, as I had expected, that the fourth bar is sung in quadruple metre. Ozawa is obviously feeling comfortable with the addition of one beat to the last note in the bar. At the same time, this very comfortableness made me wonder if he is singing this song basically in triple time, and the gentle wavering of his body imaginable by his singing in an unstrained manner suggested a long tradition of duple time singing at parties.

It was around the mid-1980s that people used to move on to karaoke bars after the height of festivities at various parties and sing songs to a pre-recorded orchestral backing, which unavoidably requires singers to conform to its rhythmical pattern, key and tempo.[4] Before the diffusion of this ubiquitous karaoke singing, people used to begin singing songs at parties when they ate heartily and got intoxicated, clapping their hands in time to the singing. Usually a certain participant would begin singing his favourite song and other participants would start beating time with their hands, which would then prompt another participant to sing a different song. It was also common for all participants to sing a college song or corporate anthem in unison as a gesture of solidarity. Handclapping was invariably and consistently in duple time, regardless of the time in which a song is written, with the first beat being clapped and then the hands separated at the second beat to be ready to clap at the first beat. Although I describe this in the past tense, I believe this tradition is still alive on occasions where karaoke equipment is unavailable.

This handclapping in duple time may well be easily associated, among the elderly Japanese, with the singing of *ryōka* (dormitory song) by the students (aged seventeen to nineteen) of elitist 'high-schools' of the pre-war education system. Personally, I was familiar with the singing as a primary-school student in the late 1940s, living in the vicinity of such a school. Those who graduated from these schools, which totalled about thirty and were abolished in 1950, got together annually (until a few years ago, when they became too old) in the cities where the schools were located and sang their dormitory songs in unison as they used to. One graduate recalled the following from 1977:

> The students always clapped hands when singing dormitory songs [...] The accompanying instrument was just a drum, and if it was not available, they were simply standing and clapped hands as an accompaniment as well as to cheer themselves up. This was always in duple time. When a song was in duple time or quadruple time, this worked well, but it was very inconvenient when a song was in triple time. (Bekku [1977] 2005: 190–2)

He describes the inconvenience as someone who is musically literate, but most of the students were not. When collected in one volume in 1972, the dormitory songs totalled 655, out of which fifty-two are in triple time, but these songs must have been sung in duple time. Unfortunately, no worthwhile audio examples of the singing of a *ryōka* song in triple time by the graduates of those schools can be found on YouTube. The triple-time tune of "Oka-no Danraku-ni Akugarete" (Aspiring for a Happy Circle on a Hill), one of Toyama High-School's dormitory songs (Hattori 1972: 632) sung by a group of old graduates a couple of years ago, is predominated by a bar consisting of one half-note and one quarter-note.[5] However, this bar is combined with the following bar to formulate one unit, and the whole song sways in a slowed-down 6/8 time, eventually reducing it to unhurried duple time. This unhurried duple time has long been familiar to the Japanese through songs known nationwide such as "Aogeba Tōtoshi" (Our Revered Teachers), which were sung at graduation ceremonies all around the country.

Nevertheless, the statement by a former student above called my attention back to the audio recording of a group of older people I met a few years ago.

"Kago-no Tori" in duple time

In late 2007, I visited a daycare centre called Slow-Life Care in Neagari, Ishikawa Prefecture for people in their late seventies, eighties and nineties, in order to see if those who should be more familiar with "Kago-no Tori" than younger people would add one more beat at the end of its fourth bar. Some twenty females and males sang along to this song with their hands clapping, watching the handwritten lyrics on a large piece of paper and without being accompanied by the piano upon my request, and sure enough they lengthened the last note in the fourth bar of Tottori's composition. The result made me simply contented at that time, but now I transcribe the way they sang the tune repeatedly in accordance with the first two verses in Figure 2.3. The key is changed here to D minor in order to make it easier to compare with Figure 2.1.

The tune is sung consistently in duple time, and thereupon disappears the strangeness of the three bars in triple time being followed by a bar consisting of four beats; the oddity assumed above by hearing the old recordings of "Kago-no Tori". Then, something of much interest is detected: when the first verse comes to the end, the repeated tune structurally alters with the first note being put as an anacrusis, and all the second note in each bar of the tune is placed as the first note in the repeated tune. The alteration is caused by the identical metrical-ending of phrase A and phrase B, but the alteration is restored, when the altered tune comes to an end, by the new identical metrical-ending. This reminds me

Figure 2.3 "Kago-no Tori" sung by older people in Neagari. Transcribed by author.

of an observation made by Tomiko Kojima, a representative musicologist of Japanese traditional music, in a tripartite talk with two other colleagues in the same field: 'In Western classical music, a duple time is based on a unit of two beats with one accented and the other unaccented, but in Japanese music each beat is accented alike' (Kojima et al. 1991: 9).[6] Analytically speaking, this alteration and restoration results in the phenomenon that the original tune and its variation are combined as one, and this musical combination accompanies verses 3 and 4, 5 and 6, and so on, respectively. It should be noted that the present tune, as well as other tunes transcribed in this chapter, is transcribed in the universal notation system that was devised in accordance with the development of Western music, and a bar in duple time inevitably implies that the first beat is stronger than the second one, but in reality, the tune is free from the implication.

When hearing again Ozawa's singing of "Kago-no Tori" (1979), with this observation in mind, one finds that it is identical in its structure to the daycare centre version. At first hearing, it sounds as though he is singing in triple time, but soon the whole sway suggests that he is singing in duple time as my transcription shows (see Figure 2.4).

The tune is structurally altered when it is repeated with the first note becoming an anacrusis, and the original tune and the altered one are

Figure 2.4 "Kago-no Tori" sung by Shōichi Ozawa. Transcribed by author.

combined as a unit to go with verses 1 and 2, 3 and 4, and 5 and 6. Moreover, it is significant that the syncopated brief violin notes inserted at the end of the instrumental six-bar introduction are invariably located at the end of each combination, revealing that the violinist is obviously aware of this combination as a unit.

This revelation naturally prompts one to listen to the old recordings referred to above without the imposed preconception of triple time. For a start, take a look at the transcription of Chieko Masaki's "Kago-no Tori" recorded in 1932 with the orchestral backing in Figure 2.5. The introductory part played by the orchestra is clearly in triple time, but it changes to duple time when Masaki begins to sing, with the result being structurally the same with the versions by the daycare-centre group and by Ozawa (Figure 2.4).

Then, one finds that this structure is in common with the Ishida's "New Version of Kago-no Tori", presumably recorded in late 1924 or 1925, as well as with Yaeko Utagawa's "Kago-no Tori" recorded in 1924.

Figure 2.5 "Kago-no Tori" sung by Chieko Masaki. Transcribed by author.

In the case of the Yoshidas' "Kago-no Tori" (around 1924), which is characterized by the pizzicato insertion, the tune appears only as the altered version seen above, invariably beginning with an anacrusis (Figure 2.6). A similar treatment of the tune is given in a version sung unaccompanied by the male partner of a comic duo, Suteji Sunakawa and Yoshiko Kawachiya, as part of their dialogue titled "Manzai Shin Kago-no Tori" (Comic Dialogue: New Version of Caged Bird) (Figure 2.7), which was presumably recorded in the early 1930s. These two versions, particularly the unaccompanied version, show that the singers are evidently comfortable to sing the tune with the original stress on the first beat being moved to the second beat by singing the note/s on the first beat as an anacrusis.

This observation regarding the song composed in triple time being sung in duple time can now be discussed more generally, but, before examining this further, I will underscore the observation with an analysis of a song with a similar defect. The song, "Furusato" (Hometown) is much more famous than "Kago-no Tori" – known to almost all Japanese people – and is, remarkably, a decade older than "Kago-no Tori".

Figure 2.6 "Kago-no Tori" sung by Kazuo Yoshida and Mitsue Yoshida. Transcribed by author.

Figure 2.7 "Manzai Shin Kago-no Tori" sung by Suteji Sunakawa. Transcribed by author.

"Furusato" and its duple-time singing

Some years ago, when looking for a similar defect in triple-time songs composed in Japan to see if "Kago-no Tori" is exceptional or not, I unexpectedly came upon "Furusato" as another exception. It first appeared in 1914 in one of a series of song (*shōka*) collections published as textbooks for primary schools by the Ministry of Education (reprinted in Kindaichi and Anzai 1979: 57). The G-major tune is in ABCD form, consisting of sixteen bars with four bars per phrase (Figure 2.8). While the rhythm of phrases

Figure 2.8 "Furusato" composed by Teiichi Okano (lyrics by Tatsuyuki Takano).

A, B and D is mostly based on three simple quarter-notes, that of phrase C is similar to the predominant rhythm of "Kago-no Tori". On top of that, its last bar is identical in its rhythm, with the unavoidable stress on the second beat inviting unrestrained singers to sing the note lengthened, in contrast to the last bar of each other phrase (A, B and D), which accentuates the general flow of the triple time.

This observable musical deficiency of "Furusato" has never been pointed out as far as I know; as in the case of "Kago-no Tori", this is very likely due to the way people have long been exposed to this song at school, through the radio and TV and at live performances, all of which depend upon the musical literacy of teachers and musicians who have recourse to the notation. Hence, there is a plethora of performances of this song on YouTube that are consistently in triple time, which has meant I have had to be very patient in my search for an appropriate piece of evidence in which the last note in the fourth of phrase C is elongated. Recently, I came upon one which was video-recorded at an anonymous daycare centre.[7] A group of older females sang the song in unison with a male accompaniment on a double-reed harmonica, who is leading the whole sing-along. His relaxed performance of the tune, which is at the forefront in the recording, is unmistakably in duple time, and the whole performance can be transcribed as in Figure 2.9.

Figure 2.9 "Furusato" performed by a male harmonica player and sung by older women. Transcribed by author.

The last note in phrase C is lengthened with an addition of one more bar, but the duple time makes the whole flow of the tune sound effortless. This is identical to the impromptu performance that I carefully observed in 2011, of a double-reed harmonica played solo by an older baker in Ōsu, Aichi Prefecture, on a weekly TV show featuring people from various provincial regions.[8]

Around the same time, I also found another interesting example on YouTube in which the leader with an accordion is unquestionably aware that the middle-aged males and females who sing this song in unison at a sing-along café would certainly elongate the note in question and urges them with a gesture not to do so.[9] Facing the singing customers, he succeeds each time with a movement of a hand or a part of his body when the singing reaches the last note in the fourth bar of phrase C, remaining consistently sceptical. Three beats per each bar are maintained by the accordionist and a subordinate pianist, but apparently most of the customers sing, or tend to sing, in duple time (as shown in Figure 2.9).[10]

Songs in triple time sung in duple time

The tunes "Kago-no Tori" and "Furusato" have been examined in order to confirm their apparent rhythmical deficiencies through listening to them being sung by ordinary, or more or less musically illiterate, people. We have learnt that, apart from the confirmed deficiencies, it must have long been a general practice for them to sing triple-time songs in duple time. In terms of metrical structure, this singing is based on converting two bars in triple time to three bars in duple time, as can be deduced from the transcriptions shown so far. Instead of referring to these two songs that have deficiencies, we will now take a look at the song "Minato" (Port), in ABCD form, which is based on the rhythm similar to "Kago-no Tori" and to phrase C of "Furusato" (Figure 2.10).

When the two bars forming a unit as the first half as well as the second half of each phrase are sung in duple time, they turn out to be three bars when notated in Figure 2.11.

"Minato" first appeared in a book of school songs compiled in 1896 and became so popular that it has long been known to the majority of the Japanese. The compilers of a well-received collection of Japanese school songs ensure that 'this jaunty song in triple time [...] was one of the most favourite songs composed in the Meiji era [1868–1912], and it was through this song that the Japanese found [...] triple time interesting' (Kindaichi and Anzai 1977: 96). In the first extensive but often forgotten collection of popular songs in Japan compiled in 1931, this song is the first song in triple time to appear in the book. One of its compilers, Keizō Horiuchi, who was born in 1897, comments, 'this lovely tune in triple time was highly welcomed by young people' (Horiuchi and

Figure 2.10 "Minato" composed by Tarihiko Hatano (lyrics by Shinta Yoshida).

Figure 2.11 "Minato" arranged in duple time by author.

Machida 1931: 228). It is indeed written in triple time and must have been taught in triple time at schools, but my investigation suggests that many students quite possibly sung them in duple time outside the classroom, though they were not aware of the metric ambiguity.

Moreover, it is more likely that this song was sung as a tune led by an anacrusis as shown in Figure 2.12. This conjecture is not only suggested corroboratively by what was perceived in Figure 2.6 and Figure 2.7, but also by an observation found in a book on the rhythm of Japanese poetry (Sugaya 1975). When making reference to a parody version of this song that was long popular among primary-school students, the author points out that the students who parodied this song were naturally aware of the basic rhythm of this song, as exemplified in the way they emphasized the second beat of each bar in the original triple-time tune in accordance with the semantic stresses of the substituted words (ibid.: 95).

His argument takes for granted that the parody was sung in triple time, but the way the students sung can be illustrated as in Figure 2.12 (a part of the parody is shown as the second verse). The popularity of this parody itself is also mentioned in the well-received collection of Japanese school songs by its compilers (Kindaichi and Anzai 1977: 96).

Figure 2.12 "Minato" arranged in duple time by author beginning with an anacrusis.

Significantly, in 1931, Horiuchi called attention, just after his brief comment on 'this lovely tune in triple time', to the fact that 'the rhythm of this song was the precursor of the rhythmic pattern of popular songs in triple time, e.g. "Kago-no Tori" and "Shūchō-no Musume" (Daughter of the Chief)' (Horiuchi and Machida 1931: 228). It is problematical and contrary to one's expectations to assert that "Shūchō-no Musume", a comic song composed in 1930, is in triple time as far as the contemporary recordings go, but it turns out to be true that there were, in 1931, quite a few songs that became popular with the rhythm (two eighth-notes followed by two quarter-notes) that typifies "Minato" and "Kago-no Tori". Tracing back to before 1931, one finds "Umi" (Sea) (1913), "Oboro-zukiyo" (Night with a Hazy Moon) (1914), "Canariya" (Canary) (1919), "Sei-kurabe" (Comparing Heights) (1919), "Amefuri Otsukisan" (Moon in the Rain) (1925) and "Aka-tonbo" (Red Dragonfly) (1927), which remain popular up to the present day. They are not 'popular songs' in the proper sense, with the first and the sixth songs intended to be taught at primary schools and the rest being composed as children's songs, but Horiuchi had foresight because many popular songs composed in triple time with this rhythmic pattern, along with many songs for schools, appeared one after another in the following decades.[11]

Recently, in a different context, triple-time songs with this rhythmic pattern were enumerated up to 1978, along with the songs mentioned above, by Hiroshi Yasuda (1999: 54–7). Yasuda refers to a study by Tadahiro Murao, who is also in the field of music education. Murao analysed this rhythmic pattern to explain the reason why this has been favoured among the Japanese (Murao 1985). Though his metrical analysis is too meticulous to be summarized here, his conclusion can be paraphrased as follows: the Japanese have had to adhere to this rhythmic pattern in order to get used to a triple metre, which had been alien to them before they were introduced to Western music in the late nineteenth century.

At the same time, it should be emphasized that ordinary people, particularly elderly people, still sing triple-time songs with this rhythmic pattern in duple time when unaccompanied by musical instruments: outside schools, recording studios, stages and karaoke bars.[12] Moreover, even triple-time songs dominated by three quarter-notes per bar have tended to be sung in duple time in a similar situation, as demonstrated above by the singing of "Furusato". Structurally, as mentioned above, the singing of the triple-time songs in duple time in question can be reduced to a unit in which two bars in triple time are converted to three bars in duple time.

Interestingly, this unit of three bars in duple time fits precisely in the repetitious sutra *nanmyō-hōren-gēkyō* chanted at services by the priests and congregation of the Nichiren sect of Buddhism. Try chanting this simple sutra along with a singing of, say, Figure 2.11. Chanting it eight times perfectly corresponds to the whole tune. This sutra phrase, which can be traced back to thirteenth-century Japan, is in duple time, but the whole unit consists of three trochaic feet, which make up a 6/4 time or an unhurried triple time. Historical research is required to see if the correspondence is a coincidence.

Notes

1 There are several references to the cinematization and the popularity of this song. One reliable source is Kurata (2006: 139–40).
2 While the *en-* of *enka* used to be spelled in a Chinese character denoting 'deliver' (in the sense of making a speech to a lot of people), the new Chinese character for *en-* denoted something romantic, sensuous or voluptuous.
3 As to the rest of the five songs, "Ukikusa-no Tabi" (Travelling Like a Floating Weed) in AB form and "Akai Bara" (Red Rose) in ABCD form, each phrase concludes with a bar consisting of two eighth-notes and a half-note. These tunes would still sound good if converted to a tune beginning with an anacrusis.

4   For more on the spread of karaoke-singing, see Mitsui and Hosokawa (1998: 1–22).
5   "Oka-no Danraku-ni Akugarete" was uploaded on YouTube on 10 November 2010.
6   Her mentor, Fumio Koizumi (1927–83), had expressed a similar observation years before (Koizumi 1994: 335), and he also remarked: 'what should specifically be noted about Japanese [traditional] music are (1) that a coordination of a strong beat and a weak beat is inconspicuous, and (2) that a triple time and triple rhythm are non-existent' (ibid.: 342).
7   "Furusato", performed on 25 August 2010, was uploaded on YouTube on an unknown date.
8   *Kazoku-ni Kanpai* (Toast to Families), NHK, at 8:00–8.45 pm on 21 November 2011.
9   "Furusato", performed on 11 April 2010 at Kāsan-no Ie (Mother's House), a sing-along coffee house in Azumino, Nagano, with accordionist Satoshi Kubota as the leader, was uploaded on YouTube on an unknown date.
10 There is one more well-known song that has a similar deficiency as a triple-time tune: "Geisha Waltz" composed in 1952 by Masao Koga, a distinguished composer of popular songs. The fourth bar of phrase A in this ABCD form consists of one dotted eighth-note combined with a sixteenth-note and a half-note, while other three phrases are closed with a dotted half-note.
11 In Western countries, this rhythmic pattern seems to be uncommon. For instance, in a comprehensive collection of British popular tunes in the past centuries (Simpson 1966), only 116 out of 540 tunes are in triple time, and only two of those triple-time tunes use this rhythmic pattern: "The Children in the Wood, or Now Ponder Well" (103–5) and "The Country Lass" (134–6). A familiar instance might be the standard version of a well-known traditional ballad, "Barbara Allen", though the second beat of a bar is often dotted.
12 To do Murao justice, he states in a footnote, 'Even today, many aged adults sing triple meter songs in such a way as follows, especially at a Japanese style party', and gives the first four bars of "Hoshikage-no Waltz" (Starlight Walz) (1968) as an example (Murao 1985: 146). However, while the 'way of clapping hands' is notated, the 'singing of the song' itself is shown in the original triple time. The singing of this song in duple time at a party is also pointed out by Akira Higuchi in the tripartite talk mentioned above (Kojima et al. 1991: 9).

Transformation inspired by the West (3)

Dance-band music

The Taishō era was distinguished further by three musical developments.

The first was dance-band music. Japan participated in the First World War (1914–18) on the side of the Allied Forces and established diplomatic relations with the United States. Passenger and cargo liners crossed back and forth over the Pacific, importing and exporting commodities in abundance, including phonograph records. A veteran music journalist recalled that North American phonograph records by white dance bands were often played in modish, Western-style coffee-houses, which were called 'milk halls' (Noguchi 1976: 7). Moreover, when they were employed by a Japanese steamship company to perform for the passengers on its regular liner, the five graduates of the Tokyo College of Music who made up the Hatano Orchestra used to purchase the scores of popular dance music in San Francisco between 1912 and 1918. The scores included "Alexander's Ragtime Band", "Smile", "Whispering", "Three O'Clock in the Morning", "Let Me Call You Sweetheart", "Tell Me" and "Dardanella".

After leaving the liner, this small orchestra, led by Fukutarō Hatano, worked as an intermission band in theatres that featured American silent films, playing short classical pieces, pre-jazz dance music and some jazz. Then, in 1921 his orchestra performed at Kagetsuen in Yokohama, the first commercial dance hall that had opened in Japan in the preceding year. High-priced imported phonograph records were used in social-dance training schools in the late 1910s and early 1920s after the opening of Kagetsuen. Conversely, in the 1920s while their ships were lying in harbour, some passenger liner US house bands, with some jazz orientation, also often performed in hotels in Yokohama and Kobe, the two largest international seaports. (For the later development of dance-band music and jazz in Japan, see Uchida 1976, Segawa 1983 and Atkins 2001.)

Asakusa Opera

The second most important musical development in the Taishō era was an adaptation of Italian opera, which gained favour in the show business field as a new popular theatrical art. The first performance of opera in Japan took place in 1903, when the graduates and students of the Tokyo College of Music performed a Japanese translation of Gluck's *Orfeo ed Euridice*, under the direction of European instructors. In 1912, the Italian Giovanni Vittorio Rossi began giving lessons at a newly formed theatre. After this proved to be unsuccessful, some of his pupils formed troupes of their own to perform in several theatres in Asakusa, an old entertainment district in Tokyo.

The acclaim of what was called 'Asakusa Opera', named after the neighbourhood where it was performed, began in 1917, and its success was due to its transformation of operas such as Verdi's *Aida*, Bizet's *Carmen* and Suppe's *Boccacio* into the style of Japanese entertainment. The original works were invariably reduced to operettas by being abbreviated, and the arbitrariness of the abbreviation was reflected in the way the lyrics were freely translated. Thus, Asakusa Opera was a popular entertainment in which 'the stage was merrily united with the audience' (Miyazawa 1990: 1). The troupes often toured the country to make Asakusa Opera a nationwide phenomenon, which contributed to the modification of the musical sensibility of the Japanese by exposing them to Western musical idioms. At the same time, the skill of adapting Japanese lyrics to Occidental melodies was honed by those involved in the performance of the operettas; songs such as "Hab' ichi nur deine Liebe" from *Boccacio*, sung by Rikizō Taya in Japanese translation, was on the lips of many people. Asakusa Opera came to an end in 1925 due to the effects of the Great Kantō Earthquake two years before, but it served as a breeding ground for many talented people, including: Yoshie Fujiwara, who led a full-scale opera company; Teiichi Futamura, a successful recording artist; Ken'ichi Enomoto, a high-spirited comedian; Kōka Sassa, a proficient songwriter; and Takashi Iba, a popular playwright. (For more about Asakusa Opera, see Masui 1990.)

Takarazuka Revue

The Taishō era was also characterized by the emergence of 'girls' opera': a musical revue that was a Japanese adaptation of a European model produced by Hankyū (an electric train company) as the chief attraction in Takarazuka, a hot-spring resort town near Osaka, the second largest city in Japan. The first show was performed in 1914, and in 1919 the Takarazuka Girls' Opera Company was formed before the establishment, a decade later, of Japan's largest theatre, with a seating capacity of 3,000. This all-female Takarazuka Revue has been characterized by its luxurious spectacle and girlish romanticism, featuring male protagonists played by star members.

The epoch-making show was *Mon Paris*, a revue performed in 1927 and directed by Tatsuya Kishida, who learned a great deal during his eighteen-month stay in Europe. The title song of the show, "Mon Paris", in Japanese translation, became a huge hit when it was recorded and released two years later. Japan's adoration for Paris was inflamed by the show as well as by records, and was accelerated by a series of shows that insatiably romanticized the gay city of Paris. Significantly, revues by the Takarazuka Revue Company are still thriving: they are shows that 'present a pastiche of styles derived from European and American musicals and juxtaposes these against a variety of Japanese theater and dance traditions' (Brau 1990: 80). Many of the foremost accomplished actresses in Japan graduated from this theatrical company, which, since 1919, has boasted its own training school of dancing, singing and playing. (For more about Takarazuka Revue, see Robertson 1998 and Stickland 2008.)

(To be continued: see page 75 for (4).)

3

"Sing Me a Song of Araby" and "My Blue Heaven": When the production of hit songs began in the late 1920s

This is a revised version of '"Sing Me a Song of Araby" and "My Blue Heaven": "New folksong", hybridization and the expansion of the Japanese recording industry in the late 1920s', in *Popular Music History* (London: Equinox), vol. 1, no. 1, pp. 65–82 (© Equinox Publishing Ltd 2004). It was revised in Japanese for a book edited by Tōru Mitsui (2005b: 9–41), before it was presented on 17 November 2006 as a lecture in English at the 51st Conference of the Society for Ethnomusicology held in Honolulu.

1927

It was in 1927 that Benjamin Gardner, the American executive director of the newly formed Nippon Victor recording company, suggested that the production and release of new songs should be a major source of income generation for the company; a relatively novel idea to his Japanese colleagues (Morimoto 1975: 27; Uchida 1976: 80).[1]

While this model of production seems to have been already well established in the United States, the Japanese music industry had previously 'picked up and recorded songs that were already widely accepted among the public' (to use a succinct summary by a former staff songwriter of Nippon Columbia and an elderly researcher of Japanese popular songs in the late nineteenth and early twentieth centuries (Nishizawa 1990b: 7; see also Horiuchi [1942] 1948: 237). In other words, there was no system in place that specifically aimed to popularize songs through recordings. Since the introduction of the phonograph in the late nineteenth century, there had been a number of companies that had sprung up to cater for the demand for recordings (for a concise history, see

Komota et al. 1970: 61–2; and for a detailed development, Kurata 1979), but 1927 was the year in which the Japanese recording industry as we know it really began to cohere.

This was the year when three major recording companies were formed in Japan with the entry of overseas enterprises into the domestic market. Firstly, Nippon Polydor was formed as a joint venture on 30 May when Anan & Co signed a contract with Deutsche Polydor. On the same day (or 20 June, according to other accounts), Nippon Chikuonki Shōkai (Japan Phonograph & Co), which was called Nicchiku for short, executed the capital tie-up with the British arm of Columbia in May 1927, and subsequently American Columbia took part in the newly formed company, dispatching Lester H. White as the vice president. (In October 1928, Nippon Columbia was formed as a subsidiary of Nippon Chikuonki.) Then on 13 September, American Victor invested money in establishing Victor Company of Japan (Nippon Victor) with Benjamin Gardner as the top executive (RIAJ 1993: 36).

The roots of these developments lay in earlier economic factors. The 1923 Great Earthquake in the Kantō area surrounding Tokyo was a serious blow to the Japanese economy. In response, in the following year the government passed a new law to levy customs duties on imported 'luxury goods' as part of a number of policy measures designed to promote domestic production. Designated 'luxury goods' included phonographs and records, for which the rate of taxation was 100 per cent (Horiuchi [1942] 1948: 234), causing their prices to be raised substantially. Overseas recording companies 'feared the loss of the Japanese market which had been prosperous, and attempted to break down the levy barrier by setting up their factories in Japan' (ibid.: 234), while the main domestic record companies who owned the marketing rights to overseas records tried to bypass this levy by importing masters of foreign recordings instead of physically importing discs (RIAJ 1993: 35). This actual manufacturing of discs carrying foreign recordings served to facilitate much closer cooperation between Japanese recording companies and US and European companies; a situation that quickly led to overseas investment and ultimately the formation of three major Japanese companies, enabling the production of a domestically pressed record priced at 1.50 yen when an imported record was priced at 3, 5 or even 7 yen (Kurata 1979: 315). The formation of these new companies was also prompted by the use of new electric microphone recording techniques, which American manufacturers developed around 1925, under the influence of the evolution of radio technology. Indeed, for the first few years, this new process of recording with its resultant improvements in sound quality was frequently emphasized as a major selling point by being printed on the contemporary Nicchiku sleeve used for all releases.

In general, the types of popular songs that were dominant in the market were those with features that stemmed from the age before the Meiji era and also *enka* in the old sense: basically political and topical broadside songs sung by street singers. *Enka* increasingly incorporated Western musical idioms at least in its scale and the use of the violin accompaniment played in unison in a fiddle fashion. However, it was not until investment from overseas recording companies that these hybrids began to become popular among a truly mass audience.

It was from early 1928 that Nicchiku and Nippon Victor began releasing numerous records (the first release of Nippon Polydor records was in 1930), but it took nearly a year and a half for one of these major companies to have a significant hit with a song whose music and lyrics were originally composed for recording. Indeed, there were necessary developmental stages, in terms of both the market and the industry, before the massive success of Nippon Victor's "Kimi Koishi" (Yearning for You) in early 1929. I will unpack these developmental stages by considering significant hit recordings in the Japanese market within those two years. I will also discuss how these songs were written and produced and examine how the rise of new pentatonicism in Japanese popular music, the mass mediation of orchestral sound and new media forms served to produce hybrid forms of popular music that would dominate the market in subsequent decades.

'New folksong'

A notable feature in the market since February 1928, when Nicchiku began releasing new records, was that a group of *shin-min'yō* – 'new folksong' – recordings became visible. The 'new folksong' movement, with its emphasis on poetical colloquialism and a construction of locality (for a historical survey in English, see Nakamura 1991: 277–81), officially began in 1919 when a group of poets got together to compose 'indigenous new folksongs sprouted out from agricultural soil' (Komota et al. 1970: 70). The first popular recording to emerge from this movement was "Debune-no Minato" (Sea Port of Outgoing Ships) coupled with "Debune" (Outgoing Ship), which was released by Nippon Victor in February 1928.

The songs were supposed to have been 'sprouted out from agricultural soil', but the vocalist of these recordings, Yoshie Fujiwara, was trained in the tradition of Western classical music and was typically accompanied by the piano. The recording of these pieces of hybridized music was carried out at the Victor recording studio in Camden, New Jersey, on 28 and 29 January 1928, a few weeks before they were released. They were released both in the US and in Japan with the same release number (1230) and with the titles, "Sea Port" and "Outgoing Ship" for the American version (for American release numbers and other songs recorded, see Spottswood 1990: 5, 2545).[2] Fujiwara (1898–1976) was a singer in his late twenties with conspicuous Caucasian features, due to his parents being a Scottish expatriate and a *geisha*. He was a *bel canto* tenor, first trained in Asakusa Opera, a short-lived but highly successful form of musical and theatrical revue that flourished in Asakusa, Tokyo's most popular entertainment district at the time (see 'Transformation inspired by the West (3)' on Asakusa Opera, and for more, see Masui 1990). Featuring adaptations of European operettas in Japanese, Asakusa Opera's popularity made a significant contribution to the spread of the major and minor scales of Western tonality within Japan before the theatre was destroyed by the Great Kantō Earthquake of 1923. In the intervening years, Fujiwara had gained an international reputation through tours of Europe and North America and was offered an exclusive contract with American Victor in mid-1926. In late January 1928, he recorded songs as a 'Red Seal' artist (Furukawa 1993: 244–5), a gesture that was not without prestige as the Victor artists whose recordings were honoured with red labels included such renowned musicians as Fritz Kreisler and Sergei Rakhmaninov.

While being a product of the new nationalistic 'new folksong' movement, both songs were also part of the song-writing system imported from the US. "Debune-no Minato", with lyrics by Shigure Otowa (1898–1980), a staff songwriter, was set to music by Shinpei Nakayama (1887–1952), a composer who had also signed an exclusive contract with Nippon Victor a month after its formation. However, the composition of both the lyrics and music had been executed before they signed with Nippon Victor: the lyrics were originally a poem, 'Asahi-o Abite' (Basking in the Morning Sun) published in a new magazine, *King*, founded in 1925 (Ikeda 1985: 55). "Debune-no Minato", coupled with "Debune", which also became popular, sold well and was quickly followed by the success, in May, of another 'new folksong', "Habu-no Minato" (Port of Habu): composed by Shinpei Nakayama to a poem published by Ujō Noguchi, a prominent advocate of 'new folksong', in the June 1923 issue of *Fujin Sekai* (Women's World) (Ikeda 1985: 55) and sung by Chiyako Satō (1897–1968), a female singer, under an exclusive contract, who had graduated from a conservatory where Western music was taught. She also sang the song with a single piano accompaniment, this time by Nakayama himself, in the conventional style of Western vocal music. ("Uguisu-no Uta" (Nightingale Song) on the B side of "Habu-no Minato", composed also by Nakayama and Noguchi and sung by Satō, must have been unpopular because no reference is found in relevant books.)

Contrary to the statement in a history of Nippon Victor (Nippon Victor 1967: 40), Fujiwara's recording of the song preceded that of Satō, who in fact 'covered' the Fujiwara version. The latter was recorded on 3 March 1928, in Oakland, California (Spottswood 1990: 5, 2545–6), a month after Fujiwara's recording in Camden, New Jersey, when he must have been touring around the US (Furukawa 1993: 254). Fujiwara's "Habu-no Minato" – which was released with the same release number (4042) in the US and Japan (the release date in the US is unknown) – was also successful, and the sales of both Fujiwara's and Satō's discs allegedly reached 160,000 copies, with Satō's 'Black Seal' disc being priced at 1.50 yen and Fujiwara's 'Red Seal' at 2.50 yen (Daicel 1990: 4). The staff of Nippon Victor were surprised at the high sales, saying, 'we didn't expect that records would sell so many' and 'production can't keep up with the demand' (Morimoto 1975: 16–17, his source unknown). Indeed, "Habu-no Minato" was so popular that it inspired three different film companies to make silent film versions of the song (Kurata 1979: 334).

Fujiwara's "Hoko-o Osamete" (Laying Down Arms), also released in July 1928, was successful as well. It was recorded on 4 March 1928, the day after the recording of "Habu-no Minato" in Oakland, California, and was also released in the US with the same release number (4043). (Fujiwara recorded ten other songs on 3 and 4 March, and five more songs on 22 March in Oakland, before his successful performance at the Royal Albert Hall in London the following month (Furukawa 1993: 254)). "Hoko-o Osamete" was originally a poem, 'Kinsen' (Golden Fan) written by Shigure Otoawa and published in the January 1926 issue of *King*, for which Nakayama wrote the music (Ikeda 1985: 55). Meanwhile, "Asane" (Getting Up Late), the B side of "Haubu-no Minato" (lyrics by Shindai Matsubara, music by Ryūtarō Hirota), and "Sendō Uta" (Boatman's Song), the B side of "Hoko-o Osamete" (music by Yūji Itō, lyricist unknown) were clearly not as popular as no references can be found in books. For reference, in December 1928 Nippon Victor released "Debune", sung by Chiyako Satō on the flip side of a 'new folksong' titled "Tabibito-no Uta" (Traveller's Song), composed by Ujō Noguchi (lyrics) and Shinpei Nakayama (music), the sheet music of which was originally published in 1923.

These successful 'new folksongs' were noteworthy through their pentatonicism in addition to the vocal delivery based upon the Western classical tradition and its piano accompaniment. "Debune-no Minato" was basically written in a Japanese traditional scale known as the folksong scale, though with the addition of the fourth passing note. This folksong scale can be described, in comparison with tonal scales for convenience's sake, as a scale with the second and sixth notes extracted from the minor scale. "Habu-no Minato" was in another pentatonic scale with the fourth and seventh notes extracted from the minor scale, while "Hoko-o Osamete" was basically in a scale with the fourth and seventh notes extracted from the major scale.

The appropriation of Western musical forms was, in fact, nothing new for Nakayama who was already a well-regarded composer with a series of songs, the tunes of which were distinguished by his use of pentatonicism. His breakthrough success was with "Fukkatsu Shōka" (Resurrection Song) (later known as "Katyūsha-no Uta" (Katyusha's Song)), which was sung by Sumako Matsui in the successful play, *Fukkatsu* (Resurrection), an adoption of Tolstoi's novel with the same title. The tune was composed upon the suggestion of Hōgetsu Shimamura, the song's lyricist and the leader of Geijutsuza (Art Company), one of the troupes in the theatrical new wave that became active under the influence of European drama in the late 1900s. Shimamura had envisaged the song to be a self-conscious mix between Eastern and Western forms, suggesting that they aimed 'at a hybrid between a Japanese indigenous ditty and a Western *lied*', according to Nakayama in a newspaper interview in 1935 (Nishizawa 1990a: 3003–4). Recorded in 1914 by Orient Records in Kyoto, the song became very popular and was later estimated to have sold 20,000 copies (Yamaguchi [1940] 1972: 186), although the actual figure could have been 2,000 considering the limited diffusion of the phonograph at the time. That the core of the audience was students, who must have acquainted with the song orally, was apparent from various contemporary newspaper quotes such as, 'Students are singing this song enthusiastically. Those who are not singing aloud are singing under their breath' (Kurata 1979: 173). These students were obviously attracted in the beginning by the new age suggested by the name of the play's original publication and Tolstoi's latest novel, which had been translated into Japanese in 1905, six years after its original publication. Behind this intellectual thirst was a certain zeitgeist, which later became known as the Taishō Democracy (the Taishō era began in 1912 and lasted until 1926).

Sumako Matsui's unaccompanied delivery of the song sounds astonishingly amateurish to our ears, but its plaintive qualities along with its innovative use of an anhemitonic pentatonic scale, known as *yonanuki* at the time, had a broad appeal (Mitsui 2002: 743). (In the original composition, a semitone appears in the middle as a passing note.) Though the scale itself with the fourth and seventh notes extracted from the major scale was universal elsewhere, it sounded modern to a Japanese audience. The success of "Katyūsha-no Uta" is exemplified in the comment by Keizō Horiuchi, a prominent figure in the modern history of music in Japan: 'the innovative lyrics and melody marked a new epoch in the history of popular songs favoured by different social classes' (Horiuchi and Machida 1931: 246). This success led to Nakayama subsequently employing the scale again to great success in his later song "Gondola-no Uta" (Gondola Song). The song was composed in 1915 for another play, *Sono Zen'ya* (The Night Before), adapted from one of Turgenev's novels, and would go on to become popular in the early 1920s, despite the play being a flop (Komota et al. 1970: 37).

It was another pentatonic scale, however, this time with the fourth and seventh extracted from the minor scale, that was to prove the most successful with the Japanese public, perhaps because of its connotations of distress that fit with the sorrow-stricken lyrics. Nakayama made use of this uniquely Japanese pentatonicism when he composed "Kare Susuki" (Withered Silver Grass). This scale was not unfamiliar to the general public as it had been used in a popular brass-band melody, "Utsukushiki Ten'nen", also known as "Ten'nen-no Bi" (Natural Beauty), composed by Hozumi Tanaka, a naval band master, around 1900 (Horiuchi and Machida 1931: 220), although the tune was characterized by its waltz time and the closing phrase, which rather abruptly modulates to a traditional scale, *miyako-bushi*. The tune became essential as an instrumental in the repertoire of street brass bands known as *jinta* (Horiuchi 1935: 147). However, it is unknown how conscious Nakayama was of this minor pentatonic scale combined with waltz rhythm, which didn't exist in Japan at the time. Published in 1919, "Kare Susuki" became popular in subsequent years, understandably due to the success of the scale underscoring its gloomy lyrics (by Ujō Noguchi), in contrast to the slowly bouncing waltz time of "Ten'nen-no Bi" (Natural Beauty), and went on to be recorded by several record companies. It was so popular that in 1923 it was made into a movie, *Sendō Ko-uta* (Boatman's Ditty) (Komota et al. 1970: 41), which then became the alternative title of "Kare Susuki". After this success, it became common practice for the Japanese film industry to make film versions of hit songs; as is exemplified by the popularity of "Kago-no Tori" (Caged Bird) composed in 1924 by Shun'yō Tottori in the same scale and dramatized by at least two film companies (Komota et al. 1970: 42). The new pentatonic scale's popularity clearly prompted Nakayama to use it for "Habu-no Minato". Indeed, "Kare Susuki" is now generally recognized as the very foundation stone of the later genre, *enka* or hardcore *kayōkyoku* (domestic popular song).

Japanese versions of "Sing Me a Song of Araby" and "My Blue Heaven"

While the success of 'new folksongs' recorded by Nippon Victor can be connected to new nationalism and sentimentalism expressed in their lyrics and implied within the musical features, other strains can be detected within the nascent Japanese recording industry that appropriated Western musical forms in alternative ways. Perhaps most significantly, Nicchiku scored hits in May 1928 with two songs recorded with an orchestral accompaniment and released as the A and B sides of the same disc (Nipponophone 16855). Both the A side, "Aozora", a Japanese version of "My Blue Heaven", and the B side, "Arabia-no Uta", a Japanese version of "Sing Me a Song of Araby", had equal and lasting popularity. Both were so popular that they were soon covered in the same year by Nippon Victor, although the vocalist featured was the same one.

The fact that these two songs were the Japanese versions of Tin Pan Alley songs and performed by small jazz orchestras featuring vocals must have caused these recordings to be understood historically as being the first well-received jazz (or even American popular music) records in Japan, as demonstrated by two LP reissues in 1976, *Nippon-no Jazz Song* (Jazz songs in Japan) and *Nippon-no Jazz-Popular-shi* (History of jazz & popular music in Japan), but they deserve to be re-contextualized within a wider context. Writings on the history of Japanese popular songs tend to disregard the significance of songs of foreign origin in pre-war Japan, which are often discussed as 'jazz songs' separately from domestic songs or simply excluded because they were from abroad (e.g. Nippon Victor 1967, Zakō 1983, Ikeda 1985, etc; even Kurata 1979: 334). However, it is unlikely that the public were aware of "Arabia-no Uta" (Sing Me a Song of Araby) and "Aozora" (My Blue Heaven) as the Japanese versions of American songs. Even the writer of the liner notes to the LP reissues mentioned above asserts that 'No other songs perhaps surpass "Aozora" and "Arabia-no Uta" in pre-war and post-war Japan in that they were widely sung by people of all ages and both sexes as if they were Japanese songs' (Segawa 1976b: 35).

Even to me, the flexibly translated words that correspond to the first four bars of the middle eight or bridge – 'You'll see a smiling face, a fireplace, a cosy room' – of the former and those that correspond to the opening eight bars of the tune of the latter – 'When the sun sets in the desert land / Sing me a song of Araby' – used to sound much more familiar than the 'new folksongs', having been combined with the haunting melodies and the carefree, innocent-sounding delivery by a tenor, Teiichi Futamura (1900–48), who had also been trained in Asakusa Opera. I never saw the discs simply because it was by no means unusual for an ordinary family not to own a phonograph, but the songs have lingered in my memory since I was young, obviously because of their exposure on the radio. When you turned on the radio, which was in common household use in this post-war period mostly devoid of amusement, what one heard was invariably the national broadcasting company NHK, which was the only available station until the appearance of commercial broadcasting in 1951; and Radio 1 was understandably much more popular than the education channel, Radio 2. Though the radio playlists from those days are not available, one may well conjecture that the well-liked records in the past years, particularly those electrically produced since 1928, often went on the air when the number of post-war new products was comparatively limited. It should also be noted that the number of the well-liked records itself was limited because patriotic and martial songs, which had dictated the record market during the Pacific War, all disappeared from the radio waves of the defeated nation.

The lyrics of both "Sing Me a Song of Araby" and "My Blue Heaven" were translated by Keizō Horiuchi (1897–1983) from the original English language versions. Unusually for a Japanese person of that time, Horiuchi had spent time studying in the US where he received a Bachelor of Science from the Michigan Institute of Technology in 1921, a Master of Science in Mechanical Engineering from the Massachusetts Institute of Technology in June 1923 (Horiuchi 1992: 44), and also studied musical composition during this period. In his early twenties, he already had a developed interest in American music and in 1920 had published an article on ragtime, with many music illustrations, in a Japanese periodical of music (Horiuchi 1920). The piano arrangements and the lyrics of both translated songs can be found in the 19th volume of a now-forgotten colossal collection of world music, *Sekai Ongaku Zenshū*, subtitled in German, *Gesammel Tewerke der Welt Musik*. Consisting of more than eighty volumes, the collection was published between 1929 and 1936, and, while dominated by Western classical forms, covered a wide range of music. Invaluable for historians of Japanese popular music, the collection includes an independent volume of *ryūkōka*, or Japanese popular songs, titled *Meiji, Taishō, Shōwa Ryūkōka-kyokushū* (Popular songs in the Meiji, Taishō and Shōwa eras). Published in 1931, a time when both songs continued to enjoy widespread popularity amongst the Japanese public, the volume was compiled by Keizō Horiuchi himself and Kashō Machida, a pioneering field collector of Japanese folksongs. The selected 152 songs comprised of 100 songs from the Meiji era (1868–1912), thirty-eight from the Taishō era (1912–26) and fourteen from the Shōwa era. The Shōwa era had just begun in late December of 1926 and these fourteen songs became popular in 1927–29 (Horiuchi and Machida 1931).[3]

According to Horiuchi's annotation to "Arabia-no Uta", he translated the lyrics on 18 February 1928 and had the song sung by Teiichi Futamura, who had been active in the field of Asakusa Opera, and by a female vocalist, Kikuyo Amano, with the accompaniment of the JOAK Jazz Band. The song was broadcast alongside "Aozora", the lyrics of which Horiuchi also translated, at JOAK (the predecessor of the NHK) five days later (Horiuchi and Machida 1931: 256). In fact, the translation of the songs was made specifically for the purpose of broadcast as Horiuchi had begun working for JOAK in October 1926, a year and a half after its formation, as one of two employees in charge of music (Horiuchi 1935: 78). His experience in listening to music on American radio in the early 1920s as well as observing how music was orchestrated and arranged for silent-film theatres and vaudevilles in Boston was highly influential upon his work at the station (Horiuchi 1992: 53). The JOAK Jazz Band consisted of members recruited by Horiuchi from the New Symphony Orchestra, whom he regarded as 'not so good' in terms of feel but were employed because of their musical literacy (Horiuchi 1935: 78–9). The band often played jazz using the orchestral scores Horiuchi regularly imported from San Francisco (Horiuchi 1992: 53). Eventually, Horiuchi felt it necessary to feature vocals in emulation of 'the practice of overseas bands' (Horiuchi 1935: 79). "Aozora" and "Arabia-no Uta" were not, however, Horiuchi's first endeavour into adapting Western material. He had already translated and published the lyrics of "Tell Me" in 1919, in Ann Arbor, Michigan, and "Caravan", earlier in his time at JOAK in 1927. However, these previous attempts had attracted only limited attention (Horiuchi and Machida 1931: 256) and were broadcast on a very limited number of occasions (Horiuchi 1992: 68). The fact that JOAK principally broadcast instrumental performances is substantiated by a recollection that 'there were often performances of "jazz with a vocal solo" in the JOAK afternoon programmes in those days' (Ōkawa 1972: 71–2).

In contrast, "Aozora" and "Arabia-no Uta" became extremely popular with the radio audience and, less than a month after they were first broadcast, Nicchiku had both Futamura and Amano record versions of their respective numbers for release on the Nipponophone label[4] with the catalogue number 16855 ("Caravan"/"Tell Me", an instrumental record, preceded it with the number 15380). (Futamura and Amano recorded two other songs on the same date, but no further information on this is available.) This time, orchestral accompaniment was by the Red & Blue Club Orchestra, a jazz ensemble consisting of students from Keiō University (Uchida 1976: 60), an institution known for educating the sons of wealthy families. Both recordings were released two months later with "Aozora" as the lead song and "Arabia-no Uta" on the B side. It was "Arabia-no Uta", however, that seems to have proven the most popular. Horiuchi comments that the song 'enjoyed unprecedented sales' (Horiuchi and Machida 1931: 256) without putting a marked emphasis on the popularity of "Aozora", and, additionally, he placed "Aozora" after "Arabia-no Uta" in the 19th volume of the world-music collection mentioned above (Horiuchi and Machida 1931).

Having achieved fame, Futamura recorded a few songs with other bands in July and September, and Amano recorded a few in April and more than a dozen in December (Nippon Columbia 1976: 40). Meanwhile, in response to the popularity of this Nicchiku record, Nippon Victor made their own recordings of the songs, this time swapping the billing of the song so that "Arabia-no Uta" was now on the A side. Released in October 1928, this Victor version (50460) also sold well. Both songs were sung by Futamura, who had recorded both the JOAK and Nicchiku versions of "Arabia-no Uta" and "Aozora". It is somewhat unclear how it was possible for Victor to employ the same singer who had recorded for Nicchiku, but it would suggest that contractual working practices in the Japanese recording industry were at a nascent stage. However, it should be noted that the names of Futamura and Amano are absent on the label of the Nicchiku disc while Futamura's full name was clearly given on the label of the Victor disc followed by the Victor Jazz Band. In contrast, the Nipponophone label of the Nicchiku disc featured the name, the Red Blue [sic] Club Orchestra, with the vocals credited as *danjo gasshō* (mixed chorus). The Victor Jazz Band was conducted by Ichirō Ida (1894–1972), a pioneering and prominent violin and banjo jazz player, arranger and conductor who had moved to Tokyo in the spring of 1928 from Kobe, a cosmopolitan seaport city where imported music flourished. Perhaps significantly, he had already performed both "Arabia-no Uta" and "Aozora" with Futamura on stage, enjoying a favourable reception, around the time when Futamura recorded them with the Red & Blue Club Orchestra. It was 'in April that the Cherryland Jazz Band led by Ichirō Ida, consisting of young proficient jazzmen came up to Tokyo and astounded the Tokyo jazz audience with the performance of genuine jazz at Mitsukoshi Hall, and then drew great crowds since next month at Asakusa Denkikan' (Segawa 1976a: 30). Interestingly, in the newspaper advertisement for their appearance at Asakusa Denkikan, the song title "Sing Me a Song of Araby", in *katakana* characters, is spelt out instead of "Arabia-no Uta", along with the names of Ichirō Ida and Teiichi Futamura in large Gothic letters (Uchida 1976: 39).

In response to the release and subsequent success of the Victor recordings of the songs, Nippon Columbia, a subsidiary of Nicchiku reissued their Nipponophone recordings on the Columbia label (25303) in November 1928, this time giving vocal credits to Futamura and Amano. (In this month, Nippon Columbia began to release many domestically produced records.) The instrumental credits were also changed, nominally, with the Columbia Jazz Band replacing the Red & Blue Club Orchestra. Although it is unclear how much each recording sold individually during this time, Horiuchi later estimated that their combined sales were more than 200,000 copies (Horiuchi [1942] 1948: 238). Even if this was an exaggeration, a newspaper article from 1929 gives an idea about the reputation of the success of the two records: 'Just about a year ago, selling 3,000 copies [was] considered as good, and selling as much as 5,000 excellent [...] However, in less than a year the record industry grew astonishingly, and now the sales figure of a record should be 5,000 for it to be considered a success' (*Tokyo Asahi*, 13 December 1929, quoted in Kurata 1979: 333).

The mass mediation of orchestral sound

The 1931 score for "Arabia-no Uta" in the 19th volume of the world-music collection consists of the vocal melody and its piano accompaniment, credited in Japanese spelling to Fred Fisher under 'Translated by Keizō Horiuchi', along with translated lyrics by Horiuchi. Fisher (1875–1942) was a prolific composer between 1904 and 1940 (Kinkle 1974: v. 2, 911–2), whose most famous songs included "Dardanella" (1919), performed by Ben Selvin & His Orchestra in the US (Whitburn 1986: 379), which sold more than five million copies. However, "Sing Me a Song of Araby" was, and remains, completely obscure in the US. In fact, as far as I know, no reference books or history books mention any recording of the song or the title itself, and there is no trace of the original sheet music in the collection at the Library of Congress or the Center for Popular Music at Middle Tennessee State University.[5] The original lyrics are, however, shown in Horiuchi's annotation to this song (Horiuchi and Machida 1931: 256). Comparing both the Nicchiku version and the Victor version with the piano score published in Japan in 1931, one finds that both performances were quite faithfully based upon the written piano accompaniment, particular the sixteen-bar introduction, and both versions were played in F major as is designated there.[6] Whether this accompaniment could actually be attributed to Fred Fisher himself is uncertain because of the unavailability of the original sheet music or orchestral score for comparison, but, as the discussion below illustrates, the accompaniment must have essentially been written by Fisher.

The sixteen bars at the beginning, plainly longish to be the introduction, were originally intended to be the 'verse' part of the song. As Horiuchi explained: 'The original song consisted of two parts, verse and chorus, but I translated only the chorus part' (Horiuchi and Machida 1931: 256). He then had the vocalist/s sing the song's main part consisting of thirty-two bars in AABA form. Judging by the exclusive dominance of shorter tunes in the rest of this volume of Japanese popular songs edited by Horiuchi and Machida, thirty-two-bar songs must have sounded long to the contemporary audience with the exception of "Ten'nen-no Bi" (Natural Beauty) in thirty-two-bar ABCD form. The simple lyrics were literally translated in order to conform to Japanese scansion. They originally read:

> When the sun sets in the desert land / Sing me a song of Araby
> Say the words that I can't understand / Sing me a song of Araby
> Play that refrain on the harp of my heart / Vex me again with your sweet Hindu art
> Kiss me, love, and just before we part / Sing me a song of Araby

More than a dozen years later, Horiuchi recollected that a major part of the song's appeal was the fantasy and exoticism expressed in lines such as 'When the sun sets in the desert land' (Horiuchi [1942] 1948: 238). According to an account by his daughter, Horiuchi was also clearly aware that this imagery could be directly traced back to the popularity of a children's song composed several years before in 1923, called "Tsuki-no Sabaku" (Moonlit Desert), which also evoked a romanticized Arabic world (Yasui 2002: 5).

In both released versions, these relatively short and simple lyrics were effectively repeated to make them memorable to the audience, along with the straightforward delivery by Futamura. In the Nicchiku version, after the sixteen-bar introduction, Futamura runs through the lyrics before a repetition of the introductory sixteen bars. This is followed by Futamura repeating the lyrics accompanied in unison by the female vocalist, Amano, before the eight-bar break consisting of a different melody followed by a repeat of the main thirty-two-bar tune without vocals. The Victor recording lasted for 2 minutes and 35 seconds, a little shorter than the Nicchiku recording, the length of which was 2 minutes and 48 seconds. This introductory section consists of two parts, the first of which is a melody of twelve bars, not found in the piano score published in 1931, while the second part closely follows the piano score. The sixteen-bar instrumental break after Futamura's singing is also based upon the score, but the second chorus is followed without a break by an instrumental repetition of the chorus by the band.

The significance of the long instrumental introduction and the long break in both versions of the song is their contribution to exposing Japan's listening public to orchestral music in hit-record form for the first time. The sound of both versions of "Arabia-no Uta" and "Aozora" would suggest that both bands consisted of around ten members playing brass and woodwind and two or three stringed instruments. Indeed, according to Shigeya Kikuchi, the pianist and leader of the Red & Blue Club Orchestra, there were, in addition to himself, two saxophonists, two trumpeters, one banjo player, one drummer, one tuba player and one violinist (Uchida 1976: 61). There had been opportunities in Japan to hear orchestras in movie theatres where smaller ensembles performed during the showing of silent films and at intervals. Since 1910, 'orchestras were used in movie theatres to play music as something indispensable to the silence that is the fundamental defect of the silent film' (Horiuchi [1942] 1948: 149), and they were 'effective in making the public familiarized with the sound of orchestra, though they were often small in size, unskilled and played low-grade tunes' (ibid.: 248). However, such performances were limited to a small number of listeners because they were live. Similarly, the orchestral sound could be heard by a large but limited audience from the 1910s at Asakusa Opera with its orchestral performances and *bel canto* singing, and from around 1919 by bands performing in a very limited number of Western dance bands: 'The oldest social dancing may have been at Kagetsuen in Tsurumi' (Horiuchi [1942] 1948: 223).

Now, through the phonograph record, orchestral music could be heard by a mass audience. The first Japanese release of a song with an orchestral accompaniment was a 1925 recording of "Kare Susuki" (Withered Silver Grass) sung by a female vocalist, Aiko Sagara, with the Nipponophone Orchestra on the Nipponophone label; although its sales were seemingly limited. It was followed by more records performed by the Hatano Orchestra, and then the Nipponophone Orchestra on the Nipponophone label; while there were certainly imported discs with the orchestral sound, no positive reference is made on the sales of them in books on popular music in Japan. In late March 1928, when the disc "Aozora"/"Arabia-no Uta" was released, "Mon Paris" sung by the Takarazuka Revue singers was released by Nicchiku Orient in Kyoto, but 'no information has yet been found on its success' (Kurata 1979: 329).[7] It was then this electrically recorded disc, "Aozora"/"Arabia-no Uta", took orchestral music to a truly mass Japanese audience in a variety of different contexts.

This new mass-mediated listening experience was clearly accelerated by the development of a national radio network and the large-scale diffusion of radio sets. In March 1925, two years before the formation of three major recording companies, JOAK conducted a test broadcasting from Tokyo followed by stations in Osaka and Nagoya respectively, three stations that were integrated as NHK in 1927 (*Taishū Bunka* 1991: 828). The following year, this basis was expanded into a nationwide radio network. It took a couple of years before *ryūkōka* records began to be broadcast regularly and they were referred to as *kayōkyoku*, a term coined by NHK to avoid the vulgar connotation of *ryūkōka*, which was called *hayari-uta* in the Meiji and Taishō eras. It was in 1932 that JOAK began playing *ryūkōka* or *kayōkyoku* records on the air, three years after the appearance of the much-criticized but very popular "Tokyo Kōshinkyoku" (Tokyo March), which is discussed below. However, it was primarily through the radio that "Arabia-no Uta" and "Aozora" became popular. The popularity of broadcasting can be inferred from the rapid increase in the number of receiving sets: in just one year after JOAK began broadcasting, ownership rose from 5,455 to 338,204 sets (Kawabata 1990: 26). Although the record industry initially feared the competition from this new entertainment medium, the two industries eventually proved to be mutually beneficial.

Western pentatonicism

While the fact that the orchestration of the music of "Arabia-no Uta" is based on tonality, it should be pointed out that the repeated A of the structure AABA, each part of which consists of eight bars, was in a pentatonic major. As we have seen, this scale with the fourth and seventh notes extracted from the major scale had been popular since the mid-1910s, particularly through

Shinpei Nakayama's songs "Katyūsha-no Uta" (Katyusha's Song) and "Godola-no Uta" (Gondola Song), although some melodic features, particularly the rise of an octave in the fifth bar, must have sounded untypical to the contemporary audience. However, in part B (the middle eight or bridge), the tune dramatically modulates from F major into F minor, effectively underlining the words (originally, 'Play that refrain on the harp of my heart / Vex me again with your sweet Hindu art'). This chromatic drift, which would have clearly sounded novel to a contemporary Japanese audience, was followed by one more pentatonic A in the closing eight bars, thus giving a sense of relief and resolution to the listeners. At the same time, the orchestral accompaniment to the pentatonic parts must have sounded unusual to them with its tonal harmony, using the notes that are not in this pentatonic scale.

It is significant that the whole musical structure of "Aozora" is quite similar to "Arabia-no Uta". The main difference is that the introductory part of "Aozora" is much shorter than that of "Arabia-no Uta", which consists of only four bars. In the annotation to "Aozora", Horiuchi remarks with reference to the initial broadcast of the song in February 1928 that 'the original consisted of both the verse and chorus, but I only used the chorus because I translated the song with the intention that it be broadcast as part of a performance by a jazz band' (Horiuchi and Machida 1931: 256). The length of the song in this initial radio broadcast is unknown but when the song was recorded in March the whole verse part was omitted, probably so that the song would fit in the time limitations of a side of a 78 rpm single.

The musical structure is AABA in E flat major and, as with "Arabia-no Uta", part A is characterized by its pentatonicism. Part B is not chromatic but repeatedly uses the fourth and seventh notes. The freely translated lyrics that correspond to the thirty-two bars of the AABA structure are similarly simple and its catchiness is emphasized by being repeated. They originally read:

> When whippoorwills call and evening is nigh / I hurry to my blue heaven
> A turn to the right, a little white light / Will lead you to my blue heaven
> You'll see a smiling face, a fireplace, a cosy room / A little nest that's nestled where the roses bloom
> Just Mollie and me and baby makes three / We're happy in my blue heaven

The words that go with the first part of the middle eight (a free translation of 'You'll see a smiling face, a fireplace, a cosy room') were cited by Horiuchi himself later when he surmised that the lower-middle class sentiment typified in this phrase was perhaps a major part of the song's appeal, a flipside to the themes of escapism and fantasy in "Arabia-no Uta" (Horiuchi [1942] 1948: 238). In the Nicchiku recording, Futamura and Amano alternatively sing in unison and solo. All three A parts of the AABA structure are sung in unison, and part B is sung solo by Amano followed by a repeat of the AABA (after a middle eight) in which part B is sung solo by Futamura. For the Victor recording, Futamura sings solo for the entire song. The break in both recordings was orchestrated around a different tune, which consisted of twenty bars, namely, five four-bar phrases, and the repeated AABA chorus was followed by another break with another different melody with the length of eight bars. Then, in the Nicchiku recording, Futamura and Amano repeat the whole AABA chorus throughout in unison, whereas in the Victor recording, which was 2 minutes and 32-second long in contrast to the 3 minutes of the Nicchiku recording, the whole AABA chorus was completely instrumental as if Ichirō Ida and his band had boasted of their competence.

In total contrast to the obscurity of "Sing Me a Song of Araby", "My Blue Heaven" was a huge hit back in the US. Written by Walter Donaldson with lyrics by George Whiting, the song was recorded by Gene Austin and released by Victor in late November 1927. The record (20964) entered the chart on 3 December, staying there for twenty-six weeks with thirteen weeks in the top position, and selling over three million copies (Whitburn 1986: 39). In the 1931 annotation to the published version of "Aozora", Horiuchi comments that the 'song was released in 1927 and was extremely popular', but without any reference to Gene Austin (Horiuchi and Machida 1931: 256). It is unclear whether Horiuchi had really heard the record or if it was even available as an import in Japan at the time. The statement – 'The time when I translated the song was possibly in the spring of 1928, sometime after its *fu* (score) had arrived' (ibid.: 256) – seems to imply that he had heard about the popularity of the song and ordered the *fu*, which can be considered to mean either the orchestrated score or sheet music. To complicate the situation further, the music published in 1931 with Horiuchi's annotation (ibid.: 169–70) is largely different from the US arrangement (Donaldson and Whiting 1927), though Donaldson is credited as the composer. While in the original 1927 sheet music the tempo is leisurely, the music published in Japan in 1931 directs that the song is to be performed faster and livelier with distinctly clear beats by the piano. Gene Austin, whose month and year of birth happens to be the same as Futamura (June 1900, incidentally, two months after the birth of the Emperor Shōwa), sings both the verse and chorus softly in a much slower tempo accompanied only by the combination of a cello and a piano, in one of the first 'crooning' styles facilitated by the development of the microphone. In contrast to this arrangement, the Japanese versions by Nicchiku and Nippon Victor closely resemble the piano arrangement published in the 19th volume of the world-music collection.

While Gene Austin's recording had never been released in Japan, the matter is further complicated by the release of an instrumental dance-music version of the song by Don Voorhees & His Orchestra by Nicchiku on the Columbia label in January 1928 (J-356, the B side of which was "Soliloquy"), two months before the release of "Aozora". This was followed by the release of similar dance-music versions of the song by Paul Whiteman & His Orchestra and the Victor Salon Group respectively in May, and Jesse Crawford later in the year in Japan. In addition, it should be noted that all these dance-music versions had originally been released in the US before Gene Austin's hit version was out: Don Voorhee's version on 9 September 1927, Paul Whiteman's version and Victor Salon Group's version on 14 November 1927 coupled with "All by My Ownsome" by Roger Wolfe Kahn & His Orchestra (as 20828), and Jesse Crawford's version (with Wurlitzer Organ solo) on 1 November 1927 (for release dates both in the US and Japan, see Yamada 2002). It can be argued that Horiuchi was prompted to order the score of "My Blue Heaven" by its popularity through those dance-band versions. While there is a possibility that "Arabia-no Uta" was an arrangement of Fisher's original composition (that is, tune and piano accompaniment) by Horiuchi, it is more probable that the piano scores of both songs were adapted by Horiuchi from an orchestrated score. As Horiuchi's son recollected: 'as to popular tunes', his father who worked for JOAK 'had some ten jazz-orchestrated scores of them imported every month from Sherman Cray Musical Instruments in San Francisco through Yamano Musical Instruments' and 'his translations of such songs as "Arabia-no Uta" and "Aozora" were based on those scores' (Horiuchi 1992: 53).[8]

Whatever the case, "Arabia-no Uta", a Japanese version of an utterly obscure song of American origin, and "Aozora", a buoyant Japanese version of an American hit song, were both so popular that they gave birth to film versions respectively in early 1929 (Kurata 1979: 334). Both songs were also repeatedly covered by other artists and labels in later years, as evidenced by the many examples listed in a massive, though incomplete, list, compiled by Shōwakan, a Tokyo museum, of 78 rpm records released in Japan (Shōwakan 2002). They included a version of "Aozora" which was sung by Fumiko Kawabata, a female Japanese-American singer and dancer who worked in both Japan and the US, which was arranged by Ryōzō Sugita in the fashion of Gene Austin's version. Six months after its release, in June 1933, she also covered "Arabia-no Uta". In both recordings, she sang in both Japanese and English, and the English lyrics were printed in the booklet for the CD reissue collection of her records titled *Aozora* (Nippon Columbia 1976).

Songs newly produced with an eye to commercial success

The commercial achievements of those two recorded songs was highly significant in that they must have prompted the Japanese recording industry into commissioning and recording original material as a major part of their business strategies. Victor's months of groping for this bore fruit when they released another Teiichi Futamura recording with an orchestral accompaniment again by the Victor Jazz Band and again led by Ichirō Ida, using a newly composed domestic song. Released in January 1929 as the B side of 50559, "Kimi Koishi" (Yearning for You) went on to sell 200,000 copies (Kurata 1979: 33–5). The lyrics were written by Shigure Otowa, a staff songwriter of Victor and the lyricist of "Debune-no Minato" (Sea Port). He was commissioned by them to write a *ryūkōka* in a new style. However, the tune of "Kimi Koishi" had already been written seven years before by Kōka Sassa, when he was working as an Asakusa Opera composer and director (Horiuchi and Machida 1931: 180), contrary to the statement in a book on the history of Nippon Victor that 'Victor commissioned Kōka Sassa to write the music' (Nippon Victor 1967: 41) and the assertion, in a book on Japanese popular songs on discs before 1945, that Kōka Sassa set Shigure Otowa's lyrics to music (Morimoto 1975: 27). Horiuchi commented about two years after the release of "Kimi Koishi" that 'as Kōka Sassa was well versed in overseas music as one of the leading figures in Asakusa Opera while he was conversant with Japanese music, this tune was characterized by recording the melodic pattern of foreign tunes with Japanese scales' and was a new departure because 'as a whole it sounded like an Oriental dance music in the West'. He then concluded that 'although the tune was composed many years before, it was combined with new lyrics by Shigure Otowa and Victor recorded the song successfully; this is a prominent *ryūkōka* in the early Shōwa era' (Horiuchi and Machida 1931: 258).

Indeed, it is true that the lyrics were new, but Horiuchi says that 'I understand that the song was released by Nicchiku before the Great Earthquake with different lyrics' (Horiuchi [1942] 1948: 238), and the song composed 'many years before with different lyrics' was also titled "Kimi Koichi". Actually, there was a record released in 1926 with the title "Kimi Koishi" and with lyrics possibly composed by the music composer Kōka Sassa himself, which repeat the phrase 'kimi koishi' in each stanza as in the new "Kimi Koishi" at the beginning of the bridge of the tune, one of the records released in the reconstruction period after the Great Earthquake (Kurata 1979: 330). Ruby Takai (b. 1904) (Morimoto 1997: 83), who had been trained in Asakusa Opera and sang the older "Kimi Koishi" sonorously accompanied by the Nipponophone Orchestra on the record (the B side of which was "Kare Kare" (Withered and Blasted)), had already recorded at the time many songs, including "Chameko-no Ichinichi" (One Day by Chameko) and songs composed by Kōka Sassa (Shōwakan 2002). (See Hosokawa 1992b for musical analysis of both versions of "Kimi Koishi".)

The tune of the remade "Kimi Koishi", the immense popularity of which prompted five movie companies to compete for its cinematization, sounded innovative in the full Western minor scale with an AABA structure consisting of thirty-two bars, which had been established in Tin Pan Alley only a few years before (Hamm 1979: 360). It might be argued that the two songs in the same structure, "Arabia-no Uta" and "Aozora", musically reinforced the acceptance of "Kimi Koishi" by the public. Moreover, the melody of "Kimi Koishi" resembles "Aozora" in its contour, beginning at the second beat of the bar preceding the first bar, instead of at the fourth beat, and this first bar of the eight-bar phrase consists of one whole note covering the whole bar. This contour is common to the following four phrases with different pitches. The accompaniment to Futamura's straightforward delivery was arranged and conducted by Ichirō Ida, the leader of the Victor Jazz Band, and the performance is characterized by its rhythmical swing with the syncopating ensemble of the violin and brass instruments backed by a rhythm section accentuating back beats. (In October, Victor had Chiyako Satō cover "Kimi Koishi" as the B side of "Kuroyuri-no Hana" (Black Lily), written by the same writers and sung by the same singer, which turned out to be unsuccessful.)

"Kimi Koishi" was succeeded by many songs, which were later classified as *ryūkōka*, released not only by Victor and Nicchiku, but by Orient, Nittō and Hikōki (Fukuda and Katō 1994: 2–18). However, it took four months for another huge hit to appear. "Kimi Koishi" was outsold by the record "Tokyo Kōshinkyoku" (Tokyo March), released in May 1929, both the tune and lyrics of which were newly composed specifically for recording. It was released by Victor as 50755A and went on to sell 250,000 copies (Morimoto 1975: 29). The music was composed by Shinpei Nakayama, who again used the minor pentatonic scale that he had initially employed to great success in "Kare Susuki" (Withered Silver Grass) (known also as "Sendō Ko-uta"). The lyrics gave a vivid and succinct description of modern Tokyo strewn with new-fangled words such as: 'jazz', 'liquor', 'dancer', 'rush-hour', 'cinema', 'depart' (department store), all pronounced in English and phonetically spelled in *katakana*; 'chikatetsu' (underground or subway) and 'bus', the names of new public transportation systems; 'Odakyū', the abridgement of the name of a private electric-railroad company. The lyrics were written by Yaso Saijō, an ex-professor of French literature at Waseda University, who became a professional lyricist of *ryūkōka*. Prior to this song, Nakayama teamed up with Saijō in the preceding year, producing a small hit, "Tōsei Ginza-bushi" (Up-to-date Ginza Song) (released in July 1928), but Saijō's lyrics had originally been published as a poem in a magazine titled *Kuraku* (Joy and Sorrow) (Morimoto 1975: 29). Chiyako Satō's vocal delivery tends to muffle the words of the affected lyrics and the arrangement and performance of the music in the same pentatonic scale by Ichirō Ida and his orchestra lacks in spirit.[9] However the record can be taken as a preparatory step for yielding "Tokyo Kōshinkyoku" (Tokyo March). (See Hosokawa 1992a: 116–19 for an analytical description of "Tōsei Ginza-bushi" and "Tokyo Kōshinkyoku".)

The great success of "Tokyo Kōshinkyoku", which took a large step forward from "Tōsei Ginza-bushi" (see Nishizawa 1992: 25–9 for a detailed commentary on both lyrics), served more decisively to establish this uniquely Japanese pentatonicism amongst the Japanese audience. The song's structure was simpler than the thirty-two-bar AABA structure, with sixteen bars or four phrases. However, although this structure is numerically a half of "Arabia-no Uta", "Aozora" and "Kimi Koishi", each of which consists of thirty-two bars, the length depends upon the tempo designed when the song was composed as well as on the tempo when it was actually performed. In terms of the length when sung, one verse (AABA) of Victor's "Arabia-no Uta" lasts for about 35 seconds, that of "Aozora" for about 40 seconds, and that of "Kimi Koishi" for about 42 seconds, while that of "Tokyo Kōshinkyoku" lasts for about 23 seconds, with the result that the ratio is not one to two, but approximately two to three. (In this connection, the sixteen-bar of "Debune-no Minato" sung by Yoshie Fujiwara lasts for about 25 seconds and that of "Habu-no Minato" sung by Chiyako Satō lasts for about 30 seconds.) It should also be noted that the overall melodic contour of "Tokyo Kōshinkyoku" closely resembles that of "Kare Susuki".[10]

The orchestrated sound of "Tokyo Kōshinkyoku" was again arranged and conducted by Ichirō Ida, leading the Nikkatsu Orchestra. A comment, 'jaunty jazz-like melody', by a historian of jazz in Japan (Uchida 1976: 96), must have been suggested not by the melody itself, but by the skilful arrangement, and confirms that this arrangement and performance was as jazzy as "Arabia-no Uta", "Aozora" and "Kimi Koishi". The quadruple rhythm was played upon a domestic percussion instrument, the sound of which induces the audience to describe the rhythm onomatopoeically as *woon-cha-cha, cha-at-cha, woon-char, woon-char*. Backed by this rhythm, which was derived from traditional music and soon to be standardized in succeeding *ryūkōka*, Chiyako Satō, in her early thirties, sang the song both vigorously and wistfully in the voice that was trained at a Tokyo conservatory but indelibly retained a kind of squeakiness common to Japanese women before the post-war period.

This record is also significant as it marks a tightening of the links between the film and recording industries, something that was to become a defining characteristic of the Japanese music market. Rather than the film industry responding to the success of a hit record, as had been the case with songs such as "Haubu-no Minato", "Tokyo Kōshinkyoku" was more closely linked because it was a result of a simultaneous tie-in project between a record company and a film company. "Tokyo Kōshinkyoku" was originally the title of a novel written by Kan Kikuchi, which was serialized in *King*, a popular-fiction monthly magazine. The novel was so widely accepted that the film company Nikkatsu produced its movie version while Victor concurrently released the record as its theme song (Horiuchi and Machida 1931: 258). Hence the name Nikkatsu Orchestra. However, the sales of the record were poor until the release of this film, although the record had been released a month before. Accordingly, 'the public relations men of Nikkatsu flashily advertised the movie, lavishly distributing the sheet music of this song, and it did the trick, resulting in the sudden sales of 150,000 copies of the record' (*Yomiuri Shimbun*, the Evening Edition, 30 September 1929, quoted in Kurata 1979: 333). (Using the word *kōshinkyoku* (march) in song titles had been repeated occasionally after the popularity of "Dōtonbori Kōshinkyoku", released by Nittō Records in April 1928.)

Such a tie-in clearly paved the way for the advent of 'the first Japanese perfect talkie' (the phrase used in a contemporary film-theatre leaflet, 'Hongō-za Shūhō' (Hongō-za Weekly)),[11] *Madam-to Nyōbō* (Madam and Wife) in 1931, and this began the long history of records that have been associated with films for mutual advantage. Significantly enough, the director Heinosuke Gosho featured "Aozora" in this film upon the request of Keizō Horiuchi (Seki 1976: 10). Then, in the following year, JOAK began to put the record on the air, giving in to play popular songs (Hosokawa 1992b: 121) by euphemistically calling them *kayōkyoku* instead of *ryūkōka* which connotes vulgarity.[12]

Conclusion

The present discussion has suggested that these significant recordings mark the beginning of the modern recording industry in Japan. It is a period when new *ryūkōka*, later known more as *kayōkyoku*, began to dominate the Japanese record market. Indeed, it is clearly no coincidence that, at a time when the structure of the Japanese recording industry was changing towards collaboration and joint ventures with overseas companies, musical forms characterized by positive hybridization between Japanese and Western musical attributes found a mass market amongst the record-buying public. It was in the age when there emerged an unprecedented change in people's daily musical experience through the development of sound-reproduction technology and the rapid growth of other new media forms (radio and talkies). This modernization enabled the whole nation to hear the same pieces of music, turning what was regional into something national and making relevant enterprises yield profit through a tie-in sale on a massive scale. This state of affairs having, of course, never been peculiar to Japan but common to most industrialized countries, music culture was at a turning point on a global scale through its technical mediation and industrialization.[13]

Notes

1 It is stated by Morimoto (1975: 27) that "Kimi Koishi" (Yearning for You) was a song 'Shigure Otowa was commissioned to compose as a new *ryūkōka* (popular song) suitable for Victor' upon the suggestion of Benjamin Gardener who stated that, in the US, 'newly composed songs have proved a hit with the public one after another by being released as records' (a shorter version of Morimoto's statement can be found in Uchida (1976: 80)). However, it should be pointed out that Nippon Victor was formed in September 1927 while Otowa wrote the lyrics in late 1928 to a tune that had already existed. No relevant sources are given in Morimoto (1975)

and Uchida (1976). See more about "Kimi Koishi" in the 'Songs newly produced with an eye to commercial success' section on page 65.

2   It is obviously incorrect that 'January 1927' was given as one of Fujiwara's recording dates in the US by Spottswood; it should be revised to 'January 1928'.

3   The songs arranged for the piano by Keizō Horiuchi himself, which often look too elaborate, and included in this collection, were sung and recorded by many singers at the time as a part of the sound illustration of this collection (Shōwakan 2002: 322).

4   Nipponophone was the label owned by Nippon Chikuonki Shōkai, which formed a subsidiary, Nippon Columbia, in October 1928.

5   "Sing Me a Song of Araby" might have been inspired by an English song, "I'll Sing Thee Songs of Araby", composed in 1877 by Frederick Clay and W. G. Willis, as the resemblance of both titles suggests, though they are musically different. (I thank Robert Strachan for suggesting the latter.) This song published in London, by Chappell & Co, was also popular in the US (Mattfeld 1971: 156).

6   The fact that the first CD reissue of the Nippon Columbia version (25303) is in E major, virtually impossible when played by wind instruments, can be ascribed to the improper revolution of the original 78 rpm disc (reissued by Daicel Chemical Industries in 1990 as the first track in FK-0001, one disc of a sixty-set CD titled *Nihon-no Ryūkōka-shi Taikei* (Survey of Japanese *ryūkōka*)).

7   It must be noted that these developments were taking place in a context in which, even up to 1930, Western music was sometimes understood to be physically perturbing to many Japanese people (see Mitsui 1997: 153). For instance, one theatrical director described an incident when his mother, upon hearing the recorded music of Beethoven in the early 1930s, 'turned pale, her brains got reeled and she nearly fell into a swoon' (Takechi and Tomioka 1988: 65).

8   The materials left by Keizō Horiuchi were donated to Nihon Kindai Ongaku-kan (Japanese Modern Music Museum), but the scores for "Sing Me a Song of Araby" and "My Blue Heaven" are not in the possession of the museum. Then, several years after the publication of the original version of the present chapter, a stock-arrangement score of "Sing Me a Song of Araby", which Keizō Horiuchi may have purchased in early 1928 from Sherman Cray Musical Instruments in San Francisco, became available. A copy of the part scores is owned by the National Library of Australia. Edgar Pope who studies popular music in pre-war Japan found it in early 2009 and obtained its photocopy. The score arranged by Paul Van Loan in 1927 consists of part scores for a flute, a clarinet, four saxophones, two trumpets, a trombone, a tenor banjo, a piano, a set of drums, two violins, a viola, a cello and a contrabass, and it testifies that it was the basis of the two recordings of "Arabia-no Uta" in 1928 as well as its piano arrangement in volume 19, edited by Horiuchi and Machida, of *Sekai Ongaku Zenshū*. In order to ascertain that it was the basis of

the arrangement of the two recordings, in November 2009 I compiled a full score, editing all the part scores as a full score, using Finale (see Figure 3.1). Edgar Pope also obtained, in November 2010, a photocopy of the stock-arrangement of "My Blue Heaven" by Ferde Grofé from the San Jose Public Library in California, which shows that the recording of "Aozora" in 1928 was based on it. I compiled the part scores for a violin, two trumpets, a trombone, three saxophones, a piano, a tenor banjo, a contrabass and a set of drums as a full score, using Finale again (see Figure 3.2).

Figure 3.1 The first six bars of "Sing Me a Song of Araby" composed by Fred Fisher and arranged by Paul Van Loan. Part scores are compiled as a full score by author. Courtesy of Edgar W. Pope.

Figure 3.2 The first eight bars of "My Blue Heaven" composed by Walter Donaldson and arranged by Ferde Grofé. Part scores are compiled as a full score by author. Courtesy of Edgar W. Pope.

9 Two months before the appearance of "Tōsei Ginza-bushi", "Manon Lescaut-no Uta" (Song of Manon Lescaut) written by Yaso Saijō (lyrics) and Shinpei Nakayama (music) for showing the silent film *Manon Lescaut* in Japan as its theme song became temporarily popular as well. The music uses the minor pentatonic in the fashion of Victor's 'new folksongs' with vocals by Chiyako Satō accompanied by the piano.

10 As to the fact that many of the popular songwriters in 1929 and 1930 began their career as the writers of 'new folksongs', Tomiko Kojima regretted with displeasure that 'the outcome of the new-folksong movement' was 'snatched out by *kayōkyoku* records' (Kojima 1970).

11 A collection of advertising leaflets issued by such Tokyo motion-picture houses as Dōgenzaka Cinema and Ushigome-kan in the early 1930s had been preserved by Kiyoshi Mitsui and was handed over to me, his son, in the mid-1950s.

12 *Kayōkyoku*, a redundant word with *kayō* and *kyoku*, both of which mean song, though with different overtones, was coined by Kashō Machida (1888–1981; also known as Kasei Machida), who was in charge of planning song programmes at NHK. He recollected in 1970 that, as the Ministry of Communications which supervised all the broadcasting business disliked the word *ryūkōka*, he made up as a temporary expedient 'the extremely ambiguous word, *kayōkyoku*'. 'In the course of its going on the air as the occasion needed, the word became established before one knew and even now *ryūkōka* and *kayōkyoku* are apparently dealt with as synonyms' (Machida 1970: 30).

13 In a recent book, *Tokyo Boogie-Woogie: Japan's Pop Era and Its Discontents* (Harvard University Press, 2017), Hiromu Nagahara discusses the making of "Tokyo Kōshinkyoku" (Tokyo March) from a different perspective: 'While such impressive technological and industrial developments clearly worked to commercialize and standardize what was being consumed by the audience, a close analysis of [the] making of "Tokyo March" and the controversies that followed its release reveals the ways the song was recognized by its critics and advocates alike as the broader social climate that was rife with the tensions surrounding the apparent contradictions of modernity, including the specter of an impending class-based conflict that threatened to tear Japanese society apart' (Nagahara 2017: 19).

Transformation inspired by the West (4)

Ryūkōka and *kayōkyoku*

The Great Kantō Earthquake in 1923 gave a serious blow to the Japanese economy, and the government passed a new law in the following year to levy customs duties on imported luxury goods, including phonographs and records, as part of a number of policy measures designed to promote domestic production. The rate of taxation for imported phonographs and records was 100 per cent (Horiuchi [1942] 1948: 234). Main record companies who had the marketing rights to overseas records sought to bypass this costly levy by importing masters of overseas records instead of importing the discs themselves. This manufacture of discs in Japan served to facilitate much closer cooperation between overseas companies, and the situation led to the formation of three major record companies in 1927 with the entry of overseas enterprises (Polydor, Columbia and Victor). The formation of these companies was also prompted by the use of new electric microphone recording techniques, which American manufacturers developed around 1925.

In 1927, Nippon Victor was introduced by American Victor to the idea of the production and release of new songs as a major source of income generation (Uchida 1976: 80). This model, already established in the US, was relatively novel to the Japanese record industry which had previously 'picked up and recorded songs that were widely accepted amongst the public' (Nishizawa 1990b: 7). The new idea brought about the birth of the word *ryūkōka* as an alternative to *hayari-uta*, after a brief period of the in-between word *ryūkō ko-uta*.

Ryūkōka was preceded historically by *hayari-uta* (popular song). Its spelling consists of three Chinese characters, and the first part *hayari* is the same with *ryūkō* of *ryūkōka*. *Ryūkō* is the reading of *hayari* with its

Chinese-derived pronunciation. The generic term *hayari-uta*, denoting songs that were widely accepted among the public, can be traced back to the early seventeenth century,[1] and its usage extended to the early 1930s, ranging over *enka* and *gunka*, which appeared in the late nineteenth century. The term was also used to refer to such popular songs of the 1910s and 1920s as "Fukkatsu Shōka" (Resurrection Song) (generally known as "Katyūsha-no Uta" (Katyusha Song) and "Sendō Ko-uta" (Boatman's Ditty).

The first appearance of *ryūkōka* occurred on the centre label of "Shin Ginza Kōshinkyoku" (New Ginza March) issued in 1928 by Victor. Other song classifications on centre labels in the late 1920s included 'jazz song', first used to categorize the successful songs "Aozora" (My Blue Heaven) and "Arabia-no Uta" (Sing Me a Song of Araby), sung in Japanese and accompanied by an orchestra consisting of Japanese jazz musicians, before being extended to refer to songs domestically composed in the American vein, and also *eiga ko-uta* (film songs), such as "Tokyo Kōshinkyoku" (Tokyo March).

However, regardless of the finer points of these classifications, such songs produced to make profit were all conceived as *ryūkōka*, and on the centre labels on discs this appellation soon predominated, encompassing Japanese popular songs in general. However, the word *kayōkyoku* was presently coined as an alternative word to avoid the vulgarity intellectuals considered to be inherent in *ryūkō-* (be in vogue or to be broadly favoured), and the two words began to be used interchangeably for over four decades until *kayōkyoku* began to be preferred to *ryūkōka*, which gradually sounded outmoded. From around the mid-1980s, *ryūkōka* tended to be used to refer to Japanese popular songs up to approximately 1970.

As typified by one of the first hits, "Tokyo Kōshinkyoku" (Tokyo March), released in 1929, *ryūkōka* was a hybrid of modified vernacular expressions and adapted American or Occidental idioms that mirrored social and cultural changes in Japan. The song was a verbal caricature of scenes of modern Tokyo life depicted by Yaso Saijō,[2] set to a tune in a pentatonic minor (ABCEFA), with which Shinpei Nakayama had been successful before (as mentioned above), and sung by a former Asakusa-Opera vocalist, Teiichi Futamura, with a jazz-flavoured orchestral backing.

Another eminent song, "Sake-wa Namida-ka Tameiki-ka" (Is Wine Tears or a Sigh?), released in 1931, was composed by a guitarist-composer, Masao Koga, with the intention of creating something between 'jazz song' and *dodoitsu* (a love-ditty form perfected in the mid-nineteenth century). This gloomy song in a minor hexatonic scale (ABCDEFA) was sung in a crooning voice by Ichirō Fujiyama accompanied by Western string instruments: violin, cello, guitar and ukulele. Another big hit, "Oka-o Koete" (Going over the Hill), produced by Koga and Fujiyama two months later, was in the lively pentatonic major (CDEGAC) to match the cheerful lyrics and was accompanied by a mandolin orchestra. The flip side of the record, "Watashi Konogoro Yūutsu-yo" (I'm Feeling So Down These Days), was also a success. Noriko Awaya made her debut with this song, although she was severely reproached, as Fujiyama had been, by the authorities of the music institute from which she had graduated, for singing *ryūkōka*. From this woeful song of self-abandonment, she went on to develop her career in the late 1930s (Mitsui 1992: 134–5).

Western–Japanese hybrids within *ryūkōka* continued in the new decade in three contrasting types of song. In 1933, it prompted the huge popularity of the rollicking song "Tokyo Ondo" in January. *Ondo*, originally a kind of collective folk dance and song, with indigenous rhythm emphasized by a response refrain sung in chorus, was invigorated with a new melody and lyrics in traditional style performed with Western orchestration featuring traditional drums and *shamisen*. Since this big hit, many occasional and regional *ondo* songs have been produced successfully, establishing a solid genre in Japanese popular songs. Meanwhile, the singer of "Tokyo Ondo", Katsutarō Ko-uta, was the first of many *geisha* (song-and-dance female entertainers for customers at a feast) singers to become a popular recording artist. *Geisha* singers contributed especially to *ryūkōka* by incorporating *ko-uta*, a short piece of *shamisen* song standardized in the mid-nineteenth century.[3] On recordings, new *ko-uta* was performed with an orchestral accompaniment, but the arrangement retained the traditional elements, which were complemented by a typical murmur-like vocalizing in which *geisha* were trained, along with their own *shamisen* accompaniment.

Then, in early 1934, there emerged a new song type featuring lyrics about legendary wandering gamblers before the Meiji era, which was triggered by "Akagi-no Komori-uta" (Lullaby of Akagi), the theme song of a film based on a story of a gambler who died in 1850. The combination of the clear, modulated voice of Tarō Shōji trained in a Western vocal-music course, the now-established pentatonic-minor scale and Japanized orchestration with heroic tales of legendary figures was successfully repeated in the 1930s and the early 1940s, reflecting the rise of ultra-nationalism. Record companies were urged to give more priority to the morale-raising policy, and numerous martial and jingoistic songs were produced (Mitsui 2005a: 138). As has been conjectured by one historian, the appearance of these romanticized retrospective songs might well have been designed by record companies as a counter to governmental censorship of recorded songs (Nishizawa 1990b: 10).

Meanwhile, the late 1930s saw 'blues' songs launched as a new type of *ryūkōka*. They were slow-tempo songs in the harmonic minor scale with melancholy lyrics, without musical affinity with the blues proper. Their first successful period was in the late 1930s when Noriko Awaya, who debuted in 1931, became 'the queen of the blues' with such compositions as "Wakare-no Blues" (Farewell Blues, 1937), "Ame-no Blues" (Rainy Blues, 1938) and "Tokyo Blues" (1939), composed by Ryōichi Hattori, who was well-acquainted with jazz idioms. Established as one genre of *ryūkōka*, these were slow-tempo songs in minor keys with melancholic lyrics.

In 1937, following the Sino-Japanese Incident, the government ordered nationwide mobilization, which required citizens to be engaged in the war even on the home front and affected every aspect of civilian life. Thereupon, in conformity with state policy, record companies began releasing such songs as "Sen'ninbari" (Thousand-Stitch Belt) by Taneko Seki and "Jūgo-no Tsuma" (Wife on the Home Front) by Somechiyo Asakusa to raise the morale of civilians, and others like "Shingun-no Uta" (Marching Song) by the Toyama Military School Band and "Kōkoku Kesshitai" (Imperial Ready-to-die Squad) by Sō Matsubara to provide encouragement to soldiers. Thereafter, particularly after the beginning of the Pacific War in late 1941, when the government banned the music of the enemy, such songs, which partly formed the genre *gunka* as well, increased in number, and the songs in scales derived from Western tunes were regularly accompanied by the spirited performance of trumpets and drums, while non-march songs were usually accompanied by a studio orchestra. It is ironic that songs boosting national prestige were more noticeably in a Western vein, apart from the language.

Immediately after the beginning of the Pacific War, the Intelligence Division of the Cabinet and the Ministry of Home Affairs gave instructions to the public that US and British music should not be performed either live or in recorded form. Then in 1943, vexed at the general failure to follow these instructions, the Intelligence Division listed in its official weekly bulletin the catalogue numbers of all records that should not be played, asserting that they were 'a disclosure of nationalities characterized by frivolity, materialism and paying high regard to sensuality'. Arbitrarily, the songs included not only such Tin Pan Alley songs as "My Blue Heaven" and "Alexander's Ragtime Band", but also "Annie Laurie", "Home on the Range" and Stephen Foster songs (JASRAC 1990).

The new development of ryūkōka and kayōkyoku

In August 1945, Japan made an unconditional surrender and the Second World War was over. Japan was occupied immediately by the Allied Forces, which chiefly consisted of US troops.

The first post-war hit song, "Ringo-no Uta" (Song of an Apple), appeared late in 1945 as the theme song for a film, *Soyokaze* (Breeze), sung by Michiko Namiki. The song has left an indelible impression on the memory of those who lived in the post-war period. First sung on stage, broadcast live on radio, and finally recorded for Nicchiku (four months before renamed Nippon Columbia) in late December and released in January 1946, this carefree ditty about a symbolic red apple served to raise the spirits of disheartened people all over Japan. The melodious tune had an appealing gaiety despite its minor scale, and the fact that the scale was fully diatonic saved the song from possible gloominess and crassness caused by the conventional pentatonic minor.

Six months later, the fortunes of King Records were revived by a great hit, "Tokyo-no Hanauri Musume" (Flower Girl of Tokyo). Sweetly sung by Haruo Oka in medium tempo, and backed by an orchestra playing with syncopated rhythm, this depiction of a post-war street scene in Tokyo was cheerful enough to offer people a diversion. "Asawa Dokokara" (Where Does the Morning Come From?), released at the same time by Nippon Columbia, was similar in its high-spirited feel, though more cosy. The mixed duo of Aiko Anzai and Atsuo Okamoto, backed by a female chorus, contributed to the innovative and positive qualities of the performance.

While melancholic songs in the conventional pentatonic minor mode made a comeback, especially in 1947 with King Records' "Nakuna Kobato-yo" (Don't Cry, Little Dove) sung by Haruo Oka, more characteristic of the post-war period were morale-boosting songs. This tendency was underlined by a series of songs in boogie-woogie rhythm sung by a sprightly female singer, Shizuko Kasagi. Composed by Ryōichi Hattori, who had tried his hand at boogie-woogie tunes in the late 1930s before the time was ripe for them, the first of the hits to burst on the post-war scene was "Tokyo Boogie-woogie", released in December 1947 by Nippon Columbia. The lyrics, by Masaru Suzuki, were also vivacious, with *ukiuki* (buoyant) and *zukizuki* (throbbing) rhyming with 'boogie-woogie'. Thus, the prevailing feeling of depression and sense of humiliation under US occupation were swept away, if only temporarily, by the adoption of an African-American rhythm imposed as a jazz element. Hattori also succeeded with two huge hits in 1949: one was "Aoi Sanmyaku" (Blue Mountain Range) and the other was "Ginza Kankan Musume" (Kankan Girl in Ginza). At the same time, a singing prodigy, Hibari Misora (a stage name meaning a fair-sky (Misora) lark (Hibari)), was developing her extraordinary talent and had her first superlative hit, "Kanashiki Kuchibue" (Plaintive Whistle), released as her second single in September at the age of twelve. (It was followed by a succession of hits, and her stardom was consolidated in the early 1950s and continued until her death in 1989.)

The monthly product of five existing record companies in late 1947 amounted to about 900,000 discs, which was one-third of the average monthly production before the war (Kurata 1979: 481).

Passion for popular music imported from the West

Simultaneously, Japanese interest in Western popular music was rekindled in 1945, the very year that the Second World War came to an end and Japan was occupied by the Allied Forces.

Newly introduced democracy looked dazzling, with images of freedom, positivity and affluence, and this encouraged a fascination with music from the West among the young Japanese, overlapping with the post-war development of domestic popular songs. Indeed, the Japanese preoccupation with American popular music was inseparable from the presence of US occupation forces. Significantly, a radio station, WVTR (later Far East Network, abbreviated as FEN), started service in September 1945 for some 400,000 soldiers stationed in Japan. The service, with playlists of the latest release of popular music, was easily accessible to Japanese people living in the vicinity of many US bases located all over Japan. The first piece of music to be aired was "Smoke Gets in Your Eyes" (without lyrics) which gave the defeated Japanese a refreshing surprise with its bright and sweet melody, initiating a yearning for American culture among younger people (Shiga 1991: 792; for more information, see Mitsui 2018: 21–2).

In the meantime, the demand for live music to be performed at recreational facilities on US bases led the general headquarters to employ Japanese musicians (Mitsui 2018: 26–8), who improved their skill in playing US popular music to cater for the tastes of the servicemen. The musicians, including those who had been active since the pre-war days, former military-band members and music-school students, played contemporary jazz-band music, popular songs, and also Country & Western music, which was played by bands consisting of college students (Mitsui 2001). Performances were limited to the officers and soldiers on US bases, but these Japanese musicians naturally had an aspiration to attract a Japanese audience and performed outside the bases whenever an opportunity arose: at celebrations, parties and in clubs. This kind of self-apprenticeship produced talented musicians, particularly jazz musicians, who became active in the newly evolved Japanese scene of the 1950s (for example, Hidehiko Matsumoto, George Kawaguchi, Hachidai Nakamura, Hideo Shiraki and Mitsuru Ono). Toshiko Akiyoshi and Sadao Watanabe, who were also schooled on the military bases, got involved in more progressive trends and later studied in the United States.

The general headquarters also contributed to the development of a Japanese entertainment agency by ordering the government to supply a variety of entertainment, including not only music, plays and some sports but also exhibitions of such Japanese martial arts as *jūdō*, *kendō* and *karate*. To cope with this order, many new agencies were organized, and these would eventually form the basis for the subsequent expansion of the agency industry that accompanied the growth of television and the reinvigoration of show business. Additionally, dance halls were reopened in 1945 to entertain the US troops, and their doors were subsequently opened to the Japanese public in 1947 (Sanseidō 1991: 590). This led to the later developments of go-go clubs and discotheques.

Jazz was the most favoured form of imported popular music that the Japanese listened to and performed themselves in post-war years, and the term 'jazz' often referred to American mainstream popular music in general. The popularity of Country & Western music, which had been called hillbilly music until the early 1950s, was a post-war phenomenon, and was largely due to the tastes of the US troops stationed in Japan, among whom even non-southerners enjoyed the music because of its nostalgic quality. The Japanese interest in Hawaiian music dated back to the 1920s, when a strong sense of affinity had been engendered by Japanese-Hawaiian performers who were active in Japan (for example, Katsuhiko Haida and Buckie Shirakata). Tango, having also been imported before the Second World War (Savigliano 1992), was revived with Ranko Fujisawa as the female leading spirit, and chanson (*variétés*) also made a comeback with conservatory-trained Japanese chanteurs and chanteuses, who put a new emphasis on a romanticized image of Paris. In the mid- and late 1950s, Afro-Cuban mambo and cha-cha merrily reverberated from the records of Perez Prado and live performances by Japanese Latin bands.[4]

In the meantime, beginning with the Gene Krupa Trio in April 1952, foreign artists and groups visited Japan every year throughout the 1950s, in addition to those who were sent from the United States to perform exclusively on the military bases. The former included such a variety of acts as the Xavier Cugat Band, Louis Armstrong (1953), Joséphine Baker (1954), Johnny Ray, Perez Prado, Yvette Giraud (1955), Benny Goodman and His Orchestra (1957), Paul Anka (1958), the Jack Teagarden Sextet, Charles Trénet, Carlos Montoya, and the Golden Gate Quartet (1959) (Nakamura 1988: 454–6). From 1962 onwards, the number of visiting artists and groups – particularly jazz musicians at first and, later, rock musicians, including the Beatles in 1966 – continually increased in proportion to Japan's economic growth.

In the 1950s, a period of admiration and imitation, Japanese singers not only sang covers of original songs in original languages in live performances, but also sang in translation, particularly when recording them. Whereas the lyrics of pre-war covers were for the most part Japanese, these covers sandwiched original verses between translated ones, as can be heard in such successful records as Chiemi Eri's "Tennessee Waltz" and Fubuki Koshiji's "C'est Si Bon". In the late 1950s, rock 'n' roll songs were sung, with the accompaniment of strummed guitars, by young Country & Western singers, who were invariably called 'rockabilly' singers and posed as Elvis Presley, Gene Vincent, and Paul Anka, among others. This practice of performing covers was in vogue until the early 1960s. (For a book-length description of the Japanese reception of American, Latin and European popular music in 1945–75, see Mitsui 2018.)

Japanese composition in the idiom of imported music was also attempted, as in the case of successful boogie-woogie tunes by Ryōichi Hattori, quite a few tango songs in both the pre-war and post-war periods, some chansons, and a couple of Country & Western songs. However, such undertakings were not sufficiently enduring or supported to establish these genres.

Notes

1 Then, in the eighteenth-century 'Japan saw the meteoric rise of hundreds of new genres of *hayari-uta*' (Groemer 2008: 266).
2 The references to railways in "Tokyo Kōshinkyoku" are discussed in detail in the two-volume book about songs relating to Japanese railways by Matsumura (2015: vol. 1, 163–75).
3 '*Kouta* is arguably the most intimate of all Japanese chamber music genres, ideally suited for small parlours' (Groemer 2008: 278) and the 'genre remained popular until well after the Second World War' (ibid.: 275).
4 For more on Hawaiian music in Japan, see Hayatsu (2007); Latin American music, see Nishimura (2005); tango in Japan, see Savigliano (1992 and 1995), Hosokawa (1995) and Nishimura (2012); chanson in Japan, see Kikumura (1989); the presence of 'black music' in Japan, see Hosokawa (2002); Andean music in Japan, see Bigenho (2012); American country music, including bluegrass, see Mitsui (1993).

(To be continued: see page 105 for (5).)

4

Far Western in the Far East: Japanese Country & Western

This is a revised version of 'Far Western in the Far East: The Historical Development of Country and Western in Post-war Japan', in *Hybridity: Journal of Cultures, Texts and Identities* (published for the National University of Singapore by Oxford University Press), vol. 1, no. 2 (2001), pp. 64–84 (© National University of Singapore).

In post-war Japan, Japanese interest in Western popular music was rekindled with the overnight introduction of American democracy and the exclusion of militarism. This newly implanted democracy looked dazzling with images of freedom, positivity and affluence, promoting a fascination for music from the West among young Japanese, which overlapped with the post-war development of vernacular popular songs called *kayōkyoku*.

The most favoured form of imported music that the Japanese enjoyed listening to, as well as performing themselves, was what was called jazz, or more properly, mainstream American popular music. Because of the incomparable popularity of this form and because of the fact that its reception in Japan can be traced back not only to pre-war days but even to the 1910s, serious attention has been paid to the history of its development in Japan, if not exactly within academia. Yet, there was another genre, Country & Western (C&W), which also gained ardent support. It was, however, comparatively less favoured due to its original regionalism and comparative lack of musical sophistication, and therefore has thus far suffered general disregard. This chapter sheds light on the development of this genre in post-war Japan and begins by bringing into focus a made-in-Japan song, "Wagon Master". As the song in its originally recorded form can be argued to be the epitome of how C&W from the US was received and interpreted in post-war Japan, its performance, as a whole, needs to be analysed in detail: both in its obvious and conscious attempts at linguistic transplantation and in its mostly unconscious and subtle inclusion of Japanese musical parameters.

"Wagon Master" made in Japan

'Wagon master, hurry them slow mules down the trail ...', pleads the singer of this C&W song, which has enjoyed substantial popularity. Calling out to the 'wagon master' over and over throughout the song, evoking in the minds of the Japanese audience an image of a prairie schooner travelling across the plains, the song reinforces the image prevalent in Western/cowboy films imported steadily from the US to post-war Japan (Figure 4.1).

The introductory part of "Wagon Master", released in December 1954, features a plaintive fiddle accompanied by a calmly whining electric steel-guitar and supported by an insistently bouncing riff, which is produced by electric guitar picking and the mild pulse of a rhythm guitar and a plucked contrabass. In addition, the percussion of pseudo-hoofs, which might remind one of "Blue Moon" by Elvis Presley, emphasizes the riff in medium tempo, giving the distinction of a simulation of the walking pace of 'slow mules' (Figure 4.2).

Then, led by this opening sound, which typified the standard early 1950s C&W combo in the US, a young male voice hits the first notes, 'Wa-gon', and elongates the second syllable for one whole musical bar as if to demonstrate

Figure 4.1 "Wagon Master" sung by Kazuya Kosaka. Transcribed by author.

Figure 4.2 Riff in "Wagon Master". Transcribed by author.

an exemplary nasalization of C&W delivery. Indeed, this elongation, combined with the following syncopated word 'master', characterizes the song by forming an important structural element in the tune and serves as an indelible hook for the listeners:

> Wagon master, hurry them slow mules down the trail
> Wagon master, I'm bringin' my sweet girl a bridal veil
> Your wheels are turning too slow for me, there's a brand-new bride I'm dyin' to see
> Wagon master, hurry this slow movin' wagon home

The singer himself reveals his non-English-speaking origin through an occasional unnatural enunciation, exemplified by such words as 'mules down' in the line shown above, the vowels of which are pronounced in the frontal part of the mouth. It probably does not matter much, however, because the repetition of the words 'Wagon master' are very likely the only words in the English lyrics that are memorable and intelligible, if vaguely, to the general Japanese audience, while the rest of the lyrics may well have remained discursively obscure. The fact that 'my sweet girl' is 'a brand-new bride' and the wagon is 'slow movin',' and even the fact that it is drawn by mules must have been beyond the knowledge of the average Japanese listener, even though the English four-line verse is repeated after the second instrumental break.

Hybrid lyrics

After an instrumental break, the lyrics suddenly become totally Japanese, making the singer sound slightly ambivalent. While sounding at ease with his mother tongue, he seems to be aware that his C&W vocalizing, which is somewhat reminiscent of Lefty Frizzell, a contemporary C&W singer, does not always adapt itself to this language which is far removed from that for which the style was developed. The Japanese lyrics are, on the whole, a translation of the English ones, but some details are omitted due to a limited capacity of information in Japanese caused by the difference of syllabication. When first hearing this recording, a non-informed Japanese listener may feel embarrassed by a sudden appearance, after the opening 'Wagon master' in English, of Japanese words, not only because they sound completely natural, but also because all the associations aroused by any word in the mother tongue are overwhelming when compared to the far lesser immediacy conveyed by English to the general Japanese audience.

The idea of alternating English with Japanese verses was first hit upon by a King director in 1951 when he produced the recording of "Tennessee Waltz" by Chiemi Eri, who successfully debuted with this song at the age of fourteen in January 1952. When he proposed the idea of combining the original lyrics with Japanese ones, 'Some were against the idea, saying that it wouldn't come off well, but I thought it would go for a synergistic effect that, while showing her ability in singing in English, the content of the song would be grasped in Japanese by the general audience' (Yasui 2001: 5). Through the 1950s and early 1960s, it became common practice in the Japanese record industry to alternate the original lyrics with a sketchy Japanese translation when releasing 'jazz' songs, Hawaiian songs, chansons and tango songs sung by Japanese vocalists for Japanese consumers. On the other hand, live performance in small venues for a devoted audience did not require so much Japanization, which must have often sounded awkward and embarrassing. It should be noted, however, that "Wagon Master" was composed by a Japanese songwriter with lyrics presumably by an American, while the alternation of lyrics in both languages was generally not practised on songs made in Japan, but on imported songs. Therefore, "Wagon Master" could have effectively been taken as a song from the USA.

Hybrid sounds

The tune, in four-four time consisting of sixteen bars in AA´BA´ form, is characterized by a major-oriented pentatonic scale with a flattened third an octave above in the second bar of the bridge, which adds an effectual bluesy expansion to the whole. In Japan, a scale with 'gapped' fourth and seventh was devised in the late nineteenth century as a compromise between imported Western music and indigenous music, and it had generally been favoured by the Japanese, as shown by the many popular hit songs in both minor-oriented and major-oriented pentatonic scales, with slight suggestions of tonal harmony. It is not known if the composer of "Wagon Master" consciously adopted the pentatonic scale or not, but this pentatonicism must have contributed to the popularity of the tune. From my perusal of popular C&W recordings in the late 1940s and early 1950s in the US, the number of songs in pentatonic scale seems to be quite limited. Conspicuous examples might be such songs by Hank Williams as "Honky Tonk Man", "I'm So Lonesome I Could Cry" and "I Saw the Light". What is generally common to these songs is that they tend to use many falling thirds, which are often minor and sometimes major, apparently demonstrating the influence of the blues, of which falling thirds are intrinsic. This pentatonic blues tendency is also obvious in "Wagon Master", and it makes the use of the flattened third in the middle eight daintily efficacious. Moreover, the flattened third falls on the first note of a triplet consisting of three different notes, which is another characteristic of the blues, and symmetrically echoes three other lilting triplets in the tune.

The iconography of wagons

"Wagon Master" was first recorded for Nippon Columbia by nineteen-year-old Kazuya Kosaka (1935–2000), whose popularity rapidly increased with the release of the song, two and a half years after he began singing in a professional band. The band on this recording, the Wagon Masters, was the most popular among quite a few contemporary Japanese C&W bands, whose members boasted romanticized cowboy costumes, invariably wearing ten-gallon hats unanimously on the back of their heads as Kosaka himself did. This way of wearing a hat, while iconographically foreign to C&W musicians in the homeland, endured throughout the 1950s and early 1960s among Japanese C&W bands, apparently reflecting their idea of carefree stylishness in those days. The band name Wagon Masters, which must have prompted the title of the song, was obviously derived from the Chuck Wagon Boys, a Japanese band whose popularity preceded the Wagon Masters; the Chuck Wagon Boys, in turn, was named after 'Chuck Wagon Time', a one-hour programme of hillbilly records on WVTR (later FEN), the radio station of the US forces stationed in Japan (Kitanaka 2000: 102). In the USA there was just one group with this phrase as part of their name, the Chuck Wagon Gang, a Texan white-gospel group that had been active since the mid-1930s.

The sound of the words 'chuck wagon' may well have been appealing even without their meaning being properly understood, because of its phonetic crispness. Moreover, the word wagon itself had a powerful appeal, calling to mind imported Western/cowboy films, which were particularly popular in the post-war period and which charmed many Japanese with their feeling of openness and liberation, combined with a touch of rusticity. The attraction of Western/cowboy films might also have had much to do with the idea of American democracy that was suddenly being advocated by the newly converted Japanese authorities. The wagon had, in any case, been familiar to the Japanese audience of Japanese

C&W bands through the popularity of these two bands, and the familiarity was reinforced by the usage of the group name, the Wagon Masters, in the singular form, as the title of the newly introduced C&W song. As a matter of fact, the image of the wagon has never been very pronounced in US country music. One of the few examples in which a wagon does appear is Sam McGee's "When the Wagon Was New", which is included in Horstman's collection of classic country songs: 'Back in the days when I was just a kid, we [...] went to church in wagons and even on horseback' (Horstman [1975] 1986: 29). But here the wagon appears to be far removed from the Japanese romanticized image nourished by Western/cowboy films, in which the wagon is a prairie schooner driving through the Wild West.

"Wagon Master", which became practically the theme song of the Wagon Masters, was composed in 1954 by Raymond Hattori (his baptized name), a middle-aged Japanese who contributed as the composer, arranger and lyric translator to more than 100 songs recorded by Kosaka. The English lyrics, which consist of only one verse, are credited to Hars, who was American, according to Kosaka's autobiography (Kosaka 1990a: 215), and they were translated into Japanese by Ai Okuyama. The song title must have been taken from the film *The Wagon Master*, directed by John Ford in 1950 and shown for the first time in Japan in 1951, though the title was translated into Japanese as *Horo-basha* (Covered Wagon). (The 1950 *The Wagon Master* was preceded by another Western film of exactly the same name in 1929, which featured Ken Maynard.) The recording of this song by Kazuya Kosaka and the Wagon Masters was released with "Montana Moon" on its flip side by Nippon Columbia (JL-123). "Montana Moon", which was also composed by Raymond Hattori with lyrics written in English by Hars and in Japanese translation by Hattori himself, sounds brisk in three-fourths time with a clearer melodic contour, prompting listeners to imagine that the song itself, if not this recording, could have fascinated American audiences if it was exported. (Raymond Hattori wrote two more C&W songs for Kazuya Kosaka, which enjoyed much less popularity: "Texas-no Koi-uta" (Texas Love-song) sung in duet with Sonomi Nakajima and released in January 1956, and "Muteki-no Rifleman" (Invincible Rifleman), a macho song with an orchestral introduction, released in March 1961.)

The example of "Wagon Master" illustrates Japan's intersection with American C&W music. In order to comprehend the Japanese overemphasis of the then-romanticized Western aspect of American C&W, which is epitomized in "Wagon Master", a made-in-Japan C&W song, the development of C&W music in post-war Japan and its cultural context needs to be examined.

The occupation forces and the development of Country & Western

Widespread Japanese interest in American country music – still called hillbilly in the US along with the nascent appellation Country & Western – was ignited soon after the Second World War when Japan was occupied by the Allied Forces. In addition to the popularity of Western/cowboy films mentioned above, the charm of which often stemmed from their theme songs, interest was also generated by a radio station for the servicemen of the occupation forces. What was called WVTR in the beginning, and later changed to FEN, frequently played hillbilly records as well as jazz and Tin Pan Alley songs, catering to a large number of servicemen, many of whom had developed a taste for this music during their time in the army. Any Japanese could be exposed to hillbilly music by tuning in to the station, which was possible if they were in the vicinity of the military bases that were constructed all over Japan.

What induced certain young Japanese to form their own bands to perform the music at a very early stage was the big demand among servicemen for the live performance of contemporary hillbilly music. Japanese 'dance bands who were employed in the military clubs' where Ernest Tubb and Jimmy Dickens blared out from a jukebox 'were harassed with request[s] to play "San Antone!" ' (Ihara 1958a: 34). Among those who first availed themselves of the opportunity to form hillbilly bands in the late 1940s was Takehiko Toyama, along with his younger brother Hiroshi Toyama, who converted from a Hawaiian band to form a hillbilly band, the Western Melodians, in 1947 (Shinbo 1978: 40). Lacking a featured vocalist, the Western Melodians performed only instrumental pieces, but 'GIs were wild with joy notwithstanding' (Ihara 1958a: 34). Then in 1948, Hiroshi Toyama left the band to form his own group, the Western Ramblers, whose members included a fiddler, an accordionist and a steel-guitar player. They too performed regularly on the military bases in the metropolitan area.

Both the Western Melodians and the Western Ramblers wore the quasi-cowboy costume that was then fashionable among US performers, or rather a makeshift version assembled from any material to hand. They were, however, obviously unaware, as were other bands that followed them in the 1950s and early 1960s, of the kind of romanticism shared by US performers, who aspired for respectability by wearing non-southern attire, trying to shake off derogatory connotations of the genre appellation, hillbilly, and of their own southern white background. Japanese aspiration and exoticism, visually nourished by Western films with an aura of democracy, were represented symbolically by use of the word 'Western' in the names of bands, which was probably taken directly from Western/cowboy films. Though the name of a specific style – western swing – existed, there were no contemporary US groups whose names these Japanese groups could have used as models; and, indeed, there seem to have been no US groups even since then who have used 'Western' as part of their names.

Blue-blooded sons fascinated by blue-collar music

Another popular group, the Chuck Wagon Boys, made their debut on 13 November 1949 as an amateur group at a large dining hall on the campus of Gakushūin, a renowned comprehensive educational institution for the sons and daughters of the Japanese upper class. The occasion was an annual school festival and the band, consisting of students of Keiō University, performed five songs repeatedly for the whole day. These songs made up their entire repertoire and were in the only keys they knew so far: C, G and F (Ihara 1958a: 34).

The members were Biji Kuroda (Yoshiharu Kuroda, vocals and rhythm guitar), Kōji Tomono (rhythm guitar), Takatada Ihara (bass), who were all graduates of Gakushūin Secondary School, and Rauf Miftahittin (fiddle), a Turk who was born in Japan, educated at St Joseph International School, an English-speaking institution in Yokohama, and known among his friends for his natural Tokyo cockney. They were all unmistakably from quite well-off families. Kuroda had been a son of a Baron until three years before when the titled-nobility system was abolished after Japan's defeat in the war, and Ihara, coming from a plutocratic family, lived in 'a grand residence on an immense estate' (Hori 1992: 12). The blue-blooded musicians, who were fascinated by overseas blue-collar music, were wealthy and fashionable enough to order stage costumes from the US and dressed up to the nines to perform at a number of those parties. Before long, they became professional, playing at an American officers' club in downtown Tokyo in late December of the same year.

When the Chuck Wagon Boys started performing there, 'officers at the club got so wild with excitement that some of them assembled, by the telephone, their friends and acquaintances, and the club became jampacked [...]' (Ihara 1958a: 35). Having no time to get off the stage for a break, they played their limited repertoire (which had now grown to some ten songs) until very late in the evening. Even more surprised at the popularity than the band members themselves were the people from one of the post-war entertainment agencies, who arranged entertainment bookings for the military clubs of the occupation forces. The Chuck Wagon Boys were in great demand at the clubs. The key to their popularity, apart from the possible appeal of the neatly dressed look of these young gentlemen, was the fact that they featured a vocalist, at a time when 'Western' ensembles catering for servicemen were basically instrumental groups formed by converted tango and Hawaiian musicians (Wada 1969: 2). The featured vocals, furthermore, were delivered very skilfully by Kuroda, a good-looking man whose English enunciation was good, a result of his early childhood in London and his education at St Joseph International School. Then, in March the next year, the sound of the Chuck Wagon Boys was further enriched by the addition of Hiroshi Sogabe on electric steel-guitar (Ihara 1958a: 35). Sogabe was trained under a great Hawaiian steel-guitar player, Buckie Shirakata, who had been influential in Japan since the pre-war period.

Exposure to domestic audiences

While performing regularly on the military bases for American servicemen, the Chuck Wagon Boys soon began appearing in 'jazz' concerts, which featured not only jazz and Tin Pan Alley songs, but also Latin, chansons and Hawaiian numbers, and which were held frequently (nearly on a bi-weekly basis) in Tokyo. The term jazz has been widely used in Japan since the pre-war periods as an umbrella term encompassing popular music from the non-Oriental world in general, and those jazz concerts always featured the performance of such non-jazz music as well as jazz itself. The popularity of the concerts apparently reflected the aspiration among young Japanese for American and European cultures as a reaction to wartime pressures.

The appearance of the Chuck Wagon Boys came in the wake of the Western Ramblers, who first performed in such a concert at Yomiuri Hall in Tokyo, where the fourth Swing Concert was held on 21 November 1949. This was several days after the debut of the Chuck Wagon Boys on the campus of Gakushūin and was in fact the first time a 'Western' band had performed before a substantial domestic audience (Ihara 1958a: 34). The appearance of the Western Ramblers at this concert was obviously prompted by the success of their record, "Ekibasha" (Stagecoach), their seventh single, backed by "Nogamono-no Sakebi" (Cry of the Wild Goose). It allegedly became a huge national hit. The success was probably due to the immense popularity of the film *Stagecoach* itself (which showed John Wayne's gallantry), even though the musical quality of the song was judged a decade later by Ihara (1958a: 34), rather jealously, to be 'so poor that it was below criticism'. Ihara was, of course, a member of the high-spirited Chuck Wagon Boys, when the record was released by their senior competitors.

In August 1950, the Chuck Wagon Boys were featured in an independent musical show, *Utau Horobasha* (Singing Prairie Wagon), at Nichigeki, a prestigious theatre in Tokyo, inviting news reporters who poked fun at them: 'Young masters of the former nobility having a spree in performing as a band' (Ihara 1958a: 35). Their popularity led to them being featured again in May 1951 in a large-scale show at the same theatre, this time with the Western Ramblers, who adopted drums after Spade Cooley's band and Bob Wills' Texas Playboys, and who tried to capitalize visually on Western vulgarity in contrast to their dandified co-stars. The show was again a 'Western', entitled *Utau Ekibasha* (Singing Stagecoach): 'A Western saloon appeared on the stage, and, with some rowdy cowboys, who assembled there, as a background, they sang a song' (Kosaka 1990a: 96).

Undoubtedly, Kuroda was the first 'Western' star in Japan. He sang such hit songs as "Buttons and Bows", featured in the film *The Paleface* (1948), and his singing of "Tennessee Waltz" in 1951 helped cement his popularity. The recording of this song by Pee Wee King and by Cowboy Copas in 1948 was known to the Japanese if only through WVTR. This is evidenced by Nippon Victor's release of "Tennessee Waltz", covered by the Western Ramblers in 1948 with "Lovesick Blues" on its flip side (Suzuki 1972: 33), but it seems to have soon been forgotten, as it was in the US. The resurrection of the song by Patti Page in late 1950 naturally extended to Japan via FEN (former WVTR), and Kuroda quickly and successfully included it in his repertoire before the song was made popular nationwide by Chiemi Eri in 1952. The third appearance of the Chuck Wagon Boys on the stage of Nichigeki at the end of 1951 thrust Kuroda further towards stardom and inspired him to leave the limited musical style and organization of the band in order to pursue a solo career (Ihara 1958b: 42). This ambition was realized in April 1952 when Sogabe also left to form a jazz combo, and the Chuck Wagon Boys disbanded without reluctance, although the band name was inherited by other performers.

Servicemen clubs as training ground

Ihara and Rauf M. soon coalesced with the Prairie Pioneers, a student band, to form the Wagon Masters on 1 May 1952. In addition to Ihara, the leader (bass), and Rauf M. (fiddle), the members, who were mostly students at Keiō University and

Seijō University, another institution for rich kids, were Keiji Fujisawa (vocals and rhythm guitar), Makoto Harada (electric steel-guitar) and Kōichi Fujimura (rhythm guitar) (Ihara 1958b: 42). Fujisawa, the captain of the rugby team of Seijō, was known among the devoted Japanese audience as a Japanese Hank Williams, and, as a fluent English speaker, he was an asset to a band that performed in US military clubs. Harada (b. 1932), who was repeating the twelfth grade at Keiō Secondary School, was so skilled in his performance that he made Kazuya Kosaka, at his first hearing of Harada's playing, almost wonder if Harada had in fact accompanied Hank Williams when Hank recorded such songs as "Jambalaya" and "Your Cheatin' Heart" (Kosaka 1990a: 132). A few weeks after the band was formed, Fujimura was replaced by Takeo Hori (b. 1932), who soon switched to lead-guitar, probably at the time when Kazuya Kosaka, a dropout of Seijō Secondary School who was taking lessons in C&W singing from Fujisawa, joined the Wagon Masters as an apprentice vocalist. By that time, the band had already become as active and well known as the Chuck Wagon Boys had been, through regular performances on military bases and continual appearances in jazz concerts.

The clubs on the military bases of the occupation forces, where the number of servicemen had considerably increased since the outbreak of the Korean War in June 1950, remained the basic venues for the Wagon Masters as well as for other such groups as the Western Melodians, the Western Ramblers, the Country Boys, the Flower Sisters (a converted female Hawaiian group), the Green Plowboys in Yokohama and the Lovesick Cowboys in Kyoto (Ihara 1958a: 35). The popularity of the Wagon Masters at these clubs grew when Kosaka, a boyish teenage singer, appeared more frequently and Matsuko Kihara, a violin student at Kunitchi College of Music, replaced Rauf. Animated hoedown pieces such as "Orange Blossom Special" produced by this tiny young woman were irresistible (Ihara 1958b: 42). Even more important was that the clubs served for the performers, and particularly for vocalists, as a good training ground. The audience wanted to hear something that was close to the original, and the performers endeavoured to meet their expectations. The fact that they were performing what was originally American distinguished them on stage, along with jazz musicians, from other Japanese entertainers booked for the clubs: magicians, acrobats, boxers, strippers, masters of Japanese martial arts, monkey showmen, performers of *shintō* music and dance, etc.

The customers at the clubs for enlisted men, seamen and airmen, and those for non-commanding officers, were especially fond of 'Western' music. Recollecting his days before he joined the Wagon Masters, Kosaka describes the EM clubs filled with young GIs:

> There were so many 'Western' lovers that when we played, we got warmed and excited before we knew it. And it was always at the dressing room of an EM club that we received the biggest number of bottles of beer from the customers – those modestly paid soldiers. The customers at NCOs covered a wide range of ages, and they were often accompanied by their wives. 'Western' was equally well received there, but we sometimes got frustrated with their request for very old cowboy songs. Black soldiers didn't have a liking for 'Western', and they rarely showed themselves when we performed. Even if they came to the club, they would gather in the bar-lounge and the game-room, keeping away from the hall. (1990a: 104)

Kosaka reminisces about learning songs:

> Failing to respond to GIs' requests, I would say, 'Next week, OK?' And they said, 'OK, next week'. This was one of the English conversations at which I was very good in those days. As a result, I was prompted to learn new songs. Staring at the plentifully misspelled lyrics, which GIs wrote for me, and those in a couple of recent issues of *Country Song Roundup*, my treasures which I managed to obtain through GIs, I listened to songs played on FEN; this was the only available way to learn them. (1990a: 111)

Another contribution to the development of Japanese 'Western'-music making was the existence of a certain number of C&W bands formed by American servicemen. Although little is known about them, the Drifters were the most influential, according to Ihara (1958b: 43), through their frequent appearances before Japanese audiences as well as through live regular performances on a Saturday FEN show, *Honshū Hayride*, named after the main island of Japan. The band was led by a rhythm guitarist, Chuck Berry (!), and featured a star singer, Bob Norton. Other members were Dickey Hall (electric steel-guitar, later replaced by Mac McCoy), Johnny Goodwin (vocals) and two former Chuck Wagon Boys: Takatada Ihara (bass) and Rauf M. (fiddle), who belonged to the Wagon Masters at the same time.

The domestic impact of Country & Western

In August 1953, Ihara left the Wagon Masters to work as a producer for a newly formed TV company, and was replaced by Atsutaka Torio, his younger cousin. Torio, a student at Keiō University, was born the son of a Viscount and had been a classmate of the present emperor through his Gakushūin days. According to Hori, then the lead guitarist of the Wagon Masters, there were some other classmates of the emperor who played in 'Western' bands as university students, including one of the sons of the aristocratic Shimazu family (Hori 1992: 25). Fujisawa, the senior vocalist, also left soon after he became the new leader, giving more scope for Kosaka and Keiichi Teramoto (b. 1933),[1] another pupil of Fujisawa, who had joined the band several months before. Kihara, the female fiddler, had also left by this time to join a female Western band, the Joy Sisters (Kosaka 1990a: 180), and a technician, Seiichi Fujimoto from Yokohama, took over in playing the fiddle.

The Wagon Masters remained the most eminent 'Western' band throughout, being featured in the Hillbilly Show (at Shinjuku Theatre in May 1953), the first large-scale show to be exclusively 'Western', where they appeared with other groups, including the Western Ramblers, the Country Boys, the Tokyo Western, and the New Melodians. They made another large domestic impact, later in the same year, with their appearance in the first Western Carnival (at Video Hall), which was known as the Japanese Grand Ole Opry. Then, Kazuya Kosaka, now the featured vocalist, along with the Wagon Masters, signed with Nippon Columbia through the influence of Ihara (Kosaka 1990a: 212–14).

Catering to the domestic market: The musicians' ambivalence

"Wagon Master", the first single recorded by Kosaka with the Wagon Masters, was successfully promoted through continuous live performances. Kosaka recalls in his notes to a double-CD reissue of his recordings for Nippon Columbia (Kosaka 1990b: 10):

> On January 1, 1955, the Wagon Masters appeared at the National Theatre in Asahikawa. It was the opening day of a fortnight Hokkaidō tour. [...] The tour was a 'Western' show headed by Biji Kuroda, the pioneering Japanese 'Western' singer, whom we backed – myself by strumming rhythm and sometimes with vocal harmony. I was given at every show an opportunity to sing just one song, and it was "Wagon Master". As the song was totally unknown in Hokkaidō, the audience did not show a good response. I wanted to sing such well-known songs as "Jambalaya" and "Tennessee Waltz", but followed the instructions of my seniors, and had the patience to sing only "Wagon Master" through the whole tour. I was still a submissive youngster at that time. The tour in Kyūshū in the following month went the same way, with me sticking only to that song. It is indeed good to give heed to your seniors' counsel, for the record gradually began to sell well, and, in no time, I was asked to record a second single.

The growth in the domestic popularity of 'Western' music was accelerated, around the time "Wagon Master" was released, by the emergence of what were called jazz *kissa* (jazz cafés), coffee houses that featured live performance. In the beginning, jazz cafés devoted themselves exclusively to jazz proper, but soon they became tolerant enough to accept other kinds of music that were bundled under the term jazz at the time (Kosaka 1990a: 196). The appearance of the Wagon Masters in the first jazz café, Tennessee, drew such a large audience that they were asked to perform as many as four days a week (Hori 1992: 26). The more they performed at jazz cafés, the more difficult it became for them to stick to their repertoire for US servicemen. 'A continuous performance of songs in English with simplistic melodies got the audience tired. We often had to replace them with more theme songs of Western films as well as American popular songs which were successful in Japan' (Kosaka 1990a: 202).

While jazz cafés were mostly limited to Tokyo, provincial tours by the Wagon Masters, such as those mentioned above by Kosaka, helped spread the interest in 'Western' bands nationwide. Kosaka, however, grew increasingly frustrated at the limited repertoire for those shows and the inclusion of Japanese lyrics (1990a: 223):

> For one appearance some fifteen numbers were performed, of which I sang ten, and all I had to do on every stage was to sing those ten songs. [...] Every song included lyrics in Japanese. The audience enjoyed the songs because the translation was good, and, to begin with, because it was partly sung in Japanese; I knew that, but I wondered ... 'Isn't this different from the kind of 'Western' music I used to be absorbed in? Feelings like that surged up day after day. My repertoire boasted more than a hundred songs, which I had accumulated and kept on singing in the days of performing in US military camps, but the places where I could sing those 'Western' songs in English were rapidly receding from me.

Kosaka had already felt these sentiments in 1952, when he began appearing in jazz concerts with the Wagon Masters. When he was once told by Ihara to sing "Bimbo" and "Mom and Dad's Waltz", he answered back (1990a: 136):

> 'Oh, ... but I sang them at the last concert in Hibiya'. 'Right! That's why you'll sing them again', said Ihara. 'Just keep on singing those songs at jazz concerts for some time to come. If you sing this and that, the audience won't remember any of them'.

He was certainly right, but it was very difficult for me to restrain myself, because there were many more good songs which I was good at singing. On the other hand, US military clubs gave more time to perform, and they were naturally a much more well-informed audience. You would get lots of requests [...]

The other aspect of his ambivalence was, as one might expect, associated with the rise to stardom. His success led him to record more singles, which were successively released from August to December in 1955, including "Kawliga", "Ballad of Davy Crockett", "Sixteen Tons", "Hey, Mister Banjo", "The 'A' Triangle" and "The Yellow Roses of Texas". In the following year, he even covered "Heartbreak Hotel" by Elvis Presley, among many others, a typical example of the way in which rock 'n' roll was embraced by Japanese performers. It was through the repertoire of 'Western' singers and bands that many rock 'n' roll songs by Presley, Gene Vincent, Eddie Cochran, Wanda Jackson and others were introduced into live performance in Japan.

Kosaka's popularity was, however, directed toward something that was markedly different, when he was asked to sing "Seishun Cycling" (Youthful Cycling). It was a light-hearted, bouncing song, with an orchestration whose sound was dominated by a xylophone and embellished by tremolos played on the Italian mandolin and whistling, in which he sang about the joy of cycling around the countryside. The tune was characterized by the typical major-oriented pentatonicism of the composer Msao Koga. Koga was one of the most eminent composers of Japanese popular songs, and Kosaka was both intimidated and deeply honoured to perform one of his songs, although he sighed in his heart over his further removal from 'Western' music (Kosaka 1990a: 225). This single, released in April 1957, was the most successful of Kosaka's recordings, and it prompted Nippon Columbia to have him record a series of other songs, many in a similar vein, while he continued to perform with the Wagon Masters.

Meanwhile, the Wagon Masters were largely reduced to the status of Kosaka's backing band, and Takeo Hori, the lead guitarist, left the band two months before the release of the cycling ditty, together with Keiichi Teramoto and Shōichi Tanabe, to form the Swing West. Hori says, 'Not only to cope with rockabilly, but also to pursue some musical development with more jazzy sound, we formed this band, and we tried to reflect our aim in its name' (1992: 45). This band, which debuted in late March 1957, consisted of steel guitar, fiddle, lead guitar, contrabass, drums, banjo and two rhythm guitars, with vocals provided by the banjo-player and the two rhythm guitarists. The Swing West soon became a very powerful band and topped the readers' poll in the monthly *Music Life* at the end of the year as the most popular 'Western' band, surpassing the Wagon Masters (Hori 1992: 49–50).

Far 'Western' image

By early 1957, the 'Western' music scene was vivacious, with activity by the Wagon Masters, the Swing West and other prominent groups, including All Stars Wagon, the Western Caravan, the (new) Chuck Wagon Boys, the Boots Brothers, the Sons of Drifters, the Wagon Aces, the Blue Cowboys in Osaka, the Rhythm Wagon Boys also in Osaka, the Sons of the West in Kobe and the Western Blue Rangers in Fukuoka (*Western-no Tomo* 1958). As discussed previously, the term 'Western' became established in Japan in the mid-1950s as a term that denoted hillbilly/C&W music, excluding all other possible candidates, and was unanimously used as a genre label until the early 1970s. A songbook, *Western Hyakkyoku-shū* (One Hundred Western Songs), published in 1952, is subtitled in English as *Hit Parade of Cowboy Songs* with an assortment of the theme songs of popular Western films, old and newly-composed cowboy songs and southern folksongs. The November 1957 issue of *Music Life* has a column, 'Western monoshiri-daigaku', the English title of which is given as 'Western quiz room', with a simple line-drawing of a cowboy with a bandana around his neck. On the upper right corner of the first page, 'Hillbilly's Corner' is found. The 'Western' column in *Juke Box*, a Japanese monthly of popular music published in April 1958, even had, at least in its first year of publication, '*Seibu-ongaku-eno Izanai*' (Invitation to music in the West) as a subtitle. The title was illustrated by small line-drawings of a cowboy, a ten-gallon hat, a revolver and even American Indians. Then the first book-length introduction to C&W music in Japanese, for general readers, was published in 1963 with *Western Ongaku* as its title and a coloured photograph, on the cover, of grazing cattle shepherded by cowboys on plains somewhere in the US; although the author, Hiroyuki Takayama, did not fail to mention the American South as the geographical and cultural origin of C&W music while mostly engaging himself in maintaining the image of the West.

To get a general idea of how this 'Western' genre was situated in the contemporary field of popular music practised by the Japanese, the classification of musical genres in the 1958 readers' popularity poll (Top Ten list) for best musicians in *Music Life* can be quoted: Hawaiian Bands, Chūnambei Gakudan

(Latin American Bands), Western Bands, Combo Bands, Full Bands and Vocal Groups (*Music Life* 1958). Note that *Music Life* was launched, like *Juke Box*, as a monthly magazine that devoted itself to popular music that was not domestic in origin, without covering kayōkyoku.

It is true that the late 1950s saw a further flourishing of 'Western' among the young Japanese, but it was largely assisted by the rock 'n' roll craze, which, so to speak, eroded 'Western' music while thrusting it forward. Then, gradually, the decline of 'Western' became perceptible in the early 1960s. A contemporary observer declares exaggeratedly, perhaps due to his enthusiasm, that it 'totally disappeared around the time the Olympic Games were held in Tokyo' (Sawano 1994: 224). Besides being the year of the Tokyo Olympics, 1964 was also the year when international bullet trains began travelling, proclaiming the forthcoming Japanese economic growth along with the Olympic Games. (A detailed account of the subsequent Japanese practitioners of American country music would require the writing of another article, though they have been much less active; for an overview of the popularity of American country music in Japan, with an emphasis on old-time and bluegrass and, therefore, on its southern origin, see Mitsui 1993.)

The decline of Country & Western in Japan

Apart from the change in the general popular music scene generated by the emergence of rock 'n' roll, it can be argued that the decline of 'Western' music in Japan was caused by at least three factors. Firstly, the number of occupation military bases were markedly reduced after the Treaty of Peace with Japan was concluded in San Francisco in September 1951 and effected in April 1952. Though some of the bases have continued to exist until today, many were eliminated, leaving limited opportunities for 'Western' bands to perform before a responsive and sympathetic audience. The frustration repeatedly expressed by Kosaka as discussed above might well have been shared by other 'Western'-band members; particularly by vocalists, who immersed themselves in singing a variety of C&W songs.

Secondly, aspiration for the exotic, fantasized West declined in parallel with its increasing accessibility. Though the physical accessibility of the USA by travel did not come until later, people were becoming more and more informed about the USA through mass media, especially after 1959, when the number of household television sets increased dramatically due to the televising of the wedding parade of the crown prince and princess, the first commoner member of the imperial family. A large quantity of visual information helped revise the general image of the USA while making the country more accessible – no longer a far-off land beyond one's reach.

Thirdly, 'Western' was basically a reproduction of C&W music in the USA. There were such skilful singers as Jimmy Tokita (1936–2000), who formed the Mountain Playboys after leaving the Western Ramblers. In the final analysis, however, he might simply be comparable to any fine but obscure club singer in the US with a tasteful repertoire of miscellaneous country classics originally made popular by distinguished singers. As this comparison suggests, the reproduction of an original in the field of music survives mostly, if not only, when it is live. Imagine a universal situation in which people enjoy live performance even it is a reproduction of a recording that is played during an intermission. American GIs on the military bases enjoyed the *live* reproduction of what was not otherwise available except on record. This was also the case with the Japanese C&W fans, who enjoyed the live performance of Japanese performers but were generally reluctant to buy their recordings (Tamura 1978: 50), preferring instead to buy the originals recorded by American performers, which became available, to the delight of C&W fans, in the early 1960s when Japanese record companies began releasing those records pressed in Japan. Moreover, in the 1970s, an array of historical recordings by such legendary performers as Jimmie Rodgers, the Carter Family, Hank Williams and others was compiled and reissued exclusively in Japan (for a complete documentation of the analogue discs, see Nagai 2000).

From this perspective, one can maintain that 'Western' music practised by the Japanese began retreating in the mid-1960s, and gradually became something to be looked back on fondly by aged enthusiasts, as demonstrated by such albums as *Western All-Stars* (Toshiba EMI EP-7715) and *Nihon-no Western Kashu-tachi* (Japanese Western Singers) (Victor SPX-1034). The former, released in 1969, was an abridged reissue of two LPs titled *Western Jamboree*, which had been released in 1958–9 as the first 'Western' LPs by representative Japanese 'Western' musicians. The latter, which came out in 1976, consisted of new recordings by some fifteen Japanese practitioners who had seen better days in the 1950s. They got together at a Victor recording studio, as if they had been attending a meeting of an alumni association, to produce this album expressively subtitled 'Shinchūgun Hanayaka-narisihi-koro' (In the Lively Days of the Occupation Forces). Both albums consist of covers of C&W standards in the 1940s and

1950s and are complete with the composite imagery of a cowboy with his boots, revolver and horse dominating the sleeves.

A mythical West condensed in "Wagon Master"

Among all those recordings and a number of singles released in the heyday of Japanese 'Western' music, "Wagon Master" stands out as a striking piece of sound and image that creatively condensed a mythical West constructed by the post-war Japanese. The West was, to begin with, romanticized in the homeland by C&W musicians, particularly through stage costumes, who came mostly from poor white families in the South and aspired for respectability as exemplified by having the appellation hillbilly replaced by C&W. Crossing the Pacific Ocean, this C&W underwent an alteration in the way it was received and interpreted, initially by the sons of the rich. The alteration is clearly recognizable in Japan, with the wilful adherence to the appellation 'Western', as well as in ubiquitous 'Western' and cowboy images that surrounded the music. In retrospect, however, the alteration is not particularly recognizable in the sound recordings by Japanese 'Western' artists, almost all of which are covers of American records. In that respect, Raymond Hattori's monumental contribution should never be overlooked. Along with Hars and Ai Okuyama, he had Kazuya Kosaka and the Wagon Masters encapsulate in 3 minutes and 23 seconds how C&W music was embraced in post-war Japan.[2]

Notes

1   Post-war enthusiasm over C&W in Japan from the viewpoint of Keiichi Teramoto is sketched in the article 'Y'All Come: Japan's Country Music Scene' by Yosuke Kitazawa on 11 September 2019 (https://www.pbssocal.org/country-music/yall-come-japans-country-music-scene/). This is apparently based on the author's interview with Teramoto, who was 'in elementary school in Tokyo when the teacher told the class the news that Japan had entered the war' and 'by that time already had a taste for Western pop culture in the form of a head-to-toe cowboy suit his parents had brought back from a trip to the US'.
2   In 2008, seven years after this 'Far Western' article was published, there appeared 'American Country Music in Japan: Lost Piece in the Popular Music History Puzzle' by Michael Furmanovsky (2008) which 'attempts to expand on' this,

using 'interviews with some of the pioneers of the music in Japan'. Then, a film titled *Far Western* was released in November 2016 in the Netherlands. This documentary 'that tells the phenomenal story of the transplant of American country music to post-World War II Japan' was directed by James D. Payne and presented by This Land Films, with its title being taken from this 'Far Western in the Far East' article.

Transformation inspired by the West (5)

Conversion to *kayōkyoku*

More significantly, a number of performers who began their careers as imitators of imported music tried their hand at, and often converted to, Japanese music, especially *kayōkyoku*, bringing in some Western elements.

Dark Ducks (Mitsui 1992: 629), Duke Aces and Bonny Jacks are longstanding male quartets, all dressed in tuxedos, who have been strong in Russian folksongs, African-American spirituals and children's songs, respectively. They have an additional repertoire of school-taught Japanese songs, as well as some jazz songs, which they specialized in when they were formed in the mid-1950s. Some Hawaiian bands and Latin bands became successful with songs composed for their musical genre, in which a male chorus and the steel or *requinto* guitar were featured.

Similarly, jazz singers won renown by singing *kayōkyoku* songs, as was the case with Frank Nagai and Peggy Hayama. Nagai succeeded with songs that affirmed urban life such as "Tokyo Gozen Sanji" (Tokyo, 3.00 am) (1957), tinged with a Latin beat, and "Yūrakuchō-de Aimashō" (See You in Yūrakuchō) (1958). These songs with self-explanatory titles were in the harmonic minor scale and sung in a low crooning voice with the accompaniment of sophisticated orchestration. Hayama's name became closely associated with "Nangoku-Tosa-o Atonishite" (Leaving Tosa, My Southern Home) (1959), a song of nostalgia in the representative pentatonic minor (ABCEFA). 'Rockabilly' singers also achieved success with *kayōkyoku*, exemplified most remarkably by Hiroshi Mizuhara, whose "Kuroi Hanabira" (Black Petals) (1959) in the minor scale with a rhythm typified by a triplet for each quadruple beat was immensely popular. It was written by the song-writing team of

Hachidai Nakamura, a jazz pianist, and Rokusuke Ei. The 1960s was characterized, inter alia, by songs in much less vernacular and more Western-oriented styles, beginning with "Ue-o Muite Arukō" (I Look Up When I Walk) (1961), another song written by Nakamura and Ei. It was sung by another 'rockabilly' singer, Kyū Sakamoto, and became Japan's only international chart-topper under the title "Sukiyaki" (Mitsui 1991: 259). The song heralded a move away from the confines of *kayōkyoku* with its more Western-oriented style. The basic part of the tune in the pentatonic major is accompanied by a harmonic progression that makes use of non-pentatonic notes as well, and it is effectively contrasted with the bridge, featuring a chromatic progression accompanied by polished orchestral strings. The chromaticism was lavishly developed in another hit "Miagete-goran Yoru-no Hoshi-o" (Look Up the Stars in the Sky), composed by Taku Izumi with lyrics by Rokusuke Ei and sung by Sakamoto (Mitsui 1992: 2179).

Combined with such a new tendency, mainstream *kayōkyoku* remained vigorous during the 1960s with the Record Awards, which was modelled on the Grammy Awards in 1959, and with some television shows that emphasized conventional singers and songs in contrast to others that catered for younger and urban tastes, as discussed afterwards.

Commercial song

The first commercial song, "Boku-wa Amateur Cameraman" (I'm an Amateur Cameraman), appeared in 1951 when commercial radio stations were formed in Japan for the first time, although radio commercials tended to use existing tunes in the public domain. This song was far ahead of the times in the way it was used to promote a company and its products without mentioning them by name. It was a precursor of typical commercial songs with its light-hearted tune in major scale and heart-warming comical lyrics; in contrast to contemporary popular songs, which tended to be in minor scale. In the 1950s, its composer, Torirō Miki, with his commercial song-writing team, towered over the new field, which soon emphasized brand names and firm names in songs, while also expanding into television broadcasting in 1953.

'Commercial song' (often abbreviated as 'CM song'), used as an English phrase, is a song inserted in or combined with a commercial, an advertisement on Japanese radio or television. It is a complete piece of song-writing, however short in duration, and thus different from a jingle and a fragmentary accompaniment to a vocal message or visual image. Commercial songs increasingly caught the fancy of the public, resulting in an amateur singing contest of commercial songs becoming a regular TV show in the early and mid-1960s. The fact that the contestants included many children suggested that the repetition of the firm/brand names made the songs catchy, and they largely had nothing to do with adult man–woman relationships, to the relief of parents. The further tendency to incorporate rhythmical and melodic elements from overseas popular music was evidenced by Taku Izumi, who was a protégé of Torirō Miki. Izumi, who successfully found his way into writing popular songs as well, used commercial songs as a testing ground for integrating new Western musical elements into his composition of popular songs.

Merging the new trend of popular songs into commercial songs continued into the late 1960s and early 1970s, resulting in commercial songs being written in the styles of contemporary popular songs, including folk, rock and *enka*. Use of the major pentatonic scale was on the increase, among other musical changes, though the regular major scale still predominated. In the lyrics, reliance on the portrayal of a situation was replaced by a growth in introspection. The eminent figure in the field of commercial songs in the 1970s was Eiichi Ōtani, who was also active in the field of popular songs. While assimilating the elements of such music as New Orleans jazz, 1950s rock 'n' roll and 1960s pop, he produced his own sound after the model of Phil Spector's 'wall of sound'. (For the first twenty-five years of commercial songs, see Zen-Nihon CM Kyōgi-kai: 1978.)

A new age of commercial songs began in the mid-1970s when sponsors, advertising agents and the music industry began presenting the 'images' of a firm and its goods in ways that placed more emphasis on visual and auditory aspects of the commercial. The names of firms or goods tended not to be mentioned in the lyrics of many songs, which were later called 'image songs'. These songs favoured the minor scale with their lyrics having a propensity for a man speaking romantically to a woman, or a woman to a man, reflecting a new trend labelled 'new music' (discussed later in 'Transformation inspired by the West (8)'), in which a singer-narrator was mostly introverted, paying high regard to his or her private life. Image songs, which were for the most part understandably tied to cosmetic firms, were gradually adopted in the 1980s by other categories of business and the types of music used also became wider ranging.

There has appeared since the later 1980s what is called in Japanized English a 'tie-up song', representing a synergy between advertisers and the music industry. The association of its lyrical contents with what was advertised was weaker than in image songs and often became insubstantial. Eventually, a tie-up song turned out to be a complete independent song, even though it was tied up with a commercial or with a serial drama on television. The year 1991 saw the first two great hits produced through using a song as a theme song of a TV drama: Kazumasa Oda's "Love Story-wa Totsuzen-ni" (Love Story Starts Abruptly) was the theme song for *Tokyo Love Story* and Chage & Aska's "Say Yes" was used for *Hyaku-ikkai-me-no Propose* (One Hundred-and-First Proposal). While prototypical commercial songs endure and image songs persist, the Japanese music industry has now taken for granted the promotion of the sale of their recorded songs through having them widely publicized on television. (For the history of commercial songs in Japan, see Hayashi et al. 1984 and Ogawa et al. 2005.)

(To be continued: see page 125 for (6).)

5

Music and protest in the late 1960s: The rise of underground folk

This is a revised version of 'Music and Protest in Japan: The Rise of Underground Folk Song in "1968"', in *Music and Protest in 1968*, edited by Beate Kutscheke and Barley Norton, and published by Cambridge University Press, pp. 81–96 (© Cambridge University Press 2013).

In 1968, underground folk songs in Japan became popular on a national scale. Emerging from student singer-songwriters in the Kansai region, underground folk songs were influenced by currents of folk song in the USA and were intimately connected to New Leftist student activism and protest. Hence, the word folk used hereafter is different from 'folk-' of 'folksongs' proper, which appear in the preceding chapters. In this chapter, I chart the rise of the underground folk-song movement through analysis of the most important songs in 1968 and highlight how these songs were a medium for student protest as part of campaigns that opposed the Vietnam War.

The emergence of the underground folk-song movement was part of a broader range of musical change and experimentation in Japanese popular and art music in the late 1960s. In the field of contemporary art music, avant-garde composers were breaking new boundaries through collaboration with independent film producers and participation in the *shō-gekijō* (little theatre) movement in Tokyo (Nihon Sengo Ongakushi Kenkyūkai 2007: 445–7), which was analogous to the off-Broadway movement in New York. Liberation from conventional musical frameworks was also evident among jazz musicians who began to explore free jazz. Both avant-garde composition and free jazz, however, gained only a limited following and had a minimal cultural impact. Free jazz 'received overwhelming support from youth who aimed at reforming society' (Soejima 2002: 76), but it 'remained an extremely marginal pursuit […] and its audience was very small' (Molasky 2005: 158). In the field of popular music, young musicians who loved groups like the Beatles started to form bands that were referred to in English as 'group sounds' and quite a few songs from these bands were hits in the charts. Most of the hits, however, were composed by experienced songwriters who were already working in the music industry and who wrote songs that fused international popular styles with characteristics of mainstream Japanese popular songs, relying heavily on the minor key to convey sentimental lyrics about love.

In tandem with developments in avant-garde art music, jazz and popular song, in 1968 the New Leftist student movement intensified causing campus strife at more than a hundred universities and colleges. Music was not central to student protest during campus demonstrations, but the song "The Internationale" – which was associated with revolts in Paris in the late nineteenth century and entered Japan in 1920 via the Soviet Union (see Morita 1984: 50) – was sung in unison by students at various gatherings as a kind of anthem of resistance.

At student peace rallies, however, protest songs, which were referred to as folk song in English and presently abbreviated as folk, were very important. The English term was adopted from US records that became popular in Japan in the early 1960s. Initially, 'pop-folk' music was popular among students, particularly those who lived in the Tokyo metropolitan area, and this led to a music scene known, in English, as 'college-folk'. This scene concentrated on the reproduction of American pop-folk songs by devotees who were by and large the sons and daughters of well-to-do families. In contrast to the 'college-folk' scene in Tokyo, students in the Kansai region (which encompasses the three large cities of Kyoto, Osaka and Kobe) were more attracted to protest songs in folk-song idioms by American singers.[1] They first sang them in the original English before singing them in translation, and soon they started to compose their own songs based on American models.

The extent to which the Kansai folk-song movement caught the imagination of the nation is evidenced through several songs entering the national charts in 1968. The first song to trigger a sensation at the beginning of 1968 was a comical song with a topical theme called "Kaettekita Yopparai" (Drunkard Returned from Heaven), which was followed by other hits such as "Jukensei Blues" (Examinee Blues). Analysis of these songs in the next section is followed by discussion of how the underground folk-song movement became closely intertwined with anti-war protest and the Peace-for-Vietnam Committee in Japan. Interestingly, one of the most popular anti-war songs, "Jieitai-ni Hairō" (Let's Join the Self-Defence Forces), was at first mistakenly understood by the Japanese Defence Agency as a possible recruiting tool, rather than as a parody of the Self-Defence Forces. As exemplified by "Jieitai-ni Hairō", Japanese songwriters also attempted to revive the tradition of *enka* songs from the early twentieth century to articulate social and political protests, alongside new protest music that was influenced by the songs performed by such American musicians as Pete Seeger and Joan Baez who toured Japan in the 1960s. The most strident forms of political activism and protest were initiated by young members of the Peace-for-Vietnam Committee, who called themselves 'Folk Guerrilla' in English. Anti-war demonstrations by the Folk Guerrilla, which culminated in a series of rallies from February to July 1969, were vigorously suppressed by the police and ultimately extinguished. The last section of this chapter highlights how collective singing of anti-war songs, most of which became nationally popular in 1968, helped galvanize the Folk Guerrilla's activities and how songs were an important medium for protesting against the Vietnam War.

The Kansai folk-song movement and 'un-gra' songs

Songs from the Kansai folk-song movement that hit the charts in 1968 were labelled by the media as 'un-gra' songs. Un-gra, which is an abbreviation of underground, can be spelt as 'angura', but un-gra is closer to the way it is pronounced. Before it was used in relation to music, the label un-gra became popular in 1967 when experimental films produced by independent directors were dubbed as un-gra films (Nihon Kokugo Daijiten Henshū-Iinakai 2000: 710). Following the enormous popularity of the song "Kaettekita Yopparai", which set the trend for later un-gra songs, record companies jumped on the bandwagon and fifteen singles were released as un-gra songs in February and March 1968 (Mihashi 1979: 48). "Kaettekita Yopparai" was composed, performed and recorded by Folk Crusaders, a group of college students in Kyoto. It was released by Toshiba on 25 December 1967, and in January 1968 the song topped the weekly single charts of *Original Confidence*, which was founded in the previous year as a smaller Japanese equivalent to *Billboard*. Eventually the single sold more than 2.3 million copies (Original Confidence 1997: 286).

The song's narrative is based on the story of a man who dies as a result of driving a car while intoxicated. After his death, he ascends the long stairs to heaven, which is described in the song refrain as a place where 'wine tastes good and girls are pretty'. The song is given a comic twist by the singer using a stereotyped dialect of a country bumpkin and by the pitch of the vocal being raised, along with that of the instrumental accompaniment, by speeding up the reel-to-reel recording. God reproaches the man for his behaviour in the Kansai dialect,[2] but he continues to drink every day and finally God commands him to 'Get out!'. Banished from heaven, the man goes down the stairs leading up to heaven, but on the way, he loses his footing and falls. When he regains consciousness after the fall, he finds himself lying in a field with his life restored. The narrative of the song tapped into great public concern at the time about traffic congestion and deaths on the road, which had increased dramatically due to rapid growth in the domestic car industry and the economy in general.

The musical style of the song is influenced by commercial American folk music of the mid-1960s. Performed in D major, the verse of the song follows an eight-bar chord progression using chords I and V (i.e. D/D/D/A/A/A/A/D). The chords are played minimally by an acoustic steel-stringed guitar following the rhythm of two quarter-notes followed by four eighth-notes per bar. The six-bar refrain is more upbeat with the last two bars being 'doo-wopped'. The humorous tone of the song is maintained not only by the surreal narrative that is delivered in a comical voice, but also by other musical effects that are inserted into the song. These include the sound of an ambulance siren and rhythms played on a wood block found in Buddhist temples.

Before being released by Toshiba at the end of 1967, "Kaettekita Yopparai" had already become popular in the Kansai region as it had been released by Folk Crusaders themselves on their album *Harenchi* (Unabashed), when the idea of independent production was quite innovative. The band pressed just 300 copies of the album in October 1967 to commemorate the band members' college graduations and their disbanding. Despite the small print run of the album, the song became popular after being aired on 8 November by Radio Kansai's late-night show *Telephone Request*. Late-night radio shows were promoted with the catch-phrase 'a liberated area in the middle of the night' and they were very influential on students: 'For young listeners, many of whom were students preparing for college-entrance examinations, radio helped ease their stress [...] Late-night shows had little regulation, and DJs on these shows were keen to communicate and appeal to listeners in a different way compared with day-time shows' (Maeda and Hirahara 1993: 110–11). The popularity of "Kaettekita Yopparai" on *Telephone Request* led to it 'rising to second in the show's Top Ten within a week, and in the second week it gained the top spot where it remained for two consecutive weeks' (Hirose 1969: 215). The young listeners who were enthralled by "Kaettekita Yopparai" also had a passion for another song on the album, called "Imjin-gawa" (River Imjin). Since the mid-1950s, the River Imjin had marked the divide between North and South Korea and it is described in the song as a river 'across which water-fowls freely fly'. The mild social protest of the song lyrics is combined with a sentimental melody in F major sung sweetly in unison by the members of the band. "Imjin-gawa" was regularly played on local radio: Kinki Hōsō (Kinki Broadcasting) kept playing it for two months on their show, *Songs of This Week* (Maeda and Hirahara 1993: 87).

"Kaettekita Yopparai" and "Imjin-gawa" were soon aired by radio DJs in Tokyo as well, and the popularity of these songs prompted the interest of major record companies. Toshiba won the contract with Folk Crusaders and "Imjin-gawa" was planned to be released in February 1968 as a follow-up to the huge success of "Kaettekita Yopparai". However, in the end, Toshiba decided to cancel its release, even though 130,000 copies of the single, recorded anew in their studio, had already been pressed. This was because the General Association of Korean Residents in Japan had insisted that it be made clear that the song had originally been composed by two citizens of North Korea (Kurosawa 1992: 71), with the words written by Young-Saeng Pak and the music by Jong-Hwan Ko (Folk Camp 1969: 235). The Association also complained that the Japanese version, translated by Takeshi Matsuyama (a friend of Kazuhiko Katō, the lead guitarist and lead vocalist of Folk Crusaders) did not closely follow the original (Maeda and Hirahara 1993: 112), which reflects the viewpoint of the Democratic People's Republic of Korea. Matsuyama and Katō had assumed that the song was a traditional Korean folksong (Kokita 2002: 19).[3] Nonetheless, Toshiba successfully released another lyrical song by Folk Crusaders, "Kanashikute Yarikirenai" (I'm Too Sad to Bear), with "Kobu-no Nai Rakuda" (Camel without Humps) on the B side. This single reached number six in the charts and sold 259,000 copies (Original Confidence 1997: 286). After three more singles were released, the band finally disbanded in October 1968 as they had announced at the time of their signing to Toshiba.

Apart from Folk Crusaders' songs, the other most popular un-gra song in 1968 was "Jukensei Blues" (Examinee Blues), as performed by Tomoya Takaishi. The lyrics were written in 1967 by Gorō Nakagawa, then a high-school student, and they were originally set to the tune of Bob Dylan's "North Country Blues". Nakagawa stated in 1969 that he wrote the lyrics in order to 'turn people's attention to the ordeal of students preparing for highly competitive entrance-exams' and that he set it to "North Country Blues" because Dylan's song (with lyrics translated into Japanese) was already popular through being 'sung at folk song gatherings in Osaka' (Nakagawa 1969: 185–6). Nakagawa's lyrics were published in August 1967 in a mimeographed magazine called *Kawaraban*, which was obviously modelled on *Broadside* in New York. The periodical was started in Kobe by Yuzuru Katagiri, a poet and a teacher of English who supported the Kansai folk-song movement. In issues of *Kawaraban*, 'lyrics in translation by Woody Guthrie, Pete Seeger, Bob Dylan, Tom Paxton, Malvina Reynolds, Phil Ox, etc. were published' (Mihashi 1975: 233).

According to Nakagawa, Takaishi wrote a new melody for his lyrics because Dylan's melody 'sounded too gloomy for the song to spread' (Nakagawa 1969: 185). It is highly likely that the more jovial melody for "Jukensei Blues" was influenced by the popularity of "Kaettekita Yopparai", especially because Takaishi composed it in January 1968 at the time when the Folk Crusaders' song became a massive hit. Takaishi quickly recorded "Jukensei Blues" and it was released in late February, by another major label, Nippon Victor, to which Takaishi had already been signed in late 1966. The highest position of this single in the charts was number six, and it sold 113,000 copies (Original Confidence 1997: 188). Like Folk Crusaders, Takaishi mingled in Kansai folk-song circles and had moved to Osaka a couple of years before, although he was enrolled at a university in Tokyo.

The narrator/singer of "Jukensei Blues" ironically gripes about his dreary life as a high-school student preparing himself for entrance examinations for universities. Addressing the listeners, the lyrics include the lines:

Come here, everyone,
Listen to my tale,
I'm an unhappy examinee.
Listen to my tale,
It's insipid and dry as dust.

Takaishi sings the song in a light-hearted style with a tone of sarcasm. The medium-tempo, eight-bar tune in C major is cheerful and is accompanied by chords I, IV and V. The band features a five-string banjo that plays arpeggios to an eighth-note rhythm throughout.

"Jukensei Blues" provided a medium for the expression of students' unhappiness at the societal pressures imposed upon them. Resistance to such pressures is also emphasized through a brief but direct reference to the influential protest song "We Shall Overcome". At the end of "Jukensei Blues" a chorus of voices sings 'we shall overcome' in English with the lead voice also shouting 'we shall overcome' over the top of the chorus as the record fades out. "We Shall Overcome" was known to many social-minded Japanese through performances by Pete Seeger, who toured Japan several times during the 1960s, and it became an anti-war anthem at demonstrations in Japan organized by Veheiren (the abbreviation of 'Vietnam ni heiwa-o' Shimin Rengō), whose official English name was the Peace-for-Vietnam Committee.

The Peace-for-Vietnam Committee and anti-war songs

The Peace-for-Vietnam Committee, the most prominent and active anti-war organization in Japan, was formed in April 1965, two months after the United States Air Force began bombing North Vietnam. The Committee was made up of novelists, critics and academics, who organized their first anti-war demonstration march to the American Embassy in Tokyo on 24 April 1965 (Peace-for-Vietnam Committee 1974: 6), just a week after a ceasefire demonstration parade was held in Washington, DC. Japan was politically involved in the Vietnam War because its government consistently supported the American policy and many US military bases in Japan contributed to the war. Most notably, the main island of Okinawa was a key base for US fighter planes launching attacks in Vietnam. Okinawa was under direct US military government from 1945 until 1972.

Music was a prominent feature of most of the anti-war protests organized by the Peace-for-Vietnam Committee, and some other groups. Pete Seeger's tour to Japan in late 1963, which included performances of the songs "Where Have All the Flowers Gone" and "We Shall Overcome", was an important inspiration for many Japanese musicians who wrote anti-war songs, and the influence of Seeger and other American folk-singers continued through the 1960s. In January 1967, for instance, Baez was invited to anti-war meetings held by student associations in Osaka and the Peace-for-Vietnam Committee in Tokyo. The participants, who numbered more than 2,000 in Osaka and 1,200 in Tokyo (Peace-for-Vietnam Committee 1974: 188 and 518), listened to Baez singing "We Shall Overcome" and "Blowin' in the Wind" with other guest performers (Hirose 1969: 212).

It was during 1967 and 1968 that the anti-war movement in Japan gained momentum, and Tomoya Takaishi, who became nationally known in 1968 through the success of "Jukensei Blues", was a key figure in the movement. He was instrumental in setting up the Takaishi Office to help organize musical anti-war activities, and at numerous events he performed anti-war songs written by Japanese musicians, as well as Japanese versions of songs by American songwriters such as "The Times They Are A-Changin'", "What Did You Learn in School Today", "Blowin' in the Wind" and "Masters of War" (Nakagawa 1969: 180). In late July 1967, the Takaishi Office organized the first Folk Camp, a two-day event consisting of song-writing sessions, panel discussions and an outdoor concert held in Kyoto. The participants in the camp joined together for a group performance of Dylan's "Playboys and Playgirls" with new lyrics that satirized the special procurement measures that were in force due to the Vietnam War (Mihashi 1979: 34). The second Folk Camp held in November 1967 and Underground Ongakukai (Underground Concert) in March 1968 also featured many protest songs. The un-gra movement was now widely known due to the popularity of "Jukensei Blues" (Kurosawa 1992: 22; Hata 1993: 63) and the Takaishi Office adopted the word 'underground' in the title of the March concert, without having it abbreviated. The concert was 'so to speak, a trade fair of un-gra songs with television directors and music writers from Tokyo being present among the audience' (Hirose 1969: 219).

Around the same time, a concert called Folk School was held in Kyoto in early 1968. At the second Folk School concert in Kyoto on 25 February 1968, a new student singer-songwriter in the Kansai folk-song movement, Nobuyasu Okabayashi, caused quite a stir. He sang a song called "Kuso Kurae-bushi" (Go-to-hell Song) (Maeda and Hirahara 1993: 119), the lyrics of which include harsh satire and swear words. The song contains strong criticism of the pillars of society, including a company executive, a politician and a Christian minister. Okabayashi was a theology student at a university in Kyoto and his father was a Christian minister. The last verse is as follows:

> One day a holy man of religion,
> Preached a sermon to the congregation.
> Keep restraining yourself in this world,
> Then you are sure to go to Heaven.
> Liar! I don't believe you!
> You're a liar, you bastard.
> Don't tell a plausible lie,
> You, holy servant of God.

"Kuso Kurae-bushi" was scheduled for release in May 1968 by Victor with "San'ya Blues" (Doss-house Blues) on the B side, but they flinched at the original title and changed it and the lyrics were regarded as 'ideologically prejudiced' by the record ethical-code committee (Oakabayashi 1969: 111). In the end, "Kuso Kurae-bushi" was not released by Victor, and "San'ya Blues"/"Tomo-yo" (My Friends) became the single instead (Nagira 1995: 39). Both sides of this record became hits in early October. "Tomo-yo", in which the singer addresses his comrades encouragingly in a bright voice to a tune in E major ('My friends, beyond this darkness, tomorrow is shining'), was perceived to be an anti-war and anti-establishment song, and was often chosen as a sing-along song at anti-war meetings on university campuses.

Of all the anti-war songs that were written in 1968, "Jieitai-ni Hairō" (Let's Join the Self-Defence Forces) became the most popular. It was published in the July 1968 issue of the magazine *Kawaraban*, although it was not recorded in the studio until August 1969. In the long run, it turned out to be the best-known anti-war song in Japan. The lyrics to "Jieitai-ni Hairō" were written by Wataru Takada when he was a nineteen-year-old high-school student from Tokyo. Takada's lyrics were set to the tune (by Malvina Reynolds) of Pete Seeger's "Andorra". Takada first performed the song in the third Folk Camp, which was held on 9–11 August 1968 at a large Buddhist temple in Kyoto. More than 250 people participated in the camp, some of whom had come to see the popular group Folk Crusaders, who were known not only through their records but also through their television appearance (Mihashi 1979: 31). This third Folk Camp was the first opportunity for Kansai and Tokyo singers to link up with each other, and this was Takada's first visit to the Kansai region. Takada's song and singing attracted a great deal of attention at the camp (Takaishi 1969: 84). Using polite language, Takada addressed the audience with lyrics such as:

> Do you take an interest in guns, tanks and airplanes?
> Welcome to the Self-Defence Forces!
> We'll coach you with great care. [From verse 3]
> To keep the peace in Japan, guns and rockets are needed.
> With the assistance of Mr. America.
> Let's beat the wicked Soviet Union and China. [From verse 4]

The chorus has the following lines sung to a cheerful sing-along melody in the key of A major:

> Let's join, let's join, let's join!
> This world is a paradise if you join.
> Any man who is a real man,
> Joins the Forces and falls like cherry blossoms.

In a tongue-in-cheek manner, Takada mockingly invites the audience to enlist in the Self-Defence Forces. Established in July 1954, the Self-Defence Forces consist of land, maritime and air forces, and today they are 240,000 strong. It is important to note that since their inception, the legal basis of the Self-Defence Forces has often been challenged because their existence seems to contravene the Japanese Constitution.⁴ Takada's song was broadcast in August 1968 on TBS, a major television network, and it soon became the talk of the town. Once the song became well known, the Defence Agency baffled Takada when they asked him for permission to use the song to publicize their recruitment drive. Takada later reflected on this incident in a television interview: 'I wanted to write a paradoxical song [...] Isn't it strange that, despite my intention, there were some who misunderstood the song by taking it seriously? People at the Defence Agency were among them' ('Jieitai-ni hairō' 1999). Such different readings of the song's meanings highlight the ambiguity of songs as a form of protest and their susceptibility to different interpretations whatever the author's intent. In the end, however, the Defence Agency withdrew their proposal, acknowledging their failure to realize that the song was a parody. The official condemnation of the song was complete when the National Association of Commercial Broadcasters in Japan blacklisted the studio version of the song (which was released in 1969) in order to prevent it from being aired (Mori 2003: 19).

Revitalizing *enka*

The idiom in which Takada wrote "Jieitai-ni Hairō" had its roots in *enka*, a type of song that was popular from the 1880s to the 1930s.⁵ In fact, Takada also performed an *enka* song titled "Akirame-bushi" (Resignation Song) at the third Folk Camp held in August 1968, when he sang "Jieitai-ni Hairō" for the first time in public. "Akirame-bushi" was written in the mid-1900s by Azenbō Soeda who was the most prolific writer of *enka*. The performance of this *enka* song was Takada's first public attempt to resuscitate Japanese protest songs from a different era. They were songs of social and political protest, which were quite different to songs now more widely known also as *enka*.⁶ The first two stanzas of "Akirame-bushi" (Soeda 1963: 130) are as follows:

> Wealthy landowners are selfish,
> Civil servants are arrogant.
> I was born to such a world,
> I resign myself to fate.
> What have you come here for?
> To pay taxes and interests.

I was born to such a world,
I resign myself to fate.

The feeling of resignation in the song text is comical and satirical, and this is emphasized by Takada singing the words impassively to the second part of an American traditional dance-tune, "Black Mountain Rag". By setting old words to a new melody approachable to the young audience, Takada recontextualized an old protest song for a new political context. Takada's interest in *enka* was encouraged by the music journalist Kazuo Mihashi, whom he first met in the autumn of 1967. At the meeting, Mihashi showed Takada 'a book about Azenbo's *enka*' (Mihashi 1975: 64), and in correspondence Takada discussed with Mihashi which of Azenbo's song texts could be sung to melodies by Woody Guthrie (ibid.: 65).

Takada was not the only young singer-songwriter who showed an interest in *enka*. Hiroshi Iwai, a five-string banjo player and a singer-songwriter from Kyoto, recalled: 'Sometime after the Folk Camp in Kyoto in the summer of 1968, I heard Wataru [Takada] perform at Takaishi's concert at YMCA in Kyoto. He was singing the lyrics of an Azenbo's *enka* to a Woody Guthrie tune. I was also having a similar try at that [...] That made me talk with him about Woody' (Iwai 1992: 72). In September 1966, Takaishi had also performed a song by Azenbō, "Nonki-bushi" (Happy-Go-Lucky Song) (*c*. 1919), at his first public performance. He recollected in 1969 that '*Enka-no-Meiji* published by Iwanami offered me very good guidance, and on other occasions I also sang three or four *enka* songs, including "Doko Itoyasenu" (I Don't Give a Damn)' (Takaishi 1969: 95).

Two *enka* songs performed by Takada were included along with "Jieitai-ni Hairō" on a side of the first LP released by Underground Record Club (URC), an independent record label established by the Takaishi Office in February 1969 (Kurosawa 1992: 14–15). As major record companies in Japan were wary of releasing overt protest songs, URC was set up partly to avoid the self-censorship of the ethical-code committee, which had become customary practice within the mainstream music industry. In addition to the first LP, they released two singles, one of which consisted of original tracks by Trịnh Công Sơn, a distinguished Vietnamese singer-songwriter. In April 1969, URC went on to release a controversial song by Okabayashi, "Kuso Kurae-bushi", which the major label Victor had refused to release, with "Gaikotsu-no Uta" (Skull's Song) on the B side. "Gaikotsu-no Uta" was another fierce song, which Okabayashi first sang at the February 1968 Folk School concert. URC's subscription system to distribute these records was successful enough for URC to be expanded into URC Records in July 1969. In parallel with this expansion, massive anti-war rallies were held in Tokyo and songs from the folk-song movement in Kansai were sung at these rallies.

Folk Guerrilla

In late February 1969, the Tokyo Peace-for-Vietnam Committee and their supporters marched from their office to Shinjuku Station, one of the most important transportation centres in Tokyo. On the way, they sang to the accompaniment of a couple of guitars and held a singing demonstration in an open area called the Chika Hiroba (Underground Square) at the west entrance to the station. This action was motivated by young members of the Osaka Peace-for-Vietnam Committee, who participated in an indoor meeting, titled '1969 Anti-war Folk and Debate', held by the Tokyo Peace-for-Vietnam Committee on 11 January (Muro 1969: 22). The members had travelled to Tokyo several times since late 1968 and on their trips to Tokyo they held a series of singing demonstrations, which they called Folk Caravan, in the large cities of Nagoya and Yokohama (Muro 1969: 22 and 24). These young volunteers had started off by assembling in the underground shopping complex under Osaka Station to hold regular, small anti-war demonstrations, which included singing songs together. Yoshiyuki Tsurumi, one of the representatives of the Peace-for-Vietnam Committee, wrote in June 1969: 'Since February some of the young members of the Committee, who now call themselves Tokyo Folk Guerrilla, appeared every Saturday and held a meeting to sing anti-war songs together' (from Yoshiyuki Tsurumi, 'Hansen folk-ni kaigenrei' (Anti-war folk is now under martial law), *Asahi Journal*, June 1969, quoted in Tsurumi 2002: 312). In the April issue of a periodical published by the Peace-for-Vietnam Committee, a female student member of the Folk Guerrilla remarked:

> What I had in mind when singing folk songs was that the songs are a rage against, and a satire on, those who made war as if nothing were the matter. They expressed anger at those who withdraw into their shells, doing nothing while knowing that a war has broken out, and they gave us a sense of solidarity. (From Kazuko Ebata, 'Naze folk song-o utau-noka' (Why do they sing folk songs?), *Veheiren News*, April 1969, cited in Muro 1969: 26)

In the June issue of the periodical, another female student, who was one of the Folk Guerrilla organizers, reported on one of their demonstrations:

> Around six o'clock [...] suddenly two guitars began to be strummed [...] Just at that moment, a large number of people quickly drew near [...] The two guitar players were grabbled by the arm by the policemen [...] They kept playing "We Shall Overcome" and "Tomo-yo" [...] We continued to sing those songs, over and over, again and again – they had never sounded so beautiful before. I felt my heart tightening with deep emotion [...] We moved around, singing, and arrived at the east entrance [...] While singing there for a while, we were informed that singing had been resumed at the west entrance. And this time three guitar players headed there. (From Miyo Takano, 'Nishiguchi Hiroba-wa dare-no mono' (To whom the west square belongs?), *Veheiren News*, June 1969, cited in Muro 1969: 14–15)

It was during a demonstration on 17 May at the Chika Hiroba in Shinjuku Station, held after three months of guerrilla activity, that the Tokyo Folk Guerrilla reached the headlines. A reporter of a major newspaper who must have arrived there around the time that the guitar players headed to the west entrance gave the following description of the demonstration:

> Suddenly three young men took out guitars and were at once surrounded by a large circle of people [...] Fifty policemen in uniform were on patrol, and the very moment the three young men began to play the guitars they were held by thirty policemen and taken away. Protesting against this use of force, about a hundred members of the Peace-for-Vietnam Committee, being joined by passers-by, yelled out at the policemen in chorus, 'Get back, get back!' It was followed by mass singing of "Tomo-yo", and thereupon a hundred riot policemen, who had waited in readiness in the car park, were ordered out to prevent their singing. (From a report in *Yomiuri*, 18 May 1969, cited in Muro 1969: 12)

It was estimated that the crowd of protestors and spectators at the Chika Hiroba numbered about 2,000. At later demonstrations in May, the crowd swelled to around 5,000 people and this escalated further during demonstrations in June and July. Several days after a large demonstration on 12 July, when some 7,000 people gathered, the Metropolitan Police Department changed the sign Chika Hiroba (Underground Square) to Chika Tsūro (Underground Passage). This re-designation meant that holding a meeting there was a violation of the Road Traffic Act. On the day of the next demonstration on 19 July, 2,000 riot policemen were sent out to prohibit it. A large number of people were arrested, and this finally put an end to the regular Folk Guerrilla rallies at the station (Tsurumi 2002: 313).

In the insider observations and the agitated press coverage that reported the guerrilla activities, occasionally specific songs were referred to, but no importance was attached to the songs' origins. The writers in Tokyo seemed to be unaware that the songs performed at Folk Guerrilla rallies drew on the Kansai folk-song movement. However, as shown in reports by student activists and the press, the songs performed by the Folk Guerrilla in 1968 included the very songs discussed so far in this chapter. Moreover, in addition to songs such as "We Shall Overcome", "The Internationale", "Tomoyo", "Imjin-gawa" and "Jieitai-ni Hairō", the Folk Guerrilla also adapted some songs, making them directly relevant to the demonstrations they were involved: for example, "Jieitai-ni Hairō" (Let's Join the Self-Defence Forces) was modified to become "Kidōtai-ni Hairō" (Let's Join the Riot Police). The lyrics for this song were as follows:

> Do you dislike demonstrations?
> You're welcome to join the Riot Police!
> With truncheons, tear bombs and a water truck,
> Let's obstruct the demos.

Another song performed at the demonstrations, "Kidōtai Blues" (Riot Police Blues), was a variation of "Jukensei Blues" (Examinee Blues) with the narrator becoming a riot policeman:

> Come here, everyone,
> Listen to my tale,
> I'm an unhappy riot policeman,
> Listen to my tale,
> It's insipid and dry as dust.
> [...]
> Alas! At noon we go to the park,
> It was packed with demonstrators.
> As I'm unpopular with girls,
> I threw a stone in despair.

Conclusion

Protest songs in Japan around the year 1968 were strongly influenced by songs from America, and the songs suitable for singing in unison at anti-war rallies were mainly the product of student singer-songwriters who were part of the Kansai underground folk-song movement. The year 1968 in Japan was therefore marked by an outpouring of youthful musical creativity and protest in the Kansai region. One of the main motivations for those young musicians in the underground movement was the desire to compose protest songs that commented on both domestic and international events. Many of these songs drew on models provided by American singers such as Pete Seeger, Bob Dylan and Woody Guthrie, and some became popular hits across Japan. As well as incorporating Western influences, however, the Kansai folk-song movement also looked for historical models of protest within Japanese music and recontextualized *enka* songs of protest from the early twentieth century. Young Japanese singer-songwriters, then, looked for both new and old musical forms for inspiration in their attempts to form a musical culture of protest in 1968.

Notes

1. The Kansai region has a less rigid cultural hierarchy than in Tokyo, which became highly centralized after the government relocated from Kyoto to Tokyo in 1868. This is a possible contributing factor to the differences in the student music scenes in the Kansai region and in Tokyo in the 1960s.
2. The Kansai dialect has humorous association for Japanese listeners mainly due to its widespread use among Osaka entertainers on radio and television.
3. Matsuyama first heard the original sung at a Korean school in Kyoto as a junior-high-school student around 1961 and Katō learnt it orally from Matsuyama about five years later.
4. Article 9 of the Constitution states that 'the Japanese people forever renounce war as a sovereign right of the nation and the threat or use of force as means of settling international disputes' and in a later section notes that 'land, sea, and air forces, as well as other war potential, will never be maintained […] The right of belligerency of the state will not be recognized' (Department of Laws and Institutions 2010 [1946], vol. 1, p. 4). Reflecting critically on Article 9 of the Constitution and the Self-Defence Forces, Charles Lummis, who was a member of the Peace-for-Vietnam Committee and taught political thought at a Japanese university, succinctly remarks that 'the notion that the clear renunciation of the right of belligerency is not a renunciation of the right to establish a military for self-defence is absurd' (Lummis 1993: 168).
5. A history of the early form of *enka* songs by Tomomichi Soeda, who was the son of Azenbō Soeda, was published in 1963 as *Enka-no Meiji-Taishō-shi* (History of the

Meiji and Taishō eras through *enka*). It includes the texts of 157 songs, forty-five of which are complete with melodies.

6   The term *enka* re-emerged with a new usage in the late 1960s, denoting a genre that is assumed to be typically Japanese in its musical and lyrical attributes, and in the early 1980s it became a mainstay of Japanese popular music.

Transformation inspired by the West (6)

Rock

Following the 'rockabilly' craze in the late 1950s and early 1960s, the group Ventures from the United States, who visited Japan in May 1962, generated what was called 'eleki' boom in which young males flaunted electric guitar performance. This instrumental-oriented music was soon combined with vocals influenced by the Beatles and other British beat groups. Promoted by evolving artist agencies, the groups consisting of four to seven male singers who played electric guitars and drums, wore loud costumes and wore their hair long became a phenomenon called 'group sounds' in English.

    At first, they modelled their own songs on those of the British groups as well as imitating them, but most of their hits resulted from yielding to *kayōkyoku*, composed by experienced songwriters who fused Western styles with characteristics of mainstream Japanese popular songs, relying heavily on the harmonic minor to convey sentimental lyrics about love. The fad grew with Spiders' "No No Boy" and followed by Blue Comets' "Aoi Hitomi" (Blue Eyes) in 1966, the year when the Beatles performed in Tokyo. In the following year, the Blue Comets succeeded with a bigger hit, "Blue Château", a song in minor scale, characterized by the strange exoticism of the lyrics, not to mention the sound of electric guitars and vocal harmony. At the same time, many more groups, including Tigers, Golden Cups, Jaguars, Carnabeats, and Tempters, appeared and expanded the trend in different directions. However, 'group sounds' bands quickly disappeared in 1970 as the music industry was more interested in promoting the groups' pretty-boy image for teenyboppers. However, their music was significant in emphasizing beat and vocal harmony as well as in underscoring the idea of music 'for youth by youth', which was first suggested by 'rockabilly', a genre expanded from rockabilly in the United States.

Some former members of 'group sounds' bands turned to what were called art-rock and psychedelic music, forming such bands as Flower Travellin' Band, Powerhouse and Blues Creation. The most influential band in the early 1970s was Happy End, who contributed to the expansion of the scope of rock in Japan with experiments in sound and style, including, among others, adherence to Japanese lyrics. In terms of resistance to the Establishment, Zunō Keisatsu (Brain Police) and Murahachibu (Ostracism) were more representative of hard-rock bands that spoke for disaffected youth. The commercial success of Japanese rock bands, first achieved in the mid-1970s by Godiego singing in English to a Japanese sound and Sadistic Mika Band singing in Japanese to a British sound, was underlined in the late 1970s by Carol, who specialized in rock 'n' roll, and Downtown Boogie-Woogie Band, who performed Japanese boogie-woogie songs. Then in the early 1980s, while Yellow Magic Orchestra succeeded with its electronic instrumentation and the success of Southern All Stars whose "Itoshi-no Ellie" (Ellie, My Love) was later covered by Ray Charles, many indie labels appeared for obscure bands that emerged under the influence of imported punk and new wave music. (For more detail on Japanese rock, see Inoue 2009; Inoue and Nanba 2009a, 2009b; Cope 2007; and Bourdaghs 2012: 85–194.)

Folk

Running parallel with 'group sounds', Japanese contemporary folk music evolved when the North American folk revival was introduced to Japan.

The term 'folk song', which was later shortened to 'folk', was adopted from the United States without being translated into Japanese. It was in early 1959 when 'pop-folk' was first introduced to Japan through the record "Tom Dooley" by the Kingston Trio. This was followed a few years later by the popularity of Peter, Paul and Mary's version of Bob Dylan's "Blowin' in the Wind" and by tours of Japan by Pete Seeger in 1963 and the Brothers Four in 1964. The young audience was so alienated from domestic folk music that the American folk revival never triggered a Japanese parallel.

'Pop-folk' was popular among students, particularly those who lived in the Tokyo area, and this led to a music scene known in English as 'college-folk'. This sing-it-yourself acoustic music was popular particularly among young urbanites, but it was not commercially remarkable except for "Bara-ga Saita" (Roses Are Out), a gentle song composed in the typical major scale by a *kayōkyoku* songwriter in 1966 and sung by Mike Maki.

In contrast to the 'college-folk' scene in Tokyo, students in the Kansai region (encompassing Kyoto, Osaka, and Kobe) were more attracted to protest songs in folk-song idioms by American singers such as Woody Guthrie, Pete Seeger and Bob Dylan, and around 1966 started to compose and sing their own songs of a socially and politically committed nature, which were based on American models and intimately connected to New Leftist student activism. The words, which were often ill-fitted to Western melodies, were a deviation from *kayōkyoku* in their rhythm and vocabulary, and therefore composing one's own songs was in itself a positive aspect of this movement. In 1968, the movement caught the national imagination through several songs by student singer-songwriters entering the charts. The first song to trigger a sensation at the very beginning of 1968 was a comical song with a topical theme called "Kaettekita Yopparai" (Drunkard Returned from Heaven), a million-seller, by Folk Crusaders. This funny song about the story of a man who dies as a result of driving a car, which reflected rapid growth in the domestic car industry, was followed by a hit by Tomoya Takaishi, who was active in the Kansai region. The narrator of "Jukensei Blues"'(Examinee Blues) ironically gripes about his dreary life as a high-school student, and the story is told in the way of many narrative folksongs in the English-speaking world, beginning with 'Come here, everyone, listen to my tale, I'm an unhappy examinee'. The cheerful tune in C major was accompanied by a five-string banjo that plays arpeggios to an eighth-note rhythm throughout.

Then, in the summer of 1968 in Kyoto appeared "Jieitai-ni Hairō" (Let's Join the Self-Defence Forces) by nineteen-year-old student Wataru Takada, which eventually became the most popular of all the anti-war songs. Using the tune (composed by Malvina Reynolds) of Pete Seeger's "Andorra", he mockingly invited the audience to enlist in the Self-Defence Forces. The idiom in which he wrote the song had its roots in *enka*, which flourished in the early twentieth century, and he was not the only young singer-songwriter who showed an interest in *enka* to articulate social and political protest and re-contextualize it. The Kansai movement soon extended to Tokyo and provincial areas, and an annual festival on a massive scale was held in the summer of 1969.

The Nakatsugawa Folk Jamboree lasted for three years. Less visible but equally significant was a grass-roots aspect of the movement during a time of political and social turmoil (the 1960s' campaigns against the Vietnam War and campus disputes, among others), and a group of anonymous singers with guitars led the singing of protest songs by those who rallied to political meetings and those who regularly gathered at public squares. (For a detailed examination of songs in the Kansai folk movement and how important they were as a medium for protest against the Vietnam War in 1969, see Mitsui 2013.)

The season of political involvement came to an end around 1970, corresponding with such events as the automatic renewal of the Japan–US Security Treaty, the conclusion of the Okinawa Reversion Agreement (concerning the return of the Okinawa islands and the Daitō islands to Japan), the calming of the campus strife and the opening of the World Exposition in Osaka, which represented Japan's post-war economic growth. Reflecting the entailing emergence of a disenchanted generation, social-minded songs began to be replaced in the early 1970s with introspective songs. The titles of such well-received songs are self-explanatory: "Sekishoku Elegy" (Red Colour Elegy) (1972) by Morio Agata, "Kekkon Shiyō-yo" (Let's Get Married) (1972) by Takurō Yoshida, "Kasa-ga Nai" (I Haven't Got an Umbrella) (1972) by Yōsui Inoue, and "Haha-ni Sasageru Ballad" (Ballad Dedicated to My Mother) (1973) by Tetsuya Takeda.

Folk represented the musical and lyrical sensibility of the new generation of singer-songwriters, who expressed themselves in singing their own songs, in contrast to the conventional outlook represented by *kayōkyoku*, which was the product of the music industry based on the division of work in which singer, composer, lyricist, arranger, orchestra and so on are mutually dependent. At the same time, folk came closer to *kayōkyoku* in its commercialization. Major record companies showed more interest in contracting new singer-songwriters (the songs mentioned above by Yoshida and Inoue were released by CBS-Sony and Polydor respectively), and new labels specializing in folk (the songs mentioned above by Agata and Takeda were released by Bellwood and Elec respectively) were formed. Commercialization was also reflected in the use of studio musicians who were trained to command new idioms. This new tendency soon evolved into a new amorphous category called 'new music'.

Idol-*kayō*

In the late 1960s, *kayōkyoku* songs noticeably influenced by Western popular music steadily increased and such songs as "Tenshi-no Yūwaku" (Angel's Temptation) sung by Jun Mayuzumi, "Blue Light Yokohama" sung by Ayumi Ishida in 1968, and "Yoake-no Scat" (Scatting at Dawn) sung by Saori Yuki in 1969 enjoyed great popularity. In the early 1970s, the number of songs combining Western musical idioms with Japanese styles and tastes increased markedly, as demonstrated by such hits as "Shiretoko Ryojō" (Traveller's Melancholy in Shiretoko) sung by Tokiko Katō in 1970 and "Seto-no Hanayome" (Bride in Seto) sung by Rumiko Koyanagai in 1972.

Meanwhile, in the early 1970s 'idol-*kayō*' appeared: a type of *kayōkyoku* for young people who found it difficult to identify with music based on imported music, such as adapted rock and folk, but also impossible to be free from Western musical idioms. With three young male singers from the early 1960s (including Kazuo Funaki, who first succeeded with "Kōkō San'nensei" (Twelfth Grade)) as its precursors, idol-*kayō* arose out of the popularity of another three young male singers among teenyboppers: Gorō Noguchi, Hideki Saijō and Hiromi Gō. It soon, however, developed a more feminine aspect with the advent of three girl singers, Saori Minami, Masako Mori and Rumiko Koyanagi, who made their debuts at around the same time and established an image of purity and innocence. The success of this image was instantly bolstered by another trio of female singers who, independently of each other, had won a television talent scout show, *Star Tanjō* (Star is Born), which had begun in 1971 and was followed by two similar shows.

In the mid- to late 1970s, idol-*kayō* underwent changes when Momoe Yamaguchi (Mitsui 1992: 2745) and the elaborately choreographed performances of two girl groups, Candies and Pink Lady, added an element of sexuality. Moreover, Seiko Matsuda (Mitsui 1992: 1641), who replaced Yamaguchi, following her retirement, as the leading star in the 1980s, stressed her feminist lifestyle by challenging the conservative concept of wife and mother while retaining her assumed innocence. At the same time, the popularity of boy idols was revived with the emergence of groups such as the Tanokin Trio and the Hikaru Genji. These changes occurred in parallel with musical deviation from *kayōkyoku* conventions, as significantly suggested by a book entitled *Dorobō Kayōkyoku* (Robbing kayōkyoku). This fully annotated list of 190 songs, alleged to be partly emulated from North American and European originals, consists of compositions of 'new music', folk, rock and 'group sounds', as well as many idol-*kayō*, although all are categorized under the umbrella of *kayōkyoku* (Datahouse 1987). (For a sociological examination of idols in later years, see Inamasu [1989] 1993, and for a comprehensive examination of idols in Japan, see Galbraith and Karlin 2012.)

(To be continued: see page 145 for (7).)

6

Japan in Japan: Looking for inexpensive potential stars from abroad

> This is a revised version of 'Japan in Japan: notes on an aspect of the popular music record industry in Japan', in *Popular Music 3: Producers and Markets*, edited by Richard Middleton and David Horn, and published by Cambridge University Press, pp. 107–20 (© Cambridge University Press 1983).

The record and tape sales figures of the Japanese record industry have exceeded those of the industries of all other capitalist nations, except the USA, since the mid-1970s. In 1980, Japan's share amounted to 13.9 per cent of all sales in the capitalist sphere according to surveys by *Billboard*. The USA had 35.8 per cent, West Germany 11.6 per cent, the UK 11.6 per cent and France 7.3 per cent (Kawabata 1977: 22; 1982: 91, 199). The output of foreign records in Japan is, however, without parallel among culturally developed countries. For the past fifteen years, the ratio of domestic records, recorded and pressed by Japanese companies, to foreign records, pressed by Japanese companies from masters recorded by foreign companies primarily for their own consumers, has been about three to two. A good many of these foreign records are of American and European popular music, and in this field one can perceive a new and interesting tendency to promote and succeed with artists who are or were less successful in their own country. This tendency, the background of which I will discuss here, started in the mid-1970s: one of the early examples is provided by Kiss, a New York group, who were shrewdly promoted and achieved wide popularity in Japan before succeeding nationwide in America.

Japanese economic growth led foreign enterprises to penetrate the Japanese market

Since the end of the Second World War and especially since 1960, various Japanese industries have developed rapidly as a result of the amazing growth in the economy. The record industry, which has quite a long history with many twists and turns,[1] was one: its growth resulting from the liberalization of foreign trade, the rise in the Japanese standard of living, the expanded youth market, the spread of stereo equipment and tape-recorders, and other factors. According to surveys by the Association of Record Companies in Japan (see Kurata 1979: 484; Kawabata 1982: 82), the number of discs produced in Japan in 1946 was 3,420,000. It more than doubled the next year to 8,847,000, and then increased to 11,961,000 in 1948. It was at 24,003,000 in 1960, 59,594,000 in 1963, and doubled again in the next five years to 120,430,000 in 1968. In 1973 it was 172,261,000, and 194,943,000 by 1980.

Japanese economic growth naturally led foreign enterprises to try and penetrate the Japanese market, and after Japan joined the OECD in April 1963, they constantly demanded a more liberal policy on foreign capital investment. The Japanese government gradually eased restrictions and in 1967 finally decided to free foreign investment completely, but only for the types of industry that would not substantially affect the Japanese economy. This included the record industry. The law was carried into effect on 1 July 1967, and, in March 1968, the first joint venture in the record industry, CBS Sony, was established, by Sony of Japan and CBS Columbia of the USA, which had just ceased to deal with Nippon Columbia. Nippon Columbia had long been connected with CBS, pressing and releasing CBS records for the Japanese market, but had declined CBS's offer of affiliation.

CBS Columbia was the first foreign major to form a joint venture with a Japanese company. In 1969, Toshiba Musical Industries was transformed into Toshiba EMI by affiliating with EMI in England, and in the following year, two more joint ventures were established: Nippon Phonogram, formed by Phonogram International and the Matsushita Group, and Warner Pioneer, comprising the WEA Group and Japanese Pioneer. Then, five years later, Nippon Victor and Victor Musical Industries (a subsidiary formed in 1972) finally formed a joint venture, RVC, with American RCA, who had been kept waiting for more than eight years. (According to Shigeru Kawabata, author of a vocational guide to the record industry, RCA was actually the first foreign company to propose a joint venture with Victor, who had long been connected with RCA, but Victor decided that the time was not quite right, though they did set up an RCA Record Planning Section as a division in their own organization.)

What attracted foreign companies to joint ventures was not only the high percentage of Japanese record output occupied by foreign records, but even more, the general increase in overall output. For gross earnings, after the deduction of label royalty, are distributed according to capital investment ratio. Thus, a foreign parent company, in a joint venture, profits by the sales of both foreign records, pressed from their own masters, and domestic records, in addition to label royalty. For Japanese organizations, there are two marked advantages in forming a joint venture. One is that trading with a major foreign label promises stability, dispensing with worries over contract renewal and rises in label royalty. For example, before the formation of RVC, Victor Musical Industries had a licensing deal with RCA, which was based on a three-year contract; every three years they were confronted with a rise in label royalty, together with a demand for an increased advance on royalty (even if, at least until CBS parted from Nippon Columbia, gentlemen's agreements between Japanese and foreign companies prevented contracts in this situation being taken over by some other company). Once Victor's RCA Record Planning Section was transformed into RVC, it enjoyed a steady and unlimited supply of masters from RCA, with a lower rate of label royalty. The other advantage of a joint venture is an international extension of the market for the Japanese company's domestic records and artists, as exemplified by the case of Isao Tomita.

As the internationalization of the record industry in the capitalist world accelerated, two more joint ventures were organized in 1980 – Polyster (Polygram and Japanese Polydor) and Epic Sony (Epic and CBS Sony) – and at last, in September 1981, there emerged a firm with 100 per cent foreign capital. This was London, established by Polydor International and started with masters supplied by English Decca and French Barclay. The number of record companies formed with foreign capital in Japan now amounts to eight, comprising around one-third of all the members of the Association of Record Companies in Japan (minor independent labels, such as those found in the USA, are almost nil in Japan).

The hot competition to acquire profitable foreign labels

As most of the major foreign labels are monopolized by these eight joint ventures (except MCA, which has continued to renew its contract with US Victor), the remaining, purely domestic companies, including Victor, King, Teichiku, Crown, Tokuma, Trio and Canyon, have been placed in a more difficult position than before, as far as the business of foreign records is concerned. They have struggled, in competition with the joint ventures, to acquire contracts with smaller foreign labels active in the Japanese market. As mentioned previously, the mode of transaction is called a licensing deal: a Japanese company is supplied with masters (either by a foreign company, or in some cases by an artist himself, if he has rights to masters and deals with different labels in other countries), on the understanding that it pays a label royalty, which includes the original artist royalty, on 80 per cent of the records it presses (Kawabata 1982: 185). The contract has long been on a two- or three-year basis in most cases, because of uncertainties on both sides. The license-holder usually tries to raise a royalty at the time of renewal, and painful negotiations ensue. Japanese companies themselves have helped to raise royalties by competitive bidding for a contract with an attractive or prominent label, and it is this trend that has grown excessively. If a company hesitates, or negotiations break down, the contract will probably be taken by some other company; and, at times, a contract moves along with the person who has been in charge of the label or artists in question.

The hot competition among Japanese record companies to acquire profitable foreign labels has brought about a chronic rise in label royalty, especially since about 1972 when many foreign labels began to raise their rates massively on the grounds of a rise in their artist royalty. While, before the emergence of joint ventures, label royalty was normally 10 per cent or thereabouts, it became 12, often 15, and even 18–20 when superstars were involved (Kawabata 1982: 253; Orita 1981: 117). This rise was naturally accompanied by a rise in the advance, which now became almost a guaranteed maximum when previously it had been a guaranteed minimum. The fact that Japanese record companies have clung to foreign labels could be explained in terms of prestige: they want to keep not only a rich assortment of records, but also well-known artists. However, as competition for foreign labels grew intense, some companies threw more energy into domestic records, the extreme case being Nippon Columbia, the oldest Japanese record company, whose sales figures in 1981 showed domestic records taking 95 per cent (Nakamura 1981: 99). After having parted from CBS, they continued to release records by minor foreign labels. 'We will not cut off foreign records', said Toshihiko Hirahara, head of the International Section, '[…] but I don't think it's advisable for companies with domestic capital to keep working in the field of foreign records in the present situation, at a narrower margin of profit and with high rises in royalty and advance' (*OC* 1980: 74).

Under these conditions, then, it is no wonder that Japanese companies, especially those with domestic capital, while competing to acquire expensive, comparatively unprofitable but well-known, established stars, have constantly sought foreign labels and artists who are inexpensive, suit a Japanese market and will produce good results. First, and most importantly, lesser-known artists are inexpensive in royalty. Second, there is no challenge from imported records to worry about.[2] Third, a company with domestic capital can conduct a much more concentrated and long-term promotion than a joint venture, which is always influenced by the parent organization: for instance, it might not be possible to neglect a certain artist to whom the parent organization attaches importance. A company with domestic capital can push an artist as much as possible, if they find him promising, without giving much consideration to their other artists and records, and they can rather easily have the artist come to Japan for promotion. 'It is particularly desired', commented Ichirō Fukuda, a music journalist who is well versed in the ways of the record industry, 'that the artist or record in question is not affected by American and English hit charts.' If the record is not in those charts, one is not vexed by its popularity and the resulting hopes and fears, and can make and carry out a careful long-term sales campaign in one's own way (Fukuda 1982). The record companies in Japan, especially those with domestic capital, inevitably began to take chances, and the method of making a deal with a foreign label after examining its existing catalogue became outmoded. Now Japanese companies, when making a contract, often judge an independent foreign label by how promising the artists seem to be for the Japanese market or by the ability of the owner/producer, without considering very much how popular the artists are in their own domestic market. And this tendency is even leading to speculative or forward buying.

Very successful examples promoted roughly in this way are Arabesque, a female disco-style trio from West Germany, and Richard Clayderman, an easy-listening pianist from France. Arabesque, having been skilfully promoted for the market developed by ABBA, first made the Top Ten Charts in West Germany with "Hello Mister Monkey", which reached number eight in the Japanese chart in 1978, selling 388,000 copies. All their songs must have been suited to this market, for they were continuously successful in the charts. The sales figures of their singles and LPs during 1981 ranked them as the sixth most successful group of all the artists whose records were released in Japan, including domestic artists. Richard Clayderman was promoted as a major artist to replace top easy-listening conductor Paul Mauriat. (The Frenchman Mauriat had been very popular in Japan since he first toured with his orchestra in 1969.) Clayderman's *The Best*, an LP compiled in Japan, reached number eleven, staying in the chart for eighty-six weeks and selling 245,000 copies, before Clayderman successfully toured Japan, attracting a large, mostly female audience (*OC* 1982a: 29–30). More interesting, however, is another example, a five-member (later four-member) British rock group named Japan. While other artists who were made stars or superstars had been more or less saleable, or not altogether unknown, in their own countries, Japan were an utterly obscure group when a Japanese record company made a contract with their label. Moreover, they have made supposedly non-hit-oriented, ambitious music without trying to cater for popular taste, and have succeeded well enough in the Japanese market at the same time. Ichirō Fukuda admiringly described their anonymity-to-star career as alchemy practised by their Japanese record company (Fukuda 1982). In the next section, as an example of the tendency discussed in general terms above, I will describe the marketing of this group, formed in the spring of 1977, in Japan.

How the group Japan was marketed in Japan

According to Akira Yokota, the A&R man who had been in charge of Japan, and who works for Victor's International Record Division, he first received a demo-tape of Japan along with a promotion photograph of the group late in 1977. Yokota thought them a potential replacement for the Bay City Rollers, whose popularity was declining in Japan. He was interested in their visual appearance, not only the startling prettiness of their made-up faces but also a certain gloominess, a kind of decadent atmosphere suggested by their photograph, which seemed to him to symbolize present-day London and that would, he thought, have a refreshing appeal to young audiences who had become used to seeing cheerful and vivacious pop idols. British punk rock was not much talked about in Japan at the time, and it was not on Yokota's mind.

Yokota got hold of Japan's first album, produced by their West German company Ariola Hansa. In the meantime, the Japanese music publisher, Taiyō, had also been approached by Ariola Hansa (a common practice on the part of foreign labels targeting the Japanese market). After a meeting between the president of Taiyō and Yokota, Yokota decided to buy the Japanese rights to Japan. A contract was signed in May 1978, between Ariola Hansa and Victor, the deal including distribution of the records of two other groups whose music Yokota had already heard: one resembling the Nolans; the other, the Bay City Rollers.

Surprisingly enough, a Japan fan club was formed before their first album was released in Japan in September 1978. This enthusiasm can be traced back to April of the same year, when one of the fan-oriented Japanese monthly magazines dealing with American and British rock music, *Ongaku Senka*, organized a trip to Britain and provided the tour members, who were mostly girls in their late teens, with a party sponsored by EMI. The members of Japan were present, and the made-up good looks of the unknown group fascinated the Japanese teenyboppers. Photos taken by the girls and by the magazine people were featured in its June issue along with the news that Victor had signed with Ariola Hansa, while the resident London photographer of another fan-oriented Japanese rock monthly *Music Life* also sent home pictures. Japan became a sensation among many of the readers of these magazines through their visual images, and a fan club was formed without their music having been heard at all (though one song, possibly their first single, may have been played on a radio programme; see Shibuya 1978).

The aesthetic sense behind the visual enthusiasm for Japan is one shared by a majority of Japanese girls and is chiefly derived from *La Rose de Versailles* by Riyoko Ikeda, a best-selling girls' romance that tells the story of Oscar, a beautiful aristocratic French girl masquerading as a man who strives to save Marie-Antoinette at the time of the French Revolution. This story was first serialized in *Margaret*, a girls' comic weekly, in the early 1970s and then published in multi-volume book form, the parts selling in the millions for several years. The main characters are, naturally, Westerners: whether male or female, they are typically slim and refined in figure, with long, flowing, curled hair, exaggeratedly soft eyes, and a slightly distressed, sweet and delicate mouth. This style, which was itself rooted in the tradition of girls' comics, was soon taken up by teenage girls and still dominates their drawing styles. There had, of course, been no lack of flowing-haired handsome pop idols, but none could have more satisfactorily corresponded with these images than the almost unprecedentedly pretty, made-up faces of the boys who formed Japan. Perhaps the portraits drawn by the fans best show the way they reacted to their looks: the faces are invariably moulded into the conventional girls' comic styles (see Figure 6.1).

The group's name, apparently chosen on a whim, was also attractive to Japanese audiences, and, to help excite their curiosity even more, the band's first promotion poster showed one member holding a Japanese sword, and the design of their first album sleeve featured a rising sun, a symbol of the country of Japan.

This album, which had originally been released in England in February 1978 under the title *Adolescent Sex*, was finally issued in Japan, differently titled in Japanese (as is common practice), in the September. It immediately became a hit, reaching number fifty-eight in the Confidence Top LP 100 (which covers

Figure 6.1 Portraits of members of Japan by their fans, printed in the second issue of the fan club's magazine, *Japan* (June 1979).

domestic and international popular music LPs released in Japan) in the first week, and number twenty in the second; it stayed in the chart for eleven weeks (*OCAR* 1979).

The recording of their second album, *Obscure Alternatives*, had already been reported in the liner notes to the first, by a reporter from *Music Life*, who had attended the recording sessions in London to interview them (more on the subject of make-up than that of music) (Minakami 1979). Victor released it, again with a different title in Japanese, two months after the first, as a follow-up, and it was equally successful. In the week after its release, it jumped up to number thirty-five, and then to twenty-one in the chart, staying there for thirteen weeks (*OCAR* 1979, 1980). Each album sold about 65,000 copies, which was probably more than ten times as many as the English releases. According to the market research conducted by Victor, some 90 per cent of the purchasers were teenage girls, and instead of shrinking from the music, which was unlike the catchy tunes of their usual pop idols, they apparently tried to understand the more serious ideas that their new idols were trying to express. Victor had refrained from putting emphasis on these musical qualities when first promoting Japan, knowing that it might be counter-productive with record buyers, who tend to refuse to be easily imposed upon. In fact, *Music Life*, in cooperation with Victor, held a lyric translation contest, along with a competition for visual images suggested by Japan and their music. The four winning lyrics were sent to London to be read by David Sylvian, the lead vocalist, under the guidance of a Japanese interpreter. The tape, edited by Victor but still unintentionally funny, with many strange pronunciations and intonations, was issued as a sono-sheet given free to each purchaser of the second album. And the best five illustrations were used, as promised, on the covers of Japan's next five Victor singles.

In October, soon after the first album was released in Japan, the A&R man, Yokota, flew to London to meet Japan for the first time to discuss their future in the Japanese market. He had in mind further promotion and the possibility of a tour of Japan. Such a tour in fact materialized in March the following year. Their performance was not very successful though, being viewed critically as immature (see, for example, Ōtaka 1979). They were not used to such large audiences, nor to the shrieks and aggressive attentions of their teenage fans.

Late in that year, their third album, *Quiet Life*, which showed a definite change in their style, was released in Japan, a month after its release in England, and it repeated the previous success, starting at number twenty-four and staying in the chart for nine weeks (*OCAR* 1980, 1981). It led to a more serious appreciation of their music, owing to a rather speculative, long article by Tōyō Nakamura, a well-established, influential music journalist, in his *Music Magazine* (formerly *New Music Magazine*), a monthly that is clearly distinct from other popular music magazines in its non-idol-orientated posture (Nakamura 1980). While looking with suspicion at the enthusiasm of teenyboppers, *Music Magazine* had already rated Japan's previous albums highly, and had published a couple of articles on new European groups, which referred favourably to Japan (Nakamura 1979; Aikura 1980). Nakamura's new article described *Quiet Life* as a dispassionate but intense statement of Japan's view on the present apparently gloomy state of things in the West, and it seems to have been decisive in increasing Japan's musical reputation. A second Japanese tour followed, in March 1980. Again, the venues were thronged, again mainly with teenage girls, though there was a slight increase in the male audience.

It was much later in the year that Japan began to attract attention in England, where new fashions and labels, such as New Romantics and Futurists were appearing. In that respect, Japan were more than two years ahead of the times: according to bass guitarist Mick Karn, Spandau Ballet and Visage, popular groups in the new trend referred to Japan as forerunners; though in terms of music, Japan were quite different (Jansen and Karn 1981: 71). On the whole, the English music press had neglected or criticized them. The comment on *Quiet Life* by Maxim Jakubowski was representative: 'A touch of the Roxy Music's, a zest of heavy metal, a pinch of fashion and chic images, stir thoroughly and you're suddenly big in Japan' (*RYB* 1981: 116). Japan switched from Ariola Hansa to Virgin in August 1980, complaining that their former company was too commercially minded and unsympathetic. Virgin released their fourth album, *Gentlemen Take Polaroids*, in November, and for the first time Japan made a profit from an album released in England (Jansen and Karn 1981: 73). In December 1980, they performed at the Lyceum, and in February 1981, at the Hammersmith Odeon, both times to full houses. In May, a single, "The Art of Parties", entered the British singles chart at number seventy-five and stayed in the chart for five weeks. In September, another single, the title cut from *Quiet Life*, reached number nineteen in the chart, and stayed for nine weeks, while *Assemblage*, an album consisting of six tracks from the first three albums and released by Ariola Hansa, made number sixty-three in the Top LP 100. In early November, "The Visions of China" from the forthcoming album, *Tin Drum*, entered the single charts, and then *Tin Drum* skyrocketed to number twelve, probably succeeding more, in chart terms, than in Japan. In the midst of this, in December, Japan toured nationwide in England; the tickets were allegedly sold out two days after they went on sale.

Meanwhile, Japan remained as popular as ever in Japan in spite of a slight decrease in the number of teenage girl fans. *Gentlemen Take Polaroids*, released by Victor in December 1980, stayed in the Top LP 100 for eight weeks, a third Japanese tour took place in February 1981 and in March, *The Singles*, a compilation of six singles including "Life in Tokyo" was released. *Tin Drum*, which depicted the group's experiences and images of the Orient, especially those of China, in a musical style owing something to Sylvian's friend Ryūichi Sakamoto (Mitsui 1992: 2179), and to the Yellow Magic Orchestra, with whom Sakamoto plays, was successful too: the gender ratio of purchasers was now fifty/fifty. An art exhibit, 'Japan's Art of Parties', sponsored by a fashion corporation, featured eighteen sculptures by Karn, some fifty photographs by Steve Jansen, several photo-poems by Sylvian and video films of Japan. Karn and Jansen joined the recording sessions of a female Japanese singer, Akiko Yano, and Jansen also joined a domestic tour by Yukihiro Takahashi, another member of the Yellow Magic Orchestra, while Sylvian recorded a single, "Bamboo House", with Sakamoto, in London, which was released in late summer 1982, both in England and Japan. Sylvian topped the 'Mr Valentine' poll of a pop magazine, with Jansen, his younger brother, seventh and Karn eighteenth (*Viva Rock* 1982: 35).

Though they had been discontented, after a while, with the response of Japanese girls, who had been more interested in them visually than musically, Japan were well aware of their indebtedness to the Japanese market. When interviewed in early 1981, one of the members said that the group would have been disbanded if it had not been for the Japanese market, which was at one time substantially their only financial support (Jansen and Karn 1981: 73).

The contract is signed even before any records have been released

As suggested earlier, the development of unknown foreign potential hit-makers, like Japan, gives domestic companies scope for scouting, choice, promotion and creativity, in striking contrast to the problems joint ventures suffer in handling foreign products. According to the president of Victor, the staff of their International Record Division

> has endeavoured to look for labels whose artists, hopefully, will suit the Japanese market [...] This kind of business is more interesting to me. You can take initiative and be more creative. When you are affiliated with a foreign major, you inevitably rely on them, waiting for the products they make, and these products tend to dominate your repertoire or catalogue. Certainly, they are secure, and you feel safe because the artists are powerful. That kind of business is OK in its

> own way. But such companies as ours scout, make and sell an artist on their own, and if the artist suits and appeals to the Japanese market, the business can be extremely enjoyable. So, I will give a good deal of encouragement to this aspect of our business [...] Many overseas labels contact us to sell their products, and the world is large; we will choose and look for something of good quality and try to make a hit of it. This can be no less interesting than scouting for a Japanese singer and placing him on the market in Japan. (*OC* 1982b: 93)

This is echoed by Yasutaka Torio, a director of Polydor, when he describes the latest kind of licensing deal, in which the contract is signed even before any records by the artist have been released, under an agreement that he or she should record, say, two LPs within three years: 'It is almost identical with the way the domestic division of a company contracts a domestic producer on condition that his new singer should record a certain number of records within three years – except that the recording is done in Japan' (Nakamura 1981: 101).

Since early 1981, there even emerged several domestic labels that record and make masters of foreign artists in Japan. One is Sound Design, a subsidiary of Trio, and another is Video Audio Products, derived from Nippon TV Music, a master-production company, who have recorded an English singer named Nico Ramsden at least three times so far, without making a deal with any foreign label. 'It might be more constructive to have a foreign artist come to Japan, record him here, and sell him to a foreign market than to deal with foreign labels', said Masakazu Sunadoi, a director of VAP.

> We asked a Japanese producer who knows the overseas scene well to look for a promising artist, and he found this singer, Nico [...] His voice is OK, his looks are good, and well, it's a go. The album was first released in Tokyo, and we are now trying to get it released in London [...] We'd like to keep on operating this way, selling at least one artist a year. (Ibid. 99)

An established company, Canyon Records, also entered this field in 1982, and succeeded with an American adult-oriented rock (AOR) artist, Eric Tagg.

Meanwhile, the tendency towards excessive offers in order to acquire foreign stars has waned recently, for rising royalty rates have made such deals less profitable. There are even several foreign companies whose contracts remain unrenewed. One of the reasons for this change could be the influx of imported records, as explained before. And there is a wider background, in which home-taping along with some other important factors has checked the increase in annual record production in Japan. The peak was in 1976, when it was 199,752,000, but as the dissemination of tape-recorders caught up with and outdid that of record-players, the figure declined, falling to 166,371,000 in 1981 (Kawabata 1982: 82, 94). Home-taping has been boosted by the rental record stores, which have mushroomed throughout Japan since June 1981, and which have tacitly encouraged the copying of records, although the record companies countered them by tightening the regulations soon after. The decline has hit the foreign record business disproportionately, as the ratio of domestic records and foreign records manufactured in Japan during 1970–81 indicates: 53 to 47 in 1970, 58 to 42 in 1975–7, 62 to 38 in 1978 and 64 to 36 in 1981 (ibid.: 83). This change is presumably due to a changed market, in which many more consumers buy both domestic and foreign records, while once there was a clear distinction between purchasers of domestic records and purchasers of foreign records, and also to the growing internationalization of style in domestic youth popular music. The number of foreign labels dealt with by Japanese companies went up from 206 in 1977 to 226 in 1978 and 235 in 1979 before falling to 200 in 1980 and 190 in 1981 (ibid.: 249).

Under these circumstances, the international divisions of Japanese record companies are likely to concentrate more of their efforts on looking for inexpensive, potential stars from abroad. And this tendency is bound to significantly affect the nature of the music they produce.[3]

Notes

1 The first Japanese company to make discs, predecessor of the present Nippon Columbia, was formed only a few years after US Victor at the beginning of this century. Indeed, the first tin-foil phonograph, invented by Edison in 1877, was introduced to Japan the very next year, by a twenty-four-year-old English professor of physics at the Imperial University of Tokyo, who manufactured a reproduction on the basis of newspaper reports. Thereafter, cylinders were imported and sold, and some were recorded in Japan to be pressed in the USA (Kurata 1979: chapters 1 and 2).

2 Imported records, available at many record stores and mail order houses throughout Japan, have, since a rapid appreciation of the yen in the mid-1970s, generally been cheaper than those pressed in Japan, which are technically unparalleled in sound quality, but more expensive for several reasons. These include a retailing system that is quite different from those in other countries, and the supposed necessity of attaching liner notes by a Japanese writer, with translated lyrics. Moreover, in 1979, Tower Records of California, famous for their

discount prices, set up a wholesale house for American records in Tokyo, and gave a franchise to several record stores in other large Japanese cities. Tower Records Shibuya, the thirty-second Tower chain-store, established in Shibuya, Tokyo, in March 1981, boasts numerous and varied imports along with new hit records that are sent by air mail. Tower Records Sapporo and Tower Records Yokohama followed the next year. If an artist or group is not well known, however, it is unlikely that their records will be in stock or easily available or will affect the sales of the records pressed by a Japanese company.

3   In addition to written sources, material has also been drawn from interviews, by author, in person and by telephone, with Minoru Ishijima, director of the Second International Section of RVC, author Shigeru Kawabata and Akira Yokota, Japan's A&R man.

Transformation inspired by the West (7)

New *enka*

In the early 1970s, *kayōkyoku* was given fresh impetus. Mainstream *kayōkyoku* had remained vigorous during the 1960s with the Record Awards, which were founded in the manner of the Grammy Awards in 1959, and with some television shows that emphasized conventional singers and songs in contrast to others that catered for younger and urban tastes. Meanwhile, there were many older people who felt themselves marginalized by music for the young – rock, folk and idol-*kayō* – and demanded their own type of music.

What filled this void was a new trend, in the mid- to late 1960s, beginning with female singers such as Harumi Miyako, Sayuri Ishikawa and Mina Aoe, male singers such as Saburō Kitajima, Shin'ichi Mori and Masao Sen, and composers such as Tadashi Yoshida, Tōru Funamura and Minoru Endō. Then, in 1970, the trend labelled *enka* found wider acceptance when Keiko Fuji's song, "Keiko-no Yume-wa Yoru-hiraku" (Keiko's Dream Unfolds at Night) became a huge hit. The despairing sadness and self-denying forbearance that permeated these songs harked back, in terms of both lyrical and musical characteristics, to "Sendō Ko-uta" (Boatman's Ditty), the extremely popular song of the early 1920s. Following "Keiko-no Yume-wa Your-hiraku", a series of hits in the similar vein appeared, and shortly *enka* secured a footing in the music industry as a hardcore type of *kayōkyoku*, with the term being extended to encompass earlier songs of the similar tendency. While integrating the vocal style of *naniwabushi*, it was sustained by the 'queen of *kayōkyoku*', Hibari Misora. This versatile vocalist, who started her career in the late 1940s, became closely associated with *enka* (Mitsui 1992: 1709; for more about Misora, see Tansman 1996 and Shamoon 2009).

The new usage of *enka* first appeared with a different spelling of *en-* in the Chinese character, denoting something or someone romantic, sensuous or voluptuous. According to Ryōgetsu Kaminaga, the first *enka* violin player, the word *enka* with this spelling appeared as early as the mid- or late 1910s to denote old *enka* sung with the violin accompaniment (Kaminaga 1970: 41). The usage took on a new connotation, however, when Hiroyuki Itsuki used it as the title of his short story published in 1966 (Itsuki 1966). Its protagonist was modelled on the A&R man of Nippon Crown Records, a company established in 1963 which specialized in songs that were later classified as *enka*. Tetsurō Hoshino then wrote a song entitled "Enka" based on Itsuki's original idea, which became a hit for Kiyoko Suizenji in 1968. This usage of *enka* was backed by young intellectuals who favoured the New Left and songs representing the feelings of those who were socially oppressed. This conception was also reflected in the first two books on *enka* in the early 1970s, the titles of which were in this spelling: *Jazz Sandogasa: Enka-eno Michi* (Jazz Wandering: Road to *Enka*) (1970) by Naritasu Oku and *Enka-eno Shien* (Personal Resentment at *Enka*) (1973) by Agumu Nozawa. (For a discussion in English about new *enka*, see Yano 2002 and Wajima 2019.)

New *enka* songs commonly tell stories about tragic love, heart-rending partings, homesickness, moral obligation and strong emotional feelings. Words such as tear, cry, heart, dream, rain, *sake* and seaport are often used in the lyrics. Narratives are frequently in the first-person, set in a cold northern region and focus on a single grief-stricken person who returns to or visits that area, away from the hubbub of a big city. As is not uncommon in various Japanese popular music genres, new *enka* songs are sometimes cross-gendered when performed: a song in the female first person is sung by a male singer and vice versa (see Nakagawa 1999). There are a large number of female new *enka* vocalists, and stage costumes often include expensive *kimono*.

The songs are accompanied by an orchestra that often includes strings, wind instruments, percussion, piano, electric guitar and bass, and, on some occasions, *shamisen* and *shakuhachi*. Scales commonly used are a major scale minus fourth and seventh notes (CDEGAC when the root note is C) and a minor scale minus fourth and seventh notes (ABCEFA when the root note is A), although songs occasionally use, in addition to these pentatonic scales, hexatonic or even heptatonic scales. These scales, which were relatively new in Japan when they were introduced, share some features of indigenous ones in that they tend to limit themselves to stepwise motion without depending on harmonic considerations. The vocal style is characterized by the use of many vibratos and melismata, while the vocal delivery, in those parts that tend to be speech-like, reflects the rhythmic feel of the Japanese language, characterized by uniform stresses with no imabi or trochees (Okada 1991: 287–9).

Meanwhile, *enka* used to be connected closely with drinking, as is suggested by the emergence of karaoke in bars in the early 1970s where *enka* provided the main repertoire, and also by the fact that *enka* was popularized by cable radio. The music programmes of this new medium, which began service in the early 1960s, were so enjoyed by bar customers that record companies eventually linked up with cable companies to boost their new *enka* singles. Thus, *enka* became the mainstream of *kayōkyoku*, even though the popularity of *kayōkyoku* began to be eclipsed by the pervasive 'new music' in the mid-1980s. This reversal was also reflected in the changing preferences of karaoke customers as generations moved on and as the karaoke box was introduced (Mitsui and Hosokawa 1998: 41–2).

(To be continued: see page 169 for (8).)

7

Nurturing the Japanese version of an American tradition: Music from the South

This is a revised version of 'The Reception of the Music of American Southern Whites in Japan', in *Transforming Tradition: Folk Revivals Examined*, edited by Neil V. Rosenberg and published by University of Illinois Press, pp. 275–93 (© 1993 by the Board of Trustees of the University of Illinois).

A bluegrass concert given in Fukuoka in 1988

In April 1988, I saw for the first time a certain young girls' group, the Nakashima Family Band, playing bluegrass music. The band, which consisted of four sisters ranging from eight to twelve years of age, had been talked about, although not widely, among bluegrass enthusiasts in Japan. The girls, whose costumes were complete with cowboy hats, bright-coloured chequered shirts and blue jeans (the youngest in a pair of overalls), are, of course, Japanese by nationality.

The band astonished me with several songs, especially "Raw Hide", a fast, instrumental number that requires advanced technique. If one listened to the musicians carefully, one could hear that they were inexperienced and rough-edged, because it had been only a year since they had begun to learn how to play the banjo, fiddle, mandolin and guitar, respectively. The vocals, led by the youngest with a guitar that looked enormous because of her small size, were also unstable, and to me their English pronunciation had an embarrassingly thick Japanese accent. The exception was "Turkey in the Straw", a tune so familiar even in Japan that it has Japanese lyrics. This enabled the girls to deliver much more easily, although there is always a certain strangeness even to me, a Japanese, in hearing the Japanese language accompanied by a typical bluegrass sound. The feeling one got from the whole performance was, however, very pleasant.

They were the most attractive and most applauded band at the bluegrass concert in Fukuoka. The band was formed and rigorously trained by the proud father of its members, who had been playing bluegrass and old-time music in Japan since his college days in the late 1960s and early 1970s. The girls were usually supported as an ensemble by a bassist, their mother, who has been playing since her junior-college days.

After their own performance, the girls were joined by a gentleman, Tsuyoshi Hashimoto, who sang a couple of songs including "Cindy", backed by them and accompanied by his own banjo. The age contrast was visually conspicuous because the banjo player, a managing director of a newly formed company in Fukuoka, is even older than the girls' parents and his performing activities dated back to his college days in the late 1950s and early 1960s. His interest extended back even further, to the days when, as a high-school student, he was first charmed by bluegrass music after becoming a fan of Tommy Collins, Hank Williams and other mainstream Country & Western favourites of the time. It is an interesting coincidence that at around the time when a handful of teenagers in Berkeley, California, including Neil Rosenberg, became interested in bluegrass music (Rosenberg 1983), a few Japanese teenagers across the Pacific Ocean were attracted to the same music. Tsuyoshi Hashimoto was an old college classmate of mine. In 1958–61, we were fellow members of a dance combo that played Country & Western, rockabilly, Hawaiian and Tin Pan Alley. It was through him that I was invited to speak at a forum about the music of American southern whites that preceded the concert.

That afternoon we reunited as a duet, and as the eldest group performing on the occasion, we sang a couple of old-time songs accompanying ourselves with guitar and Appalachian dulcimer. It was our first public performance in twenty-six years, the last one being in early 1962, with banjo and guitar, at a New Year's party of the Japan–America Society of Fukuoka. That party was held in an officers' club on one of two US military bases then located in the suburbs of Fukuoka.[1] There were several other entertainers at the gathering, including a female group playing Japanese traditional music. It was backstage there that I first realized how the sound of a banjo string, when it is being tuned up, resembles that of a *shamisen*, which uses a head made of cat-skin instead of calf-skin, and twine instead of steel strings. The time we spent backstage was also memorable in that, when we were practising in the dark outside the backstage door to avoid having the sound of our instruments mingle with the wailing of the *shamisen* music, a smiling old American in a chequered shirt came up, possibly drawn by our music, and flattered us by saying something to the effect that we sounded like we were from Kentucky.

The other groups in the 1988 concert in Fukuoka belonged to the generation between ourselves, in our late forties, and the girls described above.[2] The span of the generations of the performers there covered roughly the entire range of the Japanese people who have come to love American bluegrass music and old-time music or hillbilly music, though such a young performing female group as the Nakashima Family Band was exceptional.

Japanese interest in the music of the American South was kindled after the Second World War

In the late 1950s, there were a few other people who became interested in bluegrass music, at least in the Tokyo area and in the Osaka area, and an article on bluegrass along with a photograph of Bill Monroe appeared in a popular music monthly as early as March 1958 (Suzuki 1958). The writer of that article and other persons who showed an interest in bluegrass at that time were obviously several years older than I, and they had been listening to Country & Western music in general and had hit upon bluegrass music among newly imported records, as was the case with my friend mentioned above. As to the bluegrass records pressed and released in Japan, by 1958 there already existed "Kentucky Waltz"/"The Prisoner's Song" by Bill Monroe and His Blue Grass Boys, the only 78 rpm Japanese single of bluegrass music, and in January 1958 "Jimmie Brown, the Newsboy"/"Cabin on the Hill" by Flatt and Scruggs was released. It was not until December 1959, almost two years later, that Flatt and Scruggs' 45 rpm single was followed by another bluegrass single, "Dixie Breakdown"/"Your Tears Are Just Interest on the Loan" by Reno and Smiley (Nagai 1975).

The interest some people had in this kind of American music, which used to be called hillbilly and later Country & Western, could have originated in late 1945 or in 1946; that is, soon after the Second World War when Japan was under occupation and the American forces brought their exotic cultures with them to the country. But even before that war, around 1934, there were quite a few hillbilly records pressed in Japan. Even the present-day Japanese followers of this music would be surprised to know that it was in fact possible to hear at that time in Japan, through Japanese labels, Vernon Dalhart, Carson Robison, the Hill Billies, Jimmie Rodgers, Ted Hawkins and Riley Puckett, Gene Autry, the Shelton Brothers, Elton Britt, W. E. O'Daniel and His Hillbilly Boys, and the Prairie Ramblers, among others (Suzuki 1972).

Therefore, it could be argued that the Japanese interest in what is called old-time music or in country music in general had sprung up not very many years after it became available in the form of phonograph records for Americans. It is very likely, however, that the interest was sporadic and quite limited because of the scarcity of published material. A book titled *Keiongaku-to Sono-Record* (Light Music and Its Records), published in 1938 (Karahata et al.),[3] includes 'Hillbilly Songs' as a section under 'Swing Music'. However, only three pages are allotted to it, with merely a dozen lines of introductory notes, which present-day enthusiasts would find amusing and almost hilarious, although they succinctly reflect how the music was accepted in pre-war Japan. The notes are indeed followed by the names of such artists as those listed above, but one wonders why Arthur Tracy ("The Street Singer") is listed as one of the most well-known hillbilly singers. That would suggest that there was limited awareness of the genre, and there is little evidence of its being performed by Japanese.

The post-war interest of some Japanese in contemporary hillbilly music was, in contrast, much more conspicuous. It was considerably stimulated by the US military radio, WVTR (the predecessor of FEN, Far East Network), which played hillbilly records along with those of other musical genres. For example, the *Honshu Hayride*, an early-afternoon show alliteratively titled after the name of the largest of the Japanese islands, was easily heard, if you were interested enough to tune in, in the Japanese homes in the vicinity of the US military bases scattered all over Japan. The broadcast continued for quite a long time and, when I was a college student, I became familiar, a little belatedly, with "The Devil's Dream", the show's instrumental theme.

Some listeners were so enthusiastic that they formed their own bands to play the contemporary hillbilly music, and a couple of them, converted tango bands, even recorded songs for Japanese labels as early as 1948. The group Western Ramblers was the most prolific (Suzuki 1972: 33–4). Interestingly enough, quite a few of these musicians came from aristocratic families. The titled-nobility system was abolished in late 1946 when the new constitution of Japan was promulgated, in English and Japanese, with the statement, 'Peers and peerage shall not be recognized', in Chapter III, Article 14. Nevertheless, many of the college students who performed hillbilly music semi-professionally in Tokyo unmistakably grew up as the sons of dukes, viscounts or barons. For instance, Atsukata Torio, the bassist of the Chuck Wagon Boys, was a son of Viscount Koyata Torio. He published his memoirs, which included an account of a mischievous nursery-school episode with 'His Majesty', just six weeks after the emperor's accession to the throne in early 1989 (Torio 1989). The sons of peers were enjoying a comparatively rich life when most other people were generally suffering from hunger as a consequence of Japan's defeat in the Second World War. It must have been their relative affluence that enabled them to purchase musical instruments and pseudo-cowboy costumes, and to have enough time to enjoy listening to music and practise performing it. They were also educated enough to have a liking for a foreign musical culture in the first place, and to get interested in something that requires somewhat advanced knowledge of the language used.

What, then, attracted the bluebloods of Japan to the blue-collar music from the American South? It was presumably the very exoticism of the music, the feeling of openness and liberation it yielded along with a touch of rusticity, and the romanticism of the West with its image and ideas of the Wild West, prairies, adventures and mobility. And the attraction might well have had much to do with the idea of American democracy that was suddenly advocated by the new Japanese authorities; this concept was awkwardly grafted onto the Japanese way of thinking immediately after Japan was defeated in the Second World War and the United States occupied the country. Democracy gave one the ideas of liberation with its implication of social equality, and liberation involved openness and freeness, which is suggested by the image of the West in 'Western' music.

In any event, the term 'Western' music, without being translated into Japanese, was adopted apparently soon after American country music of the mid-1940s was willingly accepted by the first generation of enthusiasts. It was associated with the popularity of the Western, a genre of film newly imported from the Unites States in post-war Japan; though Western films were not known as Western but as *seibu-geki*, the term's Japanese translation. Western, designating Country & Western music, prevailed for an unusually long time in Japan considering the fact that the term has never been fully established in the United States as an appellation for country music in general. Even the gradual replacement of hillbilly by Country & Western in the USA since the late 1940s did not much affect the Japanese tendency, as is shown by the title of a book published in 1963, *Western Ongaku Nyūmon* (Guide to Western music). The title was obviously selected by the publisher to give the book a general appeal, even though the author Hiroyuki Takayama states in the preface his awareness of the terminology in the United States and of the exceptional use in Japan.[4]

The images of cowboys and the West

A case could be made that it was not until the early 1970s that the general Japanese enthusiasts of the music became somewhat, if not sufficiently, conscious of the fact that it is from a cultural area called the South. The music, especially country music, came to Japan as a sound on disc without much of its cultural context; it was, above all, from the United States. The visual image on record sleeves, which was the only available clue to any cultural context, often had much to do with the West and cowboys, and included the Stetson hats, boots and Western shirts the recording artists wore as stage costumes. The Japanese audience was not informed enough to know that it actually represented the Western aspiration of the southern rural people who preferred the romanticized image of cowboys to the derogatory one of the hillbillies. The liner notes by a handful of writers sometimes referred to the fact that music was from the South, but this was usually used as a geographical term without much cultural implication, reflecting the writers' lack of interest in this aspect.

Bluegrass music was naturally taken as something that was from the South because it lacked the association with cowboys, except for the hats of the artists. In turn, mountaineers, who were supposed to be the performers of bluegrass music, were invariably romanticized as people who live in a rural heaven, so to speak, that can be anywhere in the Unites States. To the limited Japanese audience, the white music from the American South was, in concept, simply something fascinating from America, a land with richness, expansion, democracy and possibilities. That image of the United States seemed to have been more appropriately reflected in rural Western music than in urban jazz and Tin Pan Alley songs whose popularity preceded it, in Japan as well as in the US, not only in time but in the size of the movement.

The reception and adoption of this fascinating music from America was an urban phenomenon, as is usual with any imported trend. It was considered fashionable to have a liking for the music, not to speak of performing it oneself. The pseudo-cowboy costumes of the performers helped to strengthen the effect, because every item of clothing was exotic, coming out of a completely different culture, although European clothes themselves had penetrated Japanese culture since they were first introduced some eighty years before. There was certainly an awareness of the relative rusticity of the music, and in that respect the enthusiasm was a kind of reverse snobbery. (It is no wonder that the followers of jazz often looked down on those of Western music because of their liking for less sophisticated, simplistic music, even though it is from America.)

Thus, the younger Japanese who were so enthusiastic about Western music that they formed bands in the early 1950s, either following in the wake of their seniors or joining them, were also from well-to-do families in urban areas. They were also educated enough to be attending (mostly private) universities or colleges. This was a time when the majority of young people of their age could not afford to enjoy the benefits of higher education, which would have helped to widen their view of the world, making them more inclined to become interested in things overseas. Besides being well educated, these young enthusiasts were, thanks to their families, wealthy enough to buy not only records but musical instruments and had enough leisure time for practising these instruments and singing.

Rockabilly performers in Japan, who tried to resemble American originals in the late 1950s as members of Western bands, were also largely from the rich families who resided in the metropolitan area. As represented by the three top stars, one of whom was a singer of mixed British and Japanese parentage named Mickey Curtis, they were attracted to the music at an earlier age than their predecessors, and many gave up their studies and their access to a college education. The fact that the regular concert-hall show in Tokyo that featured their energetic performance was called Western Carnival indicates, among other things, that rockabilly was taken up by Western bands and was treated, if unintentionally, more as a derivation of or as an idiom within country music than it was in the United States.

Those who became interested in bluegrass music and tried to perform it themselves from the middle to late 1950s in Japan were, again, generally sons of prosperous families. My college classmate mentioned previously, for example, who was of the age of the rockabillies, lived in the largest city in southern Japan as a son of the vice president of one of a half dozen major electric power companies in Japan. That made it financially possible for him to develop his interest, through imported records, in such artists as Hank Thompson, Hank Williams, Bill Monroe and Flatt and Scruggs, and also such folksingers as Burl Ives, Woody Guthrie and Jean Ritchie.[5] In the late 1950s and early 1960s, usually one had to place an order to get an LP record imported from the United States because few record stores stocked imported records. An LP cost more than 2,500 yen, which is now the price one pays for a CD. In the late 1950s, this was equivalent to one-fifth of the starting monthly income of the average college graduate.

Another, slightly younger, friend of mine, Michio Higashi, grew up in Tokyo as a son of a prosperous couple born in Vancouver, Canada. As a nineteen-year-old student, he led a college band called the Ozark Mountaineers and was fortunate enough to have been funded by his father to tour around the United States. He travelled around America in the summer of 1961, staying with the late Mrs Hank Williams for about a week in Nashville, when it was just a dream for most Japanese to go abroad. He learned a lot there, especially the playing techniques of bluegrass instruments. The Japanese pioneers had learned to play through listening to records, but without any visual models their technique and handling of the instruments were sometimes very imaginative. Higashi made a guest appearance on the Grand Ole Opry, singing "Will the Circle Be Unbroken" with a guitar for which he borrowed a capo from Earl Scruggs. (It was on 7 May 1960 that Yoshio Ōno, a yodeller and a banjoist who debuted in Japan by signing with Nippon Columbia in 1957, performed on the Opry stage with Flatt and Scruggs as the first Japanese who had ever been given an opportunity to perform there (Isaji 1988).) The story of Higashi's adventure was published in the second issue of *Moon Shiner* (Inaya 1983). Since its founding in November 1983, this bluegrass monthly has periodically printed stories based on interviews with the older generation of Japanese performers of bluegrass music. The persons featured there, more than a dozen in number, also turn out to be urbanites who are middle class, if not very rich, and highly educated in the sense that they attended a college-level institution.

American folk revival

The American folk revival began to be imported in the early 1960s and became more popular in the mid- and late 1960s, helping to stimulate further interest in music from the American South among young Japanese in the same social stratum, just as it did much more extensively among urban, middle-class college students in the United States. The popularity of American folk music in its various forms was enhanced particularly in the first stage by the visit of Pete Seeger, a middle-aged interpreter of traditional songs from the South and also a left-wing protest singer-songwriter, who came to Japan for a concert tour in late 1963 for the first time. It was a couple of weeks before the shooting of John F. Kennedy, whose fame was used in publicizing Seeger as 'a former classmate of Kennedy at Harvard', though Seeger simply happened to have been enrolled there at around the same time as Kennedy, without getting acquainted with him and without graduating from the school.

During this period, I was involved in the reception of the music of American southern whites, and backstage after one of Pete Seeger's shows I met an American GI who had been drafted while a college student in Seattle and was then stationed in Fukuoka. He soon became my good pickin' and singin' mate. I thus shared an interest in performing this kind of music substantially for the first time with an American, one who came from outside the southern culture and who enjoyed exchanging information about the whole range of music covered in the American folk revival.[6] Meanwhile, Pete Seeger's visit prompted me to write a leaflet,[7] in both Japanese and English, criticizing the authenticity of performances by folk revivalists, which was handed out at the entrance of two concert halls in the area where I lived. I handed it to Seeger as well; he kindly responded to my possibly unskilled argument. I was armed with what I had learned about traditional songs and ballads through the writings of Cecil Sharp, Bertrand H. Bronson, William Entwistle and other scholars, and with what I had heard through phonograph records, especially those collected in *Anthology of American Folk Music*, compiled by Harry Smith, which I found in the library of the Fukuoka American Cultural Center, a U.S. governmental organization. Twelve days later – on 27 November – Seeger sent me a postcard from Hong Kong, writing "I think you will be interested in an article my father wrote – 'Folk Songs in the Schools of a Highly Industrialized Society' – it's in the Sing Out microfilm, Tokyo Univ. library at Ueno." His father is, of course, Charles Seeger.

While pop-folk performers such as the Kingston Trio, the Brothers Four and Peter, Paul and Mary were enjoyed transitorily as something trendy, the imported folk revival also produced, as in the United States, admirers of Bob Dylan. Dylan's songs were first introduced to the Japanese by Pete Seeger in his concerts mentioned above (although there were those who listened to Hugh Cherry's programme of folk music syndicated on FEN carefully enough to catch the name of Dylan and to hear his singing, as GIs must have done). Dylan's perspective on the society and culture in which he lived and his way of expressing it through songs were so influential that quite a few Japanese youngsters not only listened to his recordings but tried to write and sing their own compositions with their own guitar accompaniment. This tendency later brought out, in turn, a current of new, more westernized Japanese popular music, which to some extent rivals *kayōyoku*. (*Kayōkyoku* is an older form of popular music that is characterized by musical features developed out of Japanese idioms along with Western ones. Culturally, *kayōkyoku*, could be compared to modern country music in America, though it does not have a particular regionalism.)

The interest in more traditional forms of the music from the American South, which was generated by the imported folk revival in Japan, was not so prominent because it was not directed toward new developments in Japanese popular music. But it was more persistent among a limited audience. As was the case in the United States, the folk revival attracted the Japanese to such tradition-oriented performers as Doc Watson and to the string band music from the late 1920s and early 1930s through the New Lost City Ramblers and LP reissues of the recordings from the period, drawing a new audience into bluegrass music. The members of the new audience whose interest in music from the South was motivated by the folk revival – though they were usually as unaware of its southern-ness as their predecessors had been – were indifferent to and often disliked Country & Western music. Country & Western was generally considered not to include bluegrass, again in the United States, for its sound was characterized by newly composed lyrics, electric instruments, and unmistakably stylized nasal vocals, which were not compatible with the acoustic sound and the kind of argued authenticity of the revival.

The Japanese enthusiasts were educated urban people, as was the case with enthusiasts in America, and what has been observed about the revival there can be applied literally to the Japanese enthusiasts: 'it [the folksong revival that occurred in America in 1960] appealed primarily to individuals who celebrated traditions not their own [...]. I think the revival can be fairly characterized as romantic, naïve, nostalgic and idealistic' (Jackson 1985: 195). The difference was, as can be easily understood, the depth of the cultural and social gulf in the case of Japan.

Some Americans who were not of Anglo-Saxon background were enthralled by typically Anglo-American folksongs, and more conspicuously, quite a few people showed a strong interest in the blues, an African-American musical form. But however great the racial, cultural, and social-class differences were in terms of tradition, both the educated urban young people and the older, not-so-well-educated rural people whose musical traditions attracted them lived in the same land, as one nation, and, perhaps more significantly, spoke the same language as that of the songs. To the educated urban young people in Japan, not only were these musical traditions something radically different from domestic ones, but also the country in which the musical traditions existed and were 'revived' was located far across the ocean, and the language had no linguistic relation or resemblance to the one they used.

Why were the Japanese attracted to the rural music from the South?

There again arises the question of why the Japanese were attracted to rural music from the American South. As mentioned above, part of the reason was that America represented democratic ideals, although the image of the West was largely irrelevant to the newer enthusiasts. As was the case with the urban American educated young people, the newer Japanese interest was 'romantic, naïve, nostalgic': a nostalgia for something that was lost by urbanization.

Other factors included American capitalistic power in internationally disseminating American musical products, as well as educational motives, which were shared by the preceding generation. First, the English language was familiar to most Japanese due to the fact that it was and remains the predominant foreign language taught in almost all educational institutions beyond primary school, though written English has been overemphasized at the expense of oral English. Second, the Occidental characteristics of musical structures including melody, rhythm, and harmony were not at all foreign to Japanese ears. Since the late nineteenth century, music education at all levels in Japan has emphasized Western concepts and features of music, so much as to exclude from classrooms almost any music that is in Japanese indigenous idioms. Those Japanese compositions that are included are in Western idioms or are adaptations of them. This has naturally fostered an almost irrevocable tendency among the majority of Japanese to look down on domestic music and its derivations. This tendency has been conspicuous among the well-educated, and most of the enthusiasts for rural music from the American South were not exceptional in being indifferent to the music of older Japanese styles. It usually sounded antiquated and boring to the enthusiasts, and even if it didn't, the musical idioms of Japanese folk music were too different to prompt the enthusiasts of American folk music to look back on their own domestic musical traditions. Consequently, the imported folk revival had no visible influence on or relevance to Japanese folksongs, while the American folk revival noticeably led to revitalization of the domestic folk music in Britain and inadvertently contributed to the Celtic revival in Brittany while spreading to Germany among other countries. The performers and audience of Japanese folksongs were, on the other hand, not 'hip' enough to have a liking for newly imported music.[8]

Periodicals for the devotees

The extent and directions of the Japanese interest in the music of southern whites that has been surveyed above is reflected, to some degree, in the publication of a handful of more or less nationally circulated, non-professional periodicals. The most important one was *Country and Western*, which started in Tokyo in May 1963 with the subtitle 'The Magazine for Bluegrass and Country'. It was intended as an extension of a serial newsletter/programme for regular record concerts in Tokyo that were organized by C&WMS (the Country and Western Music Society: interestingly, the name in Japanese was *Seibu-ongaku Aikō-kai* (the Society of the Lovers of Western Music)) and were held from the mid-1950s to the early 1960s.[9] Later re-subtitled as 'The Magazine for Country and Bluegrass', this bimonthly sold more than 2,500 copies per issue in its heyday.[10] Then the main title was changed, in May 1978 (no. 86), to *Melody Ranch*, which was dubbed the 'Country, Bluegrass and Folk Rock Magazine'. This change was a symptom of the dispersal of interest in country music in Japan, alongside the growing tendency for country music to lose its stylistic identity, and the magazine was discontinued, with the May 1979 issue being the last edition.

Several years before the demise of *Melody Ranch*, there appeared *June Apple*, the first exclusively bluegrass magazine in Japan. This bimonthly, apparently named after the banjo instrumental by Wade Ward and launched in Tokyo in January 1974, obviously represented the inclination of the newly increased bluegrass audience to consider bluegrass music as incompatible with other forms of country music. With its heyday in the late 1970s, the magazine's title was changed in May 1981 (no. 44) to *Bluegrass Revival*. It ceased to exist after issue number 59 appeared in January 1983. However, ten months later, a new 'bluegrass journal' came out in the Kansai area, the second-largest metropolitan in Japan. This monthly, *Moon Shiner*, covers the overall bluegrass scene in Japan, and now enjoys a circulation of some 1,500 copies.[11] It is published by BOM Service (Bluegrass and Old Time Service). This import-record dealer is a Japanese version of County Sales in Floyd, Virginia, and has published a newsletter/catalogue since March 1972.[12]

Bluegrass community

BOM Service has also been active as an organizer of a bluegrass festival, and its annual Takarazuka Bluegrass Festival, the largest and oldest among many regional bluegrass festivals in Japan, enjoyed its eighteenth year in the summer of 1989 with an audience of about 1,000 people. As is the case with the devotees of other forms of country music, there are a large number of bluegrass listeners who love to hear the music performed by American recording musicians without much interest in what the Japanese musicians try to do with it, and so the number does not reflect the extent of the Japanese bluegrass scene in general. But, in any case, the festival has served as an annual reunion of some two dozen bluegrass circles scattered all over Japan. An affectionate observation on these regional circles, each of which has several performing bands, was given by Alan Senauke of Berkeley, California, who toured around Japan in October 1989, thanks to BOM Service, visiting and performing at various places:

> We [Senauke and his wife] had an unusual opportunity. Since I could work as a solo and play with local musicians, it was possible to visit many towns, to see how the bluegrass scene is the same throughout the world, yet different in each place. Some shows were in small concert halls, some in 'live spots', or smoky (sometimes, very smoky) bars. Some places had very elaborate, top of the line sound systems, some just the minimum that was necessary. Some audiences were entirely young, male students, some audiences were families and professionals nearer my own age. The music also varied greatly with each circle, some preferring traditional bluegrass, some leaning toward the most modern sounds. It occurs to me that this is all very like the noodles we ate (and we ate a lot of soba and udon, because we love it!). In each town noodles were similar in appearance, but the preparation and taste was always subtly different [...]. And also I got an overview of Japanese bluegrass. Although the scene is not so large, and maybe there is not enough money to be bringing over all the favorite bands, each circle seemed to be very solid. There were many musicians and families deeply involved and loving the music, keeping it alive in their own area. I think this is a great strength. (Senauke 1990: 10–11)[13]

With the Takarazuka Bluegrass Festival as an annual rallying point (any band can perform there) and *Moon Shiner* as a monthly forum and information centre, the regional circles of bluegrass can be said to visibly form a community, and it is, as Bruce Jackson re-evaluated the folk revival community in America, 'as legitimate as any other based on shared interest and knowledge' (Jackson 1985: 66).

In contrast, the Japanese scene of other forms of modern country music is much less visible, with an apparent decrease of the number of enthusiasts and the disappearance of a country music section (which denotes modern country music other than bluegrass) from a majority of record stores. In terms of performance, there are a handful of live spots in Tokyo and the Kansai area, which often feature Japanese performers who have seen better days. The sensibility of the younger generation long since disregarded this kind of music and was oriented to more energetic and rhythmical forms of music, in which bluegrass could be included,[14] though stylistically it is quite different from musical forms dominated by African-American elements.

Old-time music performers

However, there are still a limited number of Japanese performers of early hillbilly or old-time music, and every autumn since 1984 the annual Old-Time Party, an all-night get-together, has been held in Kobe, an international seaport and one of the three largest cities in the Kansai area. Again, there are those whose interest is in the music from the American South itself and not in what the Japanese musicians do, á la J. E. Mainer's Mountaineers, Wade Ward or Kenny Hall, and so the Old-Time Party does not give the full picture of how old-time music is received in Japan. It does, however, represent the performance scene of old-time music in Japan and the newer interest shown by the younger generation. Their interest in old-time music began sometime in the late 1970s, and some of them went straight to the homeland of the music to get lessons from native old-time fiddlers and banjoists, as was the case with Kōsuke Takaki who took a course in fiddle-playing at the Augusta Vintage Workshop in Elkins, West Virginia, in 1981 when he was twenty years old. Takaki then registered as a contestant at the Galax Old-Time Fiddlers' Convention in Virginia in the summer of the same year, and has since performed there many times, having won sixth place as a member of an old-time string band in 1984.[15]

According to a report by Mike Miller, a Reuters correspondent based in Hong Kong, a dozen bands, consisting of some thirty musicians, appeared at the Old-Time Party in 1987 with an audience that numbered about forty.[16] The background information about some of the performers, based on interviews by the correspondent (Miller 1988–9), is interesting enough, as in the case of one of them who 'started out playing guitar in the style of the Beatles and the Eagles, drifted into music of David Bromberg and eventually met some Japanese musicians who played bluegrass and old-time'. More interesting are the observations made by two American fiddling participants concerning the music-making itself. One of them, Valerie Mindel, a former member of Any Old Time, an old-time band in California, said to the reporter: 'There I was at four in the morning, when we'd been playing more and more obscure tunes all night. I turned to say something to the fellow next to me and realized that for all the tunes we had in common, we couldn't talk to each other. He didn't speak English. I didn't speak Japanese. And somehow it didn't matter.' And the other, Rob Craighurst from Virginia, made a musical comment: 'The music was just like all the great music in American music – it's not a copy. It's like if someone says, "Your Japanese is very good," that means it's not really very good – it's that good.' One of the participants at the concert, Sumio Inoue, who started with the guitar style of the Beatles and the Eagles, was actually good enough to have won ninth place in the fiddle contest at the renowned Galax Old-Time Fiddlers' Convention, in Galax, Virginia, in the preceding year. Miller reported: 'He has been playing old-time music for only seven years, and fiddle for just the past four.' And Inoue was not exceptional in winning in the convention, as Miller suggests. He was simply one of the dozen young Japanese winners here from 1979 to 1987.[17]

The Japanese version of an American tradition

This now leads us to the question of tradition. Is what is excellently performed by a Japanese musician legitimately a part of the musical tradition of the American rural South? If not, what is it? Is it just a tasteful imitation or facsimile of something original? Is it form without content? In the field of bluegrass music, from which one is able to make a living by performing in the United States, there are at least three professional musicians who were born and raised in Japan and have been active in the States for years. I was surprised when a part-time writer for a newspaper in Baton Rouge, Louisiana, told me in the summer of 1983 that he was first attracted to bluegrass music when he was impressed by an exciting performance by a fiddler named Shōji Tabuchi, who now regularly performs at his own theatre, built in 1989, in Branson, Missouri. The surprise could be compared with what I felt, nearly ten years before, when I found, in the library of the Country Music Foundation in Nashville, that the guitar a certain mountaineer musician was shown playing in the cover photography of an album of the music from the Ozarks was a Yamaha model! Akira Ōtsuka, a former member of Bluegrass 45, a disbanded Japanese group, has been with various bands in the Washington area, and plays 'brilliant mandolin' (Rosenberg 1985: 367). A banjo player, Hiro (an abridgment of Sumihiro Arita, who resides in Boston), 'knocked out' Alan Senauke by his musicianship when Senauke toured Europe with Arita and others in 1986,[18] and prompted a reviewer to describe his recorded performance as 'hot, hot banjo playing' (Blech 1989). Do these appraisals not have much to do with the traditional elements of the music?

It would perhaps be necessary, as is often said, to live the life that produced a musical tradition to get its real feeling. The late Merle Watson, the son of Doc Watson, said in the late 1970s: 'There are a lot of good musicians coming up, but they aren't going into the old-time music, or at least playing it pretty well. I think one problem is they just don't feel the music. The old traditional folk-type tunes are really a music of the people, and if you didn't grow up with it and don't know the feeling of what you're playing, it's hard to play it' (Stambler and Landon 1987: 779). This would be what makes 'folk-type' music different from Western music, especially serious music or art music, which is, as Bruno Nettl says, conceived as 'an internationally valid system, a set of techniques, which could be learned by anyone [...] It is accepted that anyone, no matter where his original home or what his native culture, given enough talent, hard work, and experience, can learn to perform Western music.'[19] That might be the reason why Seiji Ozawa is now esteemed as one of the best conductors in the world and why there are quite a few Japanese violinists, pianists, and other instrumentalists who are active in some well-known orchestras in Europe. There are even a couple of important Japanese opera singers in Italy. And it might also explain the fact that the three Japanese bluegrass musicians mentioned above are successful as players of instruments that require sophisticated performing techniques.

Indeed, the Japanese have tried to master the musical techniques of the southern rural whites and to copy American models that have been available in the form of recordings. Frequently, the closer to the models they are, the more highly they are esteemed in Japan. On the other hand, it is also true that many performers show in the music they perform that they had digested southern musical tradition in their own way. Their exposure to various performances by southern rural whites on record tracks and their own good experiences of performing in several sub-styles leads them more or less naturally to perform songs not necessarily in the fashion of some American performer, but in their version of a southern, rural, white musical style. They are much less 'yellow skin, white masks', to modify a phrase by Franz Fanon.

What has made such a development possible is the length of time the Japanese have been studying and performing the music of the American South. More than thirty years have passed since the Japanese began performing bluegrass music, nearly thirty years since they first played more traditional music from the South, and more than forty years since the first hillbilly band was formed. There was a father-and-son group, much older than the Nakashima Family Band, that appeared on the stage of the Takarazuka Bluegrass Festival several years ago. Even though Sumio Inoue, who got ninth place at the Galax Old-Time Fiddlers' Convention, only began performing old-time music in the early 1980s, it was a Japanese bluegrass group through which he was first exposed to music from American southern whites. And this bluegrass group, in turn, must have been motivated by another group, which again must have owed its existence to some senior group. That can easily be seen from the fact that many bluegrass bands were first formed as college bands who trained themselves as part of extra-curricular activities.

Years have passed since an overseas musical tradition that was captured on record was first imported to Japan, with suggestions of its cultural background in the sound itself but without its tangible milieu. Couldn't it be argued that enough years have now passed for the Japanese to fashion unintentionally, out of that tradition, a tradition of their own, as it were, or at least a recognizable derivation? To make it legitimate, there is a country music community as described above, though it is limited to bluegrass devotees and to old-time music lovers who largely overlap with the bluegrass enthusiasts. Moreover, it is significantly characterized by a lack of self-consciousness in terms of tradition.

R. Raymond Allen summed up an old-time music revivalist as 'a musician of urban, suburban, or small town (non-agrarian) background who attempts to create traditional, rural, vocal and instrumental styles of folk music which were not present in the home or community in which he or she grew up' (Allen 1981: 66). In the case of the Japanese, however, the 'attempts to recreate' have not been very conscious, whereas those of the American revivalists inevitably were. As we have seen, the American folk 'revival' did not affect the revival of Japanese folksongs, so the 'revival' has not been a revival to the Japanese, because it has been a phenomenon in a geographically and culturally far-off country. That culturally deep gulf naturally makes Japanese performances one step further removed from the performances of southern rural whites than are those of American revivalists such as Mike Seeger.

However, because the 'revival' itself is insignificant to them, the Japanese have not worried about the question of authenticity that is implied in revivalism, and thus are able to nurture their own version of an American tradition without constraint.

Notes

1 'New Year's Program' by the Japan–American Society of Fukuoka, on 13 January 1962, at Kasuga Officers' Club, Itazuke Air Base, Japan. The performances by four different groups of traditional Japanese musicians preceded 'American Folk Songs' that consisted of "Home Sweet Home", "Bile 'Em Cabbage Down", and "She'll Be Comin' Round the Mountain".
2 The Nakashima Family Band later performed in the presence of Bill Monroe in Kumamoto. Kumamoto Prefecture held a large concert of some well-known country music performers from Nashville in October 1989, and Mr and Mrs Nakashima took their daughters backstage to jam with Bill Monroe. Though the dream was not realized, the girls surprised and excited Monroe so much by suddenly starting to play when he came out of the dressing room upon request, that he clogged to their music. It was all filmed by the crew from the Kumamoto Office of NHK (Japanese Broadcasting Corporation) and was broadcast later on its satellite channel.
3 Preceding this book by four years, there appeared a small collection of cowboy songs: *Cowboy Aishōkashū* (Favourite cowboy songs). The cover obviously duplicates, with small modifications, that of *The Lonesome Cowboy Songs of the Plains and Hills* compiled by John White and George Shackley (1929), the reproduction of which can be found in John I. White (1975: 6).
4 The book consists of a short historical survey, biographies of 150 artists/groups, comments on 100 songs and an annotated list of 100 albums released in Japan. In *Jazz*, a book on American popular music that was published ten years earlier, the word 'South' does not appear at all in the four-page section on 'Western Music', though it briefly refers to 'hill-billy songs' after spending many words on 'cow-boy songs' (Shinozaki 1953: 257–60).
5 LP records of 'Folk Music' from the United States listed in the July 1959 issue of *Schwann* (Long Playing Record Catalog), which Hashimoto perused in 1959 and 1960, were more than twice as many as those listed under 'Cowboy and Hillbilly,' a subdivision of 'Popular Music'; 158–60 and 168–70 respectively.
6 Thane Mitchell, after having been discharged from military service, graduated from the University of Washington in Seattle, and has been active in the folk scene there as a performer and organizer.
7 Mitsui, 'Folksong and Folk Singer'. This 'purist' argument was repeated, in a way, in my letter to the editor of *Sing Out!* (see Mitsui 1965).
8 It was not until the mid-1970s that young Japanese showed an interest in traditional Japanese music serious enough to perform it themselves. The first were the Champloos, from Okinawa, led by Shōkichi Kina, who combined rock music with

the traditional Okinawan idioms. The Champloos were then followed many years later by the Takio Band, led by Takio Itō, who revitalized Japanese folksongs with contemporary interpretations. An appraisal of Itō by a Japanese writer, in English, was recently published in a British monthly (see Mogi 1989). It should also be noted that an obscure bluegrass trio, Anges Blanc, formed by Japanese female junior-college students in 1989, features a vocalist who used to sing Japanese folksongs in her childhood. Her powerful voice trained by singing them is quite suitable to bluegrass vocalization.

9   Telephone interview with Takashi Shinbo, who was the editor-in-chief of *Country and Western*, 9 February 1990.
10 Telephone interview with Masa'aki Yoshimura, who assisted Shinbo as an editor, 9 February 1990.
11 Telephone interview with Saburō Watanabe, the publisher of *Moon Shiner*, 1 February 1990.
12 The somewhat quantitative overview of the Japanese interest in southern white music could be supplemented with the number of sales of my books on the music published in the 1960s and 1970s. *Bluegrass Ongaku* (Bluegrass Music), the publication of which by the Traditional-Song Society was partly subsidized in 1967 by the college where I taught, sold out of the 500 copies printed within several years. Its revised and enlarged edition was published in 1975 by a commercial publisher in Tokyo, Bronze-sha, and sold 5,000 copies before the 1979 reprinting of 1,000 copies. *Eikei America Minzoku Ongaku-no Gakki* (The Instruments of Anglo-American Folk Music), another book published by the Traditional-Song Society, in 1970, sold its edition of 300 copies in several years. *Country Ongaku-no Rekishi* (A History of Country Music), which owes much to Bill Malone's *Country Music U.S.A.*, was published by an established Japanese publisher of books on music in 1971, Ongaku-no-tomo-sha. It started with 5,000 copies and had two reprintings, in 1974 and 1976, of 2,000 copies each.
13 The quote is from the original version in English titled 'A Letter to Japanese Bluegrass Lovers'. Courtesy of Saburō Watanabe, the publisher, and Gorō Tani, the editor, of *Moon Shiner*.
14 It should be noted that a new generation of collegiate bluegrass performers are often not well off. According to Saburō Watanabe, if one plays bluegrass, one can do without expensive electric and electronic instruments and equipment, although many students with money opt for this equipment.
15 Interview with Kōsuke Takaki in Kyoto, 22 March 1990.
16 Mike Miller, 'Old-Time Music in Japan' (1988–9). Note that this is a report of the Old-Time Party in 1987, not the one in 1988. This is a slightly enlarged version of what was originally written, with the title 'American Fiddle and Banjo Music Alive and Well in Japan', for *Asahi Evening News*, a Japanese English-language

newspaper, in November 1987. Miller is a Reuters correspondent, who, according to Takaki, came all the way from Hong Kong to cover the concert, because he is an old-time music enthusiast himself, playing the old-time guitar, and is now the husband of Valerie Mindel, a former member of Any Old Time, a women's old-time band in California, who is quoted in the report. The photostat copy of the report was printed in the liner notes to *Galax International*. Miller published the longer version of the report a year later in *The Old-Time Herald*, with a different title and picture, without referring to the fact that it was originally a newspaper report written in 1987.

17 See Fenton's 'Chronological List of Overseas Ribbon Winners at the Galax Old-Time Fiddlers' Convention 1935–87' in his 'Descriptive Introductory News' (Fenton 1988). As to Japanese winners at other contests, as far as I know, Kōsuke Takaki, a member of a string band, won fourth place at a fiddlers' convention in Deer Creek, Maryland, in 1981 (see ibid.: 13), and much earlier, in the summer of 1973, Noboru Morishige, who became a member of the Stonemans, a bluegrass band, won third place in the fiddle contest at a Mac Wiseman's festival in Renfro Valley (see Green 1974: 27).

18 'Alan Senauke Interview' 1989: 16. This interview is particularly interesting because it is illustrated with a photograph that shows Senauke, while training in a temple in Shizuoka Prefecture in May 1989, enjoying a bluegrass jam with a Japanese band from a neighbouring city in the temple building, wearing his zen monk's uniform and with his head shaven as a zen monk.

19 Nettl (1985: chapter 29). The 'Suzuki Method', a training method in the playing of classical violin devised by a Japanese, Shin'ichi Suzuki, has been so highly regarded as to draw people from Western countries to his school in Matsumoto.

Transformation inspired by the West (8)

'New music'

A loosely defined 'new music' arose in the mid-1970s, developing out of the music of singer-songwriters as well as out of early 1970s rock, with Yumi Arai (Yumi Mattōya since 1976; Mitsui 1992: 1644) as its initiator. Her songs in her first album *Hikōki-gumo* (Vapor Trail), released in late 1973 when she was nineteen, and sung with the accompaniment of her piano and a combo, displayed urbane sophistication and eclecticism under the influence of British music and French poetry, causing the critics to hail her as a neo-sensualist.

Supported by other trendy musicians, her kind of music became popular among young audiences. The term 'new music', used as an English term, does not denote a specific style and was soon grouped together with the newly developed music of such folk singer-songwriters as Takurō Yoshida and Yōsui Inoue (Mitsui 1992: 1230), whose careers slightly preceded Arai's, and also with that of newcomers, including Miyuki Nakajima, a gifted singer-songwriter who made her debut in 1975 (Mitsui 1992: 1791). Hence, 'new music', which appeared in the same year, was the name given to music that was difficult to categorize under the existing terms, and was all-embracing to cover newly developed Japanese rock, folk and pop, the musical self-sufficiency of which was in contrast to the division-of-work that characterized *kayōkyoku*, the mainstream popular music. The 'new music' musicians attached importance to the whole sound of a recorded song as a personal expression, often paying particular attention to sophisticated instrumentation and arrangement within the restrictions imposed by the music industry. In terms of business, this new tendency was reflected in the formation of For Life Records in 1975 by four eminent folk/'new music' singer-songwriters: Hitoshi Komuro,

Takurō Yoshida, Shigeru Izumiya and Yōsui Inoue. Starting this label enabled the artists to release records without the restrictions imposed by conventional producers. This, in turn, caused major record companies to grant more artistic freedom to potentially profitable artists.

It should be noted that this interest in composing and performing one's own material, which was first encouraged by 'group sounds' groups and then by contemporary folk singers, had much to do with the growth of the Japanese manufacturing industry for musical instruments. The manufacture of piano, harmonica, acoustic and electric guitar, electric organ and synthesizer, for example, has long flourished in Japan, popularizing these instruments amongst the Japanese. This prosperity involved an amazing increase in music lessons. Yamaha and Kawai, the two world-leading piano producers in the 1970s (Kōbundō 1991: 636), formed their nationwide network of music classes in 1954 and 1956, respectively, which expanded to accept more than a million students in the 1970s (ibid.: 121). These classes provided early training for those aspiring to a musical career, and in order to encourage them the manufacturers sponsored talent scout contests. These contests included the Yamaha Popular Music Contest, which launched the careers of such folk groups as Akai Tori and Off Course in 1969, as well as such solo singers as Miyuki Nakajima. Meanwhile, the Yamaha Corporation soon became the largest musical instrument manufacturer in the world in sales volume, with the number of overseas subsidiaries reaching more than forty in 1989 and eighty-five in early 2002. Kawai Musical Instruments, which also has subsidiaries all over the world, exports to over eighty countries.

The relative sophistication of 'new music' can be explained partly by the fact that advertising agencies cooperated with record companies from the mid-1970s onward in making many 'new music' songs successful. They did this by using them as the soundtracks for television commercials in which manufacturers of such goods as cosmetic, whiskey and coffee invested. In 1980, the sales of singles by 'new music' artists amounted to 50 per cent of all single sales, finally exceeding that of *kayōkyoku* (42 per cent) (Kōbundō 1991: 589). It should also be noted that, from the mid-1970s, the record and tape sales figures of the Japanese record industry exceeded those of the industries of other capitalist nations, except the United States. And the ratio of domestic records to overseas records, which were pressed by Japanese companies from masters recorded by overseas companies primarily for their own customers, was about three to two (Kawabata 1982: 199). A good many of these overseas records were US and British popular music.

It was in the late 1980s when the term 'new music' began to disappear gradually. The 'new' had been in direct opposition to *kayōkyoku*: not only the sales of singles, but also the sales of albums by 'new music' artists, had exceeded that of *kayōkyoku* in 1984. It might not be coincidental that Peter Manuel made a generalization, albeit a sweeping one, in the late 1980s, in *Popular Musics of the Non-Western World* that 'mainstream Japanese popular music is outside the scope of this book because, with the exception of *enka* vocal inflection, it is stylistically indistinguishable from Western popular music' (1988: vi). Concurrently, an increasing number of younger Japanese musicians began to consider those acts formerly bundled as 'new music' as their artistic roots instead of Western artists.

(To be continued: see page 185 for (9).)

8

Domestic exoticism: A trend in the age of 'world music'

This is a revised version of 'Domestic Exoticism: A recent trend in Japanese popular music', in *Perfect Beat: The Pacific Journal of Research into Contemporary Music and Popular Music* (Department of Media and Communication Studies, Macquarie University, Australia), vol. 3, no. 7 (1998), pp. 1–12.

A Japanese trend in the age of 'world music'

Since the late 1980s, young Japanese have shown an increasing interest in the kind of Japanese popular music that sound distinctly local or whose expression is largely derived from the musical vernacular. Rinken Band and Shang-Shang Typhoon can be considered as the most prominent exponents of this sound. Rinken Band are an Okinawan group whose music is heavily based on traditional Okinawan music, whereas Shang-Shang Typhoon are from the main islands and feature an amalgam of different local music styles (including Okinawan ones), together with reggae and other contemporary idioms. In terms of popularity, these bands are closely followed by Nēnēs, an Okinawan female group. Among those who are less known, but equally fascinating, are Takio Itō and his band, an ensemble that features energetic traditional-style vocals combined with a lively, hybridized style of orchestration, and Eitetsu Hayashi, known for his dynamic performance with Japanese drums.

Attracted to popular music from other Asian countries

Following an initial wave of interest in this music in Japan, Japanese youth have also, albeit to a lesser extent, begun to be attracted to popular music imported from other Asian countries. Various aspects informed and promoted this interest. Some were strategic, as in the work of Singapore's Dick Lee, who, in his earlier work at least, supported the idea of 'neo-traditional modernity', attempting to reformulate a contemporary Asian identity (Wee 1996: 498–9). Whatever the extent of the Japanese music industry's role in exporting domestic music and importing overseas music, younger people's interest in 'Asian pops'[1] has continued to develop and diversify. The vogue has encompassed music from many East Asian countries and has included singers such as Elvy Sukaesih, Rhoma Irama and Detty Kurnia from Indonesia; Freddy Aguilar from the Philippines; Jackie Cheung and Sandy Lam from Hong Kong; Teresa Teng and Lim Giong from Taiwan; Cui Jian and Ai Jing from China; and Lee Paksa and Seo Taiji and the Boys from Korea. Interest in these and other stars has been promoted by publications such as *Asian Pop Music-no Genzai* (Ōsuga 1993), *Asian Forum* (1994), *Pop Asia* (1995), *Asian Pops Jiten* (Dictionary of Asian pops) (1995) and *Asia-de Pop* (Let's pop in Asia) (1996). Significantly, several of the contributors to these publications are writers who recently converted from Anglo-American music to Japanese and Asian pop styles. At the same time, there has been an allied tendency for an increasing number of younger Japanese to prioritize other Asian countries as tourist destinations over previously prestigious locations such as Europe and the USA.[2] This preference might well be related to the fact that Japanese industries have been making more and more inroads into Asian markets, facilitating various economic and cultural communications. But what may also have motivated younger Japanese, albeit unconsciously, is the search for their own identity as an Asian people. As one aspect of the philosophical question 'Who am I?' (as a Japanese person), which is argued to have reasserted itself in the mid-1980s, young people may be wondering who they are, as a people belonging to a region that is called Asia or the East. In other words, they may be looking for values that could replace or complement the long-standing values fostered in the modern western societies; those that have been predominant but are now increasingly subject to doubt.

It should be noted, however, that the word Asia, which has now come into wide use in Japan, does not necessarily include Japan in its general (Japanese) usage. Though it appears to have been seldom, if ever, discussed, the term Asia is frequently used as if Japan did not belong to Asia. Just one of numerous examples is the headline of a newspaper article, 'A symposium on the subject of "Living Together with Asia" will be held on the 22nd' at Osaka International Peace Centre (*Asahi*, Osaka ed., 15 October 1995). This kind of usage might remind one of the people in the UK, another insular country, who often do not include themselves when referring to Europe. This misuse, which is more than inadvertent in both cases, may well stem from an arrogant feeling of supremacy over others in the same geographic region.

One of the most significant aspects of the rise in interest in Asian music in Japan is that, while undoubtedly commercially facilitated and/or triggered, it was an autonomous local phenomenon, one that occurred without the mediation of the Western music industry. This marks it out from previous, apparently similar, phenomena. Tango, for example, appealed to the Japanese in the pre-war period after being introduced to the country by a Japanese aristocrat who had become attracted to the music and dance during his residency in Paris in the 1920s (see Savigliano 1992: 239ff.). Similarly, the Japanese took a fancy to styles such as rhumba and mambo via the USA (rather than directly from Latin America). By contrast, various forms of Asian music that have proven attractive to present-day younger people have received little or no attention in the USA and Europe. It could therefore be argued that this is the first time that Japanese audiences have autonomously identified, selected and embraced forms of overseas music.

De-westernization

The principal impetus behind this specific musical de-westernization was the international popularity of what is called 'world music' (which is in itself an act of musical de-westernization).[3] The kind of music denoted by 'world music' is neither art (classical) music nor folk music (in a conventionally folklorist sense), whether alive or artificially preserved, but 'World Popular and Roots Music From Outside The Anglo-American Mainstream' (Sweeney 1991: ix). Arguably, this, primarily European, fascination with 'world music' was engendered by postmodernism, which became increasingly detectable in various cultural phenomena from the early 1980s onwards. The interest in popular and roots music from around the globe soon became manifest in, for example, the pages of the British-based magazine *Folk Roots* that, from the late 1980s, paid increasing attention to music from outside the Anglo-American mainstream.

In a similar manner to previous trends for overseas music in Japan, the initial commercial propagation of this music was facilitated via France. The first result was an interest in African popular music, records of which had originally been recorded and/or packaged and promoted in western Europe. As 'world music' grew in popularity, contemporary Okinawan music (performed with electric/electronic instruments and drums) became perceived and identified within this international framework. In this regard, its apparently semi-tropical attributes, and mostly unintelligible dialect, gave the form an exotic flavour and appeal that attracted the attention of many main-island Japanese. Prime movers in this were Rinken Band, who rose to prominence in 1990. The success of this group in turn revived interest in Shōkichi Kina and Champloos, whose electric Okinawan music had been ahead of its time when first released in the late 1970s. Simultaneously, the Japanese became interested in other artists and groups who also combined domestic elements and new sensibilities, while showing a readiness to accept popular music from other Asian countries.

What is especially notable about this trend is that it was the first time that young Japanese became prominently interested in any distinctly domestic-sounding music. This fact is significant, especially in the light of the interaction of popular music and folk music, because the music is of the kind that is industrially classified as popular while strongly characterized by vernacular or traditional elements.

In retrospect, the so-called folk revival or the folk movement in the USA, which had its heyday from the late 1950s to the mid-1960s, could have offered young Japanese the opportunity to develop an interest in domestic vernacular music. The North American folk revival was influential in encouraging an interest in traditional folk music, not only in North America, but also in Britain and, to various degrees, other European countries. However, the folk revival imported into Japan did not provide a noticeable stimulus for the Japanese to address traditional folk music.[4] Pop folk, a smooth and slick transformation of both folk and folksy materials, exemplified by the Kingston Trio, the Brothers Four, and Peter, Paul and Mary, was briefly popular in Japan, like other trends of American popular music, and generated a single local hit composed in an analogous vein ("Bara-ga Saita", written by Kuranosuke Hamaguchi and recorded by Mike Maki in 1966). However, the practice of singing songs one wrote himself, following the example of Bob Dylan, became established in Japan and represents perhaps the most productive contribution made by the folk revival. Nevertheless, the musical idioms that Japanese singer-songwriters used were basically Anglo-American, and the idioms were relatively easily incorporated by contemporary young Japanese whose musical education at schools had been almost exclusively Occidental-orientated.

Over the last couple of decades, folk music in Japan, especially vocal music, has largely been associated with singers who specialize in performing folksongs as a vocation (and who are notably less successful in commercial terms than mainstream singers). The stage performance of those singers has been stylized to the extent that they are invariably accompanied by a pair of *shamisen* (a three-stringed instrument with cat's skin on the resonator) and *shakuhachi* (a bamboo pipe) and boast stage *kimonos* dyed with loud-coloured patterns. These conventions are also often embraced by local preservation societies, which are found throughout the country. As might be imagined, the kind of music produced by such performers has not received significant attention from young Japanese. It was not until the late 1980s that they showed an appreciable interest in music with obvious vernacular elements that were outside the standard form of popular songs. This period, as mentioned above, was one when, among other factors, postmodernism became most evident in many more artistic, social and political quarters, and assisted, in the emergence of the concert of 'world music', in undermining and displacing the centralized master narratives of European culture.

The kind of domestic music that emerged was, necessarily, not something that was fossilized, but animated, breathing in the present. This innovative music, distinguished by its amplification and electronics, made its first appearance about two decades ago with the debut of an Okinawan band, Shōkichi Kina and Champloos, which featured Kina's bouncing *sanshin*, a three-stringed instrument with snake's skin membrane across the resonator, and his vigorous vocals. Rising to national prominence in 1977 with his hit single, "Haisai Ojisan" (included in the first album, *Kina Shōkichi and Champloos*, Polydor KK, 1977), Kina defined 'the Champloose Sound', in an interview in the same year, as something that gives new life to *uchina* (Okinawa) (*Mirai-eno Nostalgia* 1980: 27).

For me, the sound was precisely what I had wanted to hear in the mid-1970s, having first been inspired by Fairport Convention and then, decisively, by the Breton performer Alan Stivell.[5] The people who executed this integration were those who, in the words of the late English folksong scholar, A. L. Lloyd, 'through their experiences in the more modest regions of the folk song revival, had acquired a genuine respect for the melody and poetry of traditional folk song' (1982: 16). Innovation is nothing new to folk music, with traditions having been subject to continual change. As Philip Bohlman argued, '[r]ather than contenting ourselves with an ideology of conservatism, why not look instead at the proliferation of changing contexts for creativity in the modern world?' (Bohlman 1988: xx).

Kina apparently did not know about electric-folk music in Europe during the 1970s[6] (indeed, in the early stage of his development, one of his main foreign influences was reggae).[7] However, it was appropriate that someone on the Eastern side of the globe also produced a corresponding blend of folk music and rock-electrification. The cultural climate of Okinawa, where folk music remains intertwined with the daily life of the people, may well have been a key factor in Kina's lively fusion of elements. Kina's father was a well-established singer of Okinawan folksongs; as is the father of Teruya Rinken, the leader of Rinken Band, who debuted nationally about a dozen years later. Champloos' second album *Blood Line* (Polydor KK, 1980) included a hit single, "Hana-no Kajimaya", which featured a guitar accompaniment by US musician Ry Cooder.[8] During the production of the third album, *Matsuri* (Vap. Inc., 1982), Kina maintained, according to his recollection, that his approach was the only way to break an inferiority complex with respect to the West, which had long permeated the Japanese music scene (Haisai and Takarajima 1991: 77).[9]

Okinawan acts in the framework of 'world music'

It took several years, however, for such ardour to be embraced on more than a limited scale. The conceptual recognition of Japan as part of Asia can, to some extent, be seen to have de-westernized some Japanese popular music as the recognition deconstructed Japan's insular mentality to make the people more pluralistic. In this respect, it is significant that two important groups who became nationally popular in the early 1990s, Rinken Band and Nēnēs, were once again Okinawan acts who fitted relatively easily into the framework of 'world music'. While some aspects of their sound are familiar, young Japanese have found the exuberant rhythm and the distinctive scale (CEFGBC), among other characteristics, as exotic. On the other hand, as should be obvious, the Okinawan performers themselves, who grew up singing and hearing their native music, have never found such traditional elements exotic.

Both these groups were also associated with another prominent Okinawan musician, Sadao China,[10] who debuted in the main islands with the 1978 album, *Akahana* (Disc Akabana), which incorporated rock and reggae idioms into Okinawan folk music. His backing band, formed in 1977, became independent in 1982, as Rinken Band, with Rinkin Teruya, a *sanshin* player, as their band leader. The group debuted in the main islands with *Arigatō* (Wave Records) in

1990, a CD version of a cassette released in Okinawa three years before in 1987 by Maruetsu. Their music, which has gained a greater nationwide popularity than that of Kina's, is characterized by a lively combination of traditional Okinawan idioms (melody lines, rhythm, instruments, timbre and vocals) with new instrumentation that includes a keyboard, an electric bass and drums. The band features the leader's *sanshin*, and a female vocalist backed by a three-member male backing chorus, who play Okinawan drums on certain pieces. *Ajima* (Wave Records), their fourth album released in 1992, was recorded in Djakarta in Indonesia, Naha in Okinawa, and Tokyo, and included additional Chinese and Indonesian instruments. Its Okinawan dialect title suggests that Okinawa and the music of Rinken Band represent key intersections on the geographical and cultural map of East Asia.

In 1991, China produced another significant album, *Ikawaū* (Disc Akabana), recorded by Nēnēs, an Okinawan female vocal quartet formed in the preceding year. The distinctively Okinawan vocal style of the four sisters, who grew up playing the *sanshin* and singing domestic folksongs, was modernized by incorporating contemporary instruments, including the synthesizer. This album of Okinawan pop was commercially successful and was followed by a further series of albums, each of which reflected a different, innovative approach by China (who is well versed in both Okinawan folk music, the western classical tradition and the music of the Beatles). *Kayōkyoku* (Ki/oon Sony), the seventh album in this series, released in 1995, was recorded in Hawaii in their attempt to add some elements of Hawaiian and American country music.

It should be noted that this popularity of Okinawan pop was, to a considerable extent, inspired by a huge hit, "Shima-uta" (1992) by The Boom, a main-island hybrid pop group led by their principal composer Kazufumi Miyazawa. Debuting as a CBS Sony recording group in 1989, The Boom was characterized by its combination of ska beat, acoustic folk style and a sense of an active search for identity, which was clearly reflected in the third album, *Japaneska* (1992). The attempt to incorporate the *shamisen* and include Okinawan elements in their repertoire was strengthened in the 1993 album, *Shishunki*, from which "Shima-uta" became a hit single in the following summer along with a sister version sung in Okinawan dialect. "Shima-uta", which resulted from a conversation between Miyazawa and Kina (Kitanaka 1993: 161), featured a distinctive Okinawan-style melody and a prominent *sanshin* line, backed by a lively rock arrangement. The track expressed the band's unaffected longing for 'things Okinawan', which arose from the recognition of their insubstantial feeling of identification with 'things Japanese'.

'Pan-Asian festivity'

Another stylistic amalgam similar to that of Nēnēs has been developed on the main islands by Shang-Shang Typhoon, who are characterized by their festive approach to live performance. Starting in 1980 as Kōryū & the Himawari Sisters, and changing their name to the present one in 1986, they focussed on live appearances before finally recording the album, *Shang-Shang Typhoon* (Epic Sony, 1990). This was followed by another successful album, *Shang-Shang Typhoon 2* (Epic Sony, 1991), which more closely represents the style of music they regularly performed live. Along with two featured female singers, whose style has its roots in folk-singing, the instrumental line-up includes a *shamisen-banjo* (symbolic of the band's amalgamation of styles), an accordion, an electric bass-guitar, drums and percussion (sometimes replaced by a guitar or a *shinobue*, a non-reed bamboo flute). The ensemble performs a kaleidoscopic miscellany of pieces that incorporate, in different ways, *enka*, domestic folk music, Okinawan music, rock, jazz, reggae and Latin American music. One commentator has argued that rather than simply creating intriguing music, their intermingling of styles represents a revival of what might be called a 'pan-Asian festivity', which has largely disappeared from everyday life (Fukazawa 1993: 160). Whatever the accuracy of this characterization, the Japan Foundation financially assisted their tour around five East Asian countries in 1992, subsequent to which their CDs marketed in Hong Kong, Singapore, Indonesia, France and the USA.

The way in which various musical elements are combined in the music of Shang-Shang Typhoon is, however, undoubtedly different from that employed by Okinawan groups, due to the lack of such a solid musical vernacular that defines Okinawan pop. The domestic materials that Shang-Shang Typhoon draw upon, such as *Gōshū-ondo* (a traditional combination of dance and rapping), Okinawan music and main-island folk idioms, are deliberately adopted, rather than stemming from their own cultural background. There may even be a feeling of exoticism for the musicians in the way they come in contact with such elements. Eitetsu Hayashi, a distinguished player of contemporary Japanese drums, recalling the days when he joined Ondeko-za, a group performing Japanese drums in Sado Island, in 1969 at the age of seventeen, stated:

> I didn't feel close to or yearn after things Japanese and the Japanese themselves. See, the current of the times we grew up in were against such things – they were thrown away, though we are Japanese. The times were, you know, what you

would call 'the '60s'. If anything, 'Japan' looked distant from us, and I even felt something exotic towards *it*. (cited in Kojima et al. 1991: 124)

This sense of distance, combined with indifference or even dislike, has been shared, arguably to an increasing extent, by some generations. It obviously took more time for a hint of exoticism or a favourable slant, as referred to above, to emerge; as is shown in the case of Shang-Shang Typhoon and their audience.

Flexible and eclectic hybridization

Another kind of combination, which is as flexible and consciously eclectic as that of Shang-Shang Typhoon but without any visible trace of domesticity, can be seen in the music of Sandii Suzuki, produced under the supervision of Makoto Kubota. Born in Japan, of mixed Caucasian and Japanese parentage, Suzuki grew up in Hawaii before returning to Japan in her early twenties and beginning her professional career in 1977. Kubota began experimenting with a fusion of New Orleans music, reggae, Hawaiian and Okinawan music in 1975, with the release of *Hawaii Champloo* (Showboat), credited to Makoto Kubota and the Sunset Gang. The inclusion of "Haisai Ojisan" in this album appears to have prompted Kina, the song's composer, to record his own version, which, as previously discussed, made him famous in the main islands. A similar mixture was also attempted in the mid-1970s by Haruomi Hosono, later a founder member of the Yellow Magic Orchestra, in three albums: *Tropical Dandy* (Crown) in 1973, *Bon Voyage Co* (*Taian Yōkō*) (Crown) in 1976 and *Paraiso* (*Haraiso*) (Alfa) in 1978. However, largely due to his immersion in American popular music, his oeuvre exhibited a skewed exoticism towards Asian material.[11] This Orientalism, still unquestioned at the time of publication of Edward Said's compelling book, tinged Kubota's music as well.

Kubota's Sunset Gang, featuring Sandii, retitled themselves as Sandii and the Sunsetz in 1981 and toured for two months as the opening act for the British art-rock band, Japan. After a series of experiments on several albums in the 1980s, in which Kubota indulged in further musical eclecticism with Okinawan music, New Orleans rhythm and blues, new wave rock, reggae and East Asian music,[12] Kubota, along with Sandii, 'one of his main instruments' (Fisher 1994: 39), became more clearly Asian-orientated in the 1990s. Following *Mercy* (Eastworld) in 1990, which includes songs in several different languages and employs a variety of musical elements, Kubota began actively involving himself in producing albums by singers such as Singapore's Dick Lee and Indonesian artists such as Shampooer KD and Deity Churn. On subsequent albums, Sandii's vocal technique, especially her melismatic phrasing, showed influences from such Indonesian singers as Elvy Sukaesih. These albums – *Pacifica* (Eastwood) in 1992, another hybridization strengthened by Hawaiian factors, *Airmata* (Bomba Sushi) in 1993, consisting of covers of Malaysian and Indonesian songs, *Dream Catcher* (Epic Sony) in 1994, and *Sandii's Hawaii* (Jasrac) in 1996 – have shifted the pan-Asianism of Sandii and Kubota's music to an orientation towards the broader Pacific-rim.

Definitely domestic but totally new

Definitely domestic, without any exoticism on the part of the performer himself, is the lesser known Takio Itō, who grew up in a small community in Hakkaidō, hearing and singing songs in a living tradition. Being fed up with singing in identical vocalizing as a member of the established, preservationist circle of folk singing, he formed his own band. This developed into an exciting combination of an electrified *shamisen* and other traditional instruments backed by a synthesizer, an electric bass-guitar and drums. The first two albums were released by CBS Sony in 1986 and 1988, but Itō soon got frustrated by the inevitable restraints imposed by a major label and formed his own independent company to release his succeeding albums. As one observer commented, upon hearing Itō perform for the first time in the early 1980s:

> [...] the sound they delivered was totally new. The singer, Takio Itō, sang some old Japanese folksongs that have been boring us from our school days onwards, but the vivid and irresistible beat, the arrangements and high spirits brought a life to these dying or dead Japanese folksongs which no one could have expected. (Mogi 1989: 35)

Regrettably, such responses are not yet shared by a majority of young Japanese, but there are a couple of other acts who boast a national, albeit limited, popularity with music that is deeply rooted in the main island tradition. Kikusuimaru Kawachiya represents *Kawachi-ondo*, a traditional combination of dance and topical 'rapping', which incorporates the electrically amplified guitar and even Latin American percussion instruments. Another *ondo* from the same Kansai area, *Gōshû-ondo*, has become known largely through the performance of Tadamaru Sakurakawa with the band Spiritual Unity, whose line-up comprises a *shamisen*, an electric guitar, a synthesizer and some percussion instruments, and whose lively performances often make entire houses rise to their feet in response to their music.

It should also be noted that a variety of Japanese classical-style music has also enjoyed a major resurgence of popularity among young Japanese. Indeed, the work of a handful of eminent contemporary performers, such as Hidetarō Honjō, a *shamisen* player, and Hōzan Yamamoto, a *shakuhachi* player, has encouraged many young people to perform on such traditional instruments as *shamisen*, *koto* and *shakuhachi* themselves. An impression of this scene can be glimpsed by browsing through issues of *Hōgaku Journal*, a monthly publication, founded in 1987. They often feature covers that show a young person holding a traditional instrument in a modern setting.

In contrast to people in most other Asian countries, the Japanese have never prioritized their own traditional and classical music, possibly because of the fact that Japan has never been colonized, and consequently have never felt their national identity to be seriously endangered. After having eagerly adopted western music as part of their hasty, dedicated westernization since the late nineteenth century, and having been fascinated with American popular music, particularly after the Second World War, young Japanese people have now turned their attentions to Japan's own music traditions as distinct indigenous forms; albeit within a framework of their being domestically exotic.

Notes

1 In Japan, pop is almost invariably referred to as 'pops' in English, even among almost all music educators, musicologists and ethnomusicologists. This usage can arguably be traced back to the title of the now defunct popular-music monthly, *Pops*, issued by an established publisher of music books in Tokyo, Ongakunotomo-sha, which had its heyday in the 1960s.
2 Recently, a collection of essays by fifteen young Japanese on their travels to various Asian countries was published (Kobayashi 1995). Another, more conceptual book was published later in the same year by a single author (Shimokawa 1995).
3 The term 'world music' was chosen, in the summer of 1987, in a North London pub, after a series of meetings between 'about twenty-five representatives of

independent record companies, concert promoters, broadcasters and other individuals active in the propagation in Britain of music from around the world' (Sweeney 1991: ix).
4. For further discussion of the importance of the American revival to Japan and its consequences, see Mitsui (1993: 281–4).
5. The sense of ethnic identity shown in his music-making prompted me, in keeping with the musical directions of 'electric folk' in England and Brittany, to express my wish that the Japanese should also produce an original form of music based on their own tradition. See the brief closing remark of my early-1975 article on reggae, which had then just begun making inroads into Japan (Mitsui 1975: 39).
6. He made it apparent in an interview with an English rock musician Tom Robinson (published, in Japanese translation, in *Mirai-eno Nostalgia* 1980: 106).
7. For further reference, see his interview with reggae musician, Jimmy Cliff (*Mirai-eno Nostalgia* 1980: 116).
8. For an analysis of Cooder's collaboration with another Asian musician, see McNeil (1995).
9. Many of Kina's hits are collected in *Peppermint Tea House: The Best of Shōkichi Kina* (Luaka Bop/Warner Brothers, 1993).
10. 'Chi-' is pronounced like the 'chi-' of the word 'chin'.
11. For a different interpretation of Hosono's music, see Hosokawa (1998).
12. Achieving a minor Australian hit with the single "Sticky Music" in 1984.

Transformation inspired by the West (9)

Indigenous music compared with others

The various stylized forms of indigenous music have not been seriously threatened per se by the impulse of westernization. Despite the active introduction of Western music, many stylized forms of indigenous music have survived with established repertoires, coexisting with Western music as well as with manifold combinations of Western and Japanese musical elements. The conventional forms of Japanese music include *gagaku*, an ancient upper-class art music, originally from China; *shōmyō*, the Buddhist vocal music; *naga-uta*, the accompaniment to *kabuki* and *kabuki* dances; and the professional singing of folksongs, which was developed many years after the Meiji Restoration. The conventional indigenous music, generally called *hōgaku*, has been enjoyed more as live performance than in recorded form, but its tenacity is witnessed in the number of new record releases of the music: for example, 570 out of 10,689, the sum total of all domestic recordings released in 1998. This is comparable to the number of new releases by Japanese artists of Western classical music, which was 386 during the same period, before the world record market began to be on the decline (RIAJ 1999: 11).

Of the remainder of the new releases recorded by Japanese performers in 1998, 7,752 were recordings of popular music and 1,767 were 'educational and children's songs', 'music for animation films', and others. All of these displayed Western influences, to some degree, though many of the Western elements had been absorbed for so long that they were not always felt to be particularly Western. However, the huge number of foreign recordings released in Japan, that is, compact discs and cassette tapes of foreign origin, should be noted as a reflection of the continuing Japanese fascination with Western musical culture. The sum total of the releases of such foreign recordings in 1998 amounted to 10,265 in comparison to the 10,689 released by domestic performers. Out of the 10,265 released, 7,061 were of popular music, including film scores, and 2,986 were categorized as classical music (ibid.: 11).

J-pop

Around the time when the term 'new music' was disappearing, the term J-pop was coined allegedly in late 1988 or early 1989 by the programme planners for the FM radio station J-WAVE and by the public relations staff of major record companies. It did not, however, signify an existing movement.

The second commercial FM broadcasting station to be set up in Tokyo, J-WAVE began airing in October 1988 from Tokyo's most fashionable district. Its playlists were initially limited to overseas music with narration in English, but it planned from the outset to create a section devoted to 'tasteful' Japanese pop music intended to rival Western pop. The appellation J-pop was adopted as the name of the section, which went on air in the autumn of 1989. The prefix J-, as an abbreviation for the English word Japan, was already popular, as can be seen in the name of the station J-WAVE itself. Its first appearance may have been in 1985, when Nihon Senbai Kōsha (the Japan Monopoly Corporation) became privately owned and was consequently renamed JT (Japan Tobacco) in English. This name was not widely known, however, and it was the arrival of JR (Japan Railways) in 1987, formerly Nihon Kokuyū Tetsudō (the National Railways Corporation), that proved a decisive factor in the nationwide diffusion of the abbreviation. While some magazines began to use the term J-pop in the mid-1990s, the appearance of Japan's first professional soccer league in 1993, J-League, most likely accelerated the acceptance of the word.

Between 1991 and 1993, a new urban-oriented music style called 'Shibuya-kei' emerged. The music by such groups as Pizzicato Five, Original Love and Flippers Guitar was characterized by its incorporation of various Western influences and hence embodied J-pop as conceived by the music industry (for the characterization of 'Shibuya-kei' as a 'transnational soundscape', see Roberts 2013). The Shibuya in 'Shibuya-kei' refers to one of the bustling shopping quarters in Tokyo and it was where the spread of the CD in the early 1990s prompted foreign-affiliated record retailers, such as Tower, Wave and HMV, to open shops dealing in discs of a variety of new and old music from different countries. This musical environment gave an impetus to the formation of a number of groups, whose recordings were often put on air by J-WAVE and began to be referred to as J-pop by the media. The visual image of J-pop is well illustrated in a book on the Japanese pop music industry, written in 1998, in English, for a general readership by a North American journalist (McClure 1998). (For a social and industrial discussion of J-pop, see Ugaya 2005a.)

For young Japanese, however, what was attractive about the crisp and stylish word J-pop was that it implied that they could aspire to enjoy domestic pop in the same way as they did the Western variety. This aspiration was met when Hikaru Utada debuted in late 1998 with "Automatic". The rhythmical sense and vocal quality of this female singer, largely nurtured through hearing contemporary African-American music, were refreshingly un-Japanese, and when these elements were combined with her natural delivery of English phrases inserted in the Japanese lyrics and the topicality of her lyrics, they produced a performer of great distinctiveness. Born in New York as a daughter of Keiko Fuji, a female *enka* star-singer in the 1970s, Utada was only fifteen years old at the time of her debut. This successful single was followed in March 1999 by her first album, *First Love*, which sold an unprecedentedly high number of copies. As to the musical features of "Automatic", Yoshiaki Satō says, in the closing remarks of his commendable book of the musical analysis of Japanese songs in the past 100 years, 'I'm deeply moved by the fact that the dialogue between, and the fusion of, white music and black music carried on by twentieth-century popular music for long stretches of time creeped so profoundly into the inside of Japanese song' (Satō 2019: 249).

In 1998, the debut releases of female singers MISIA, Ayumi Hamasaki and Ringo Sheena were also highly successful. MISIA was regarded as an outstanding vocalist whose performances reached high standards of perfection. Hamasaki was particularly popular among teenage girls who emulated her clothing and make-up styles, and Sheena became known for singing about the hostile relationship of a daughter with her mother and for avoiding stereotypical themes such as heterosexual love.

By the early 2000s, J-pop was firmly accepted as a term used to describe Japanese urban pop that uses globalized musical idioms and is often accompanied by visual components. Popular artists who began their careers before 1998 also became encapsulated by the term J-pop. These included: B'z, a male duo known for their guitar riffs, American and British production style and their adroit 'cribbing' of melodies, and who are widely considered J-pop, even though they had their first top-ten hit in 1990; Tetsuya Komuro, known since 1994 as a producer and songwriter for many successful young female singers; and GLAY, a male band who debuted in 1994 and are known for the way they respect values advocated by the mainstream Japan such as diligence, decency and local patriotism. Along with being accepted as a J-pop band, GLAY are sometimes also classified as 'visual-*kei*', a name given to a type of music begun by the group X JAPAN, who combined heavy metal with flamboyant costumes.

The popularity of this J-pop is limited to the domestic market, with those who buy J-pop CDs being more than 90 per cent Japanese. The reason why 'the instant it strides over the national border, it loses support' is tentatively discussed in terms of the collective unconscious of the Japanese people by Ugaya in another book of his on J-pop (2005b). The literary analysis of J-pop by Ishihara places weight more exclusively on the lyrics of J-pop songs (2005). Also, 'the way in which J-pop, particularly in recorded form, is received outside Japan' is examined by Yoshitaka Mōri through his research 'in collaboration with the NHK international music television show *J-MELO*, from 2010–2012' (2014).

In the 2000s, the term J-pop was extended in record stores mainly to differentiate recent pop in general from folk, 'new music', *kayōkyoku* and *enka*. A historical extension of the usage to denote Japanese popular music in general has been attempted, but not commonly acknowledged.

Later development

As exemplified by J-pop, topics about the hybridization brought about by incorporating Western influences in the new century are bound to sound much more predictable. The accessibility of records through the international market, the continuous visitation of musicians from the United States and Europe to Japan, the increasing availability of information on music and musicians through media, including the internet, and the advancement of the technology of recording and producing discs have all accelerated the fusion. Western elements in Japanese popular music have already become assimilated or hybridized so much that the Japanese themselves have long tended not to consider them particularly westernized.[1]

One may find that the aural-scape of Japanese popular music has long been in parallel with the visual-scape of daily life in Japan since the late 1860s. Now one sees a great majority of people clad in *yōfuku* (Western clothes) designed in Japan and sees, as far as the eye can reach, public, corporate and private buildings constructed under the influence of Western styles of architecture. Understandably, as in the case of popular music, people are not particularly aware of this synthesis, which could be taken to be international. Note also that, when performing in public, musicians of Japanese traditional music invariably put on traditional clothes and musicians of 'serious' music adhere to dressing up in Western clothes, while musicians of popular music are sartorially unconstrained in general.[2]

Notes

1 For a concise and inclusive overview of popular music in Japan, see Stevens (2008: 38–61) and Yano and Hosokawa (2008); for a full examination of Japanese rap music, see Condry (2006); for 'how Japanese hip-hop DJs distinguish themselves in the global marketplace', see Manabe (2013); for various aspects of the underground scene, see Matsue (2008); for the portrayal of Japanese reggae dancehall practitioners, see Sterling (2010).
2 '[T]he cream of the mainstream Japanese popular music world in all its diversity, from elderly male soloists to youthful pop bands' is represented

in *Kōhaku Uta-gassen* (The Red and White Song Contest), the most important popular-music NHK-TV programme broadcasted annually on New Year's Eve. For the details of the 60th *Kōhaku* in 2009, see Brunt (2014). Two recent books need to be referred to here before the present book comes to a close. One is *The Revolution Will Not Be Televised* by Manabe (2015), which 'examines the structures that inhibit political expression, and how musicians work within or usurp the constraints of performance spaces', '[d]rawing from the author's ethnography since 2011 and interviews with key musicians and activists' in Japan. The other is *Resonance of Chindon-ya* by Abe (2018), a historical and ethnographic analysis of costumed musicians who parade through streets publicizing a business.

References

Abe, Marié. (2018), *Resonances of Chindon-ya: Sounding Space and Sociality in Contemporary Japan*, Middletown, CT: Wesleyan University Press.

Aikura, Hisato. (1980), 'Mokujiroku jidai-no speed-wa digital tokei-dewa hakarenai: Saikin-no rock-ni miru shin-kankaku' (Speeds in the apocalyptic age cannot be calculated with a digital watch: New trends in the current rock), *Music Magazine*, January: 33–41. (In Japanese.)

'Alan Senauke Interview.' (1989), *Moon Shiner*, 6 (10), 15–17. (In Japanese.)

Allen, R. Raymond. (1981), 'Old-Time Music and the Urban Folk Revival', *New York Folklore*, 7: 65 and 81.

Asia-de Pop (Let's pop in Asia). (1996), Travel Journal Asian Culture Book series, no. 3. (In Japanese.)

Asian Forum: Kikan Asian Forum. (1994), special issue on "Pop around Asia", 71. (In Japanese.)

Asian Pops Jiten (Dictionary of Asian pop). (1995), Tokyo: Tokyo FM Shuppan. (In Japanese.)

Atkins, Taylor. (2001), *Blue Nippon: Authenticating Jazz in Japan*, Durham, NC: Duke University Press.

Begenho, Michelle. (2012), *Intimate Distance: Andean Music in Japan*, Durham, NC: Duke University Press.

Bekku, Sadanori. ([1977] 2005), *Nihongo-no Rhythm* (Rhythm of Japanese language), Tokyo: Chikuma-shobō. Reprint of the 1977 Kōdan-sha edn. (In Japanese.)

Blech, Kerry. (1989), 'Review: Galax International', *The Old-Time Herald*, 1 (8) (May–July): 31.

Bohlman, Philip. (1988), *The Study of Folk Music in the Western World*, Bloomington, Indiana: University of Indiana Press.

Bourdaghs, Michael K. (2012), *Sayonara America, Sayonara Nippon: A Geopolitical Preshistory of J-pop*, New York: Columbia University Press.

Brau, Lorie. (1990), 'The Women's Theater of Takarazuka', *TDR: The Drama Review*, 34 (4): 79–95.

Brunt, Shelley D. (2014), '"The Infinite Power of Song": Uniting Japan at the 60th Annual *Kōhaku* Song Contest', in Mitsui (ed.), *Made in Japan: Studies in Popular Music*, 37–51, New York: Routledge.

Chamberlain, Basil. ([1891] 1971), *Things Japanese: Being Notes on Various Subjects Connected with Japan, for the Use of Travelers and Others*, Tokyo: Tuttle. Originally published in 1891 in London by Ka. Paul, Trench, Trubner & Co, Ltd.

Condry, Ian. (2006), *Hip Hop Japan: Rap and the Paths of Cultural Globalization*, Durham, NC: Duke University Press.

Cope, Julian. (2007), *Japrocksampler: How the Post-war Japanese Blew Their Minds on Rock'n'Roll*, London: Bloomsbury.

Daicel. (1990), *Nihon-no Ryūkōka-shi Taikei: Sōran* (Survey of Japanese *ryūkōka*: Conspectus), Tokyo: Daicel Chemical Industries. (In Japanese.)

Datahouse. (1987), *Dorobō Kayōkyoku* (Robbing *kayōkyoku*), Tokyo: Datahouse. (In Japanese.)

Department of Laws and Institutions, ed. ([1949] 2010), *Genkō Nihon Hōki* (Existing laws), Tokyo: Gyōsei. (In Japanese.)

Donaldson, Walter, and George Whiting. (1927), "My Blue Heaven", sheet music, Leo, Feist, Inc. Courtesy of Paul Wells at the Center for Popular Music, Middle Tennessee State University.

Fenton, Mike. (1988), 'Descriptive Introductory Notes' to *Galax International*, Heritage HRC 067.

Fisher, P. (1994), 'It's in the mix', *Folk Roots*, August/September, 134–5.

Folk Camp, ed. (1969), *Folk-wa Mirai-o Hiraku* (Folk opens the future), Tokyo: Shakai-shinpō. (In Japanese.)

Fujisawa, Morihiko. (1914), *Hayari-uta Hensen-shi* (Transition of popular songs), Tokyo: Yūrin-dō. (In Japanese.)

Fukazawa, Miki. (1993), 'Shang-Shang Typhoon: Han-Asia-teki shukusai geinō-no saisei' (Shang-Shang Typhoon: Regeneration of pan-Asian festive entertainment), in Takeshi Ōsuga and Asian Beats Club (eds), *Asian Pop Music-no Genzai* (Asian pop music now), 160–3. Tokyo: Shinjuku-shobō. (In Japanese.)

Fukuda, Ichirō. (1982), 'Basic operations in promoting international music', *Original Confidence*, 16: 777 (15 March): 32. (In Japanese.) (The original title in Japanese is unavailable in 2019.)

Fukuda, Shunji, and Yoshimasa Katō, eds (1994), *Shōwa Ryūkōka Sōran—Senzen-Senchū-hen* (Survey of Shōwa ryūkōka: pre-war and wartime), Tokyo: Tsuge-shobō. (In Japanese.)

Furmanovsky, Michael. (2008), 'American Country Music in Japan: Lost Piece in the Popular Music History Puzzle', *Popular Music and Society*, 31 (3): 357–72.

Furukawa, Kaoru. (1993), *Hyōhakusha-no Aria* (Aria by a wanderer), Tokyo: Bungei-shunjū. (In Japanese.)

Galbraith, Patrick W., and Jason G. Karlin, eds (2012), *Idols and Celebrity in Japanese Mass Media Culture*, Houndmills: Palgrave Macmillan.

Gondō, Atsuko. (1988), 'Meiji-Taishō-ki-no *enka*-ni-okeru yōgaku juyō' (Reception of Western music in *enka* in the Meiji and Taishō eras), *Tokyo Ongaku Kenkyū* (Studies in Music), 53: 1–19. (In Japanese.)

Gondō, Atsuko. (2001), 'Meiji-Taishō-ki-no yōgaku-kei *enka*-ni-okeru shakuyō-no mondai' (Borrwoing in *enka* in the Meiji and Taishō eras), *Elizabeth Ongaku Daigaku Kiyō* (Bulletin of Elizabeth College of Music), 21: 17–27. (In Japanese.)

Green, Douglas. (1974), 'Noboru Morishige: "I Think This Is the Only Time I Can Do What I Want to Do"', *Bluegrass Unlimited*, 8 (12): 12–28.

Groemer, Gerald. (2008), 'Popular music before the Meiji period', in Alison Tokita and David W. Hughes (eds), *The Ashgate Research Companion to Japanese Music*, 261–80, Aldershot, Hampshire: Ashgate.

Haisai and Takarajima, eds (1991), *Kina Shōkichi Champloo Book* (collected essays on Kina and Okinawan music), Tokyo: JICC. (In Japanese.)

Hamm, Charles. (1979), *Yesterdays: Popular Song in America*, New York: Norton.

Hata, Masaaki. (1993), 'Hata Masaaki Interview', in Susumu Kurosawa (ed.), *Nippon Folk-ki* ('Folk' in Japan), 54–70, Tokyo: Shinkō Music. (In Japanese.)

Hattori, Kikuo, ed. (1972), *Ryōka-wa Ikite-iru* (Ryōka is alive), Tokyo: Kyūsei-Kōkō Ryōka Hozonkai. (In Japanese.)

Hayashi, Susumu, Hiroshi Ogawa and Atsuko Yoshii. (1984), *Shōhi-shakai-no Kōkoku-to Ongaku* (Advertisement and music in the consumer society), Tokyo: Yūhikaku. (In Japanese.)

Hayatsu, Toshihiko. (2007), *Nihon Hawaii Ongaku-buyō-shi: Aloha! Mele Hawaii* (Hawaiian dance and music in Japan), Tokyo: Nagasaki-shuppan. (In Japanese.)

Heibonsha. (1985), *Heibonsha Daihyakka Jiten* (Encyclopedia Heibonsha), 16 vols, Tokyo: Heibonsha. (In Japanese.)

Hirose, Masaru. (1969), 'Aratana chikara-to hōkō-o: Kansai folk undo-no tenkai' (Towards new power and direction: Development of Kansai folk), in Kenji Muro (ed.), *Jidai wa Kawaru: Folk-to Guerrilla-no Shisō* (Times are changing: philosophy of folk and guerrilla), 207–25, Tokyo: Shakai-shimpō. (In Japanese.)

Hori, Takeo. (1992), *Itsudatte Seishun: Hori-Pro-to-tomoni 30 nen* (Always young: 30 years with Hori Production), Tokyo: Tōyōkeizai-shimbun. (In Japanese.)

Horiuchi, Kazuo. (1992), *'Ongaku-no Izumi'-no Hito, Horiuchi Keizō* (Person associated with 'A Fount of Music', Keizō Horiuchi), Tokyo: Geijutsu-gendai. (In Japanese.)

Horiuchi, Keizō. (1920), 'Ragtime-no Kenkyū' (Study of ragtime), *Ongaku-kai* (Music World), September and October issues. (In Japanese.)

Horiuchi, Keizō. (1935), *Jinta Konokata* (Since *jinta*), Tokyo: Aoi-shobō. (In Japanese.)

Horiuchi, Keizō. ([1942] 1948), *Ongaku Gojūnen-shi* (Fifty-year history of music). Enlarged edn, Tokyo: Masu-shobō. 1st edn published in 1942. (In Japanese.)

Horiuchi, Keizō. (1969), *Teihon Nippon-no Gunka* (Standard edition of *gunka* in Japan), Tokyo: Jitsugyō-no-Nihon-sha. (In Japanese.)

Horiuchi, Keizō, and Kashō Machida, eds (1931), *Sekai Ongaku Zenshū: Gesammelt Tewerke der Welt Musick*, vol. 19: *Meiji, Taishō, Shōwa Ryūkōka-kyokushū* (Popular songs in the Meiji, Taishō and Shōwa eras), Tokyo: Shunjū-sha. (In Japanese.)

Horstman, Dorothy. ([1975] 1986), *Sing Your Heart Out, Country Boy*, rev edn, Nashville: Country Music Foundation. 1st edn published in 1975.

Hosokawa, Shūhei. (1992a), 'Ryūkōka (44)', *Music Magazine*, November, 116–19. (In Japanese.)

Hosokawa, Shūhei. (1992b), 'Ryūkōka (45)', *Music Magazine*, December, 120–4. (In Japanese.)

Hosokawa, Shūhei. (1995), 'Le tango au Japon avant 1945: Formation, deformation, transformation', in Ramon Pelinski (ed), *Tango nomade*, 289–323, Montréal: Triptyque.

Hosokawa, Shūhei. (1998), 'Soy Sauce Music: Haruomi Hosono and Japanese Self-Orientalism', in Philip Hayward (ed.), *Widening the Horizon: Exoticism in Post-war Popular Music*, 114–44, Sydney: John Libbey.

Hosokawa, Shūhei. (2002), 'Blacking Japanese: Experiencing otherness from afar', in David Hesmondhalgh and Keith Negus (eds), *Popular Music Studies*, 223–37, London: Arnold.

Hosokawa, Shūhei, and Norio Okada. (1993), liner notes to *Machikado-no Uta: Shosei-bushi-no Sekai* (Street songs: the world of student songs), DA1005, Tokyo: Daidōraku Records. (In Japanese.)

Ihara, Takatada. (1958a), 'Honpō Western tanjō-ki' (Birth of Western in Japan), in *Western-no Tomo*, 34–5, Tokyo: Shinkō-gakufu. (In Japanese.)

Ihara, Takatada. (1958b), 'Honpō Western tanjō-ki (2)' (Birth of Western in Japan (2)), *Western-no Tomo*, 42–3, Tokyo: Shinkō-gakufu. (In Japanese.)

Ikeda, Ken'ichi. (1985), *Shōwa Ryūkōka-no Kiseki* (Tracks of Shōwa ryūkōka), Tokyo: Hakuba-shuppan. (In Japanese.)

Inamasu, Tatsuo. ([1989] 1993), *Idol Kōgaku* (Idol engineering). Enlarged edn, Tokyo: Chikkuma-shobō. 1st edn published in 1989. (In Japanese.)

Inaya, Shōichi. (1983), '"Bokurawa mandolin no chōgen sura shiranakatta": Bluegrass no daybreak in Tokyo' ("We didn't even know how to tune the mandolin"), *Moon Shiner*, 1 (2): 15–19. (In Japanese.)

Inoue, Takako, ed. (2009), *Nihon-de Rock-ga Atsukatta-koro* (When rock was burning in Japan), Tokyo: Seikyū-sha. (In Japanese.)

Inoue, Takako, and Hiroyuki Nanba, eds (2009a), *Shōgen! Nihon-no Rock 70's: New Rock, Hard Rock, Progressive Rock* (Witness! Japanese rock in the 1970s), Tokyo: Artes Publishing. (In Japanese.)

Inoue, Takako, and Hiroyuki Nanba, eds (2009b), *Shōgen! Nihon-no Rock 70's, Vol. 2: New Music, Punk Rock* (Witness! Japanese Rock in the 1970s, Vol. 2), Tokyo: Artes Publishing. (In Japanese.)

Isaji, Rick. (1988), 'Nihon-no Western kashutachi, Part 1: Ōno Yoshio' (Japanese Western singers, Part 1; Yoshio Ōno), *Rave On*, 7: 77–9. (In Japanese.)

Ishihara, Chiaki. *J-pop-no Sakushi-jutsu* (Art of J-pop verse making), Tokyo: Nihon-hōsō Shuppan-kyōkai. (In Japanese.)

Itsuki, Hiroyuki. (1966), 'Enka', *Shōsetsu Gendai* (Modern short stories), December issue, pages unknown, Tokyo: Kōdansha. (In Japanese.)

Iwai, Hiroshi. (1992), 'Iwai Hiroshi interview', in Susumu Kurosawa (ed.), *Nippon Folk-ki* (Folk in Japan), 72–80, Tokyo: Shinkō Music. (In Japanese.)

Jackson, Bruce. (1985), 'The Folksong Revival', *New York Folklore*, 11: 195–203.
Jansen, Steve, and Karn, Mick. (1981), interview in *Ongaku Senka*, April: 70–3. (In Japanese.)
JASRAC. (1990), 'Beiei ongaku-no tsuihō' (Expatriation of American and British music), *Shūhō* (Weekly Bulletin) by Naikaku Jōhō-kyoku (Intelligence Division of the Cabinet), No. 328 (27 January, 1943). Reproduced in *Nihon Ongaku Chosakuken-shi* (History of Rights of Authors, Composers and Publishers in Japan), vol. 2: 97–102, Tokyo: JASRAC. (In Japanese.)
'Jieitai ni Hairō: Takada Wataru'. (1999), 'Let's Join the Self-Defence Forces: Wataru Takada' (www1.linkclub.or.jp~kury/ct/abunaiuta/jieitai.html, accessed August 2011). (In Japanese.)
Kaminaga, Ryōgetsu. (1970), '*Enka* omoide arekore' (Recollections of *enka*), in Matsuo Takita (ed.), *Original-ban-niyoru Meiji-Taishō-Shōwa Nihon Ryūkōka-no Ayumi* (History of Japanese popular songs in Meiji, Taishō and Shōwa eras through the original discs), 40–2. A book accompanying a 10-LP set with the same title, ADM1001-1010. Tokyo: Nippon Columbia. (In Japanese.)
Kanai, Madoka. (1979), *Tommy-toiu-nano Nihonjin: Nichibei Shūkō Shiwa* (A Japanese named Tommy: treaty-of-amity anecdotes), Tokyo: Bun'ichi-shuppan. (In Japanese.)
Karahata, Masaru, Kōbun Nogawa, and Tadashi Aoki. (1938), *Keiongaku-to Sono-record* (Light music and its records), Tokyo: Sansei-dō. (In Japanese.)
Kasahara, Kiyoshi. (2001), *Kurofune Raikō-to Ongaku* (Black-ships-coming and music), Tokyo: Yūzan-kaku. (In Japanese.)
Kawabata, Shigeru. (1977), *Record Sangyōkai* (Record industry), Tokyo: Kyōiku-sha. (In Japanese.)
Kawabata, Shigeru. (1982), *Record Sangyōkai* (Record indsutry), rev 3rd edn, Tokyo: Kyōiku-sha. (In Japanese.)
Kawabata, Shigeru. (1990), *Record Gyōkai* (Record industry), Tokyo: Kyōiku-sha. (In Japanese.)
Kikumura, Norihiko. (1989), *Nippon Chanson-no Rekishi* (History of Japanese chanson), Tokyo: Yūzan-kaku. (In Japanese.)
Kindaichi, Haruhiko, and Akiko Anzai, eds (1970), *Nihon-no Shōka* (*Shōka* in Japan), vol. 1, Tokyo: Kōdan-sha. (In Japanese.)
Kindaichi, Haruhiko, and Aiko Anzai, eds (1977), *Nihon-no Shōka: Meiji-hen* (Japanese *shōka*: in the Meiji era), Tokyo: Kōdan-sha. (In Japanese.)
Kindaichi, Haruhiko, and Akiko Anzai, eds (1979), *Nihon-no Shōka: Taishō-Shōwa-hen* (Japanese *shōka*: in Taishō and Shōwa eras), Tokyo: Kōdan-sha. (In Japanese.)
Kinkle, Roger D. (1974), *The Complete Encyclopedia of Popular Music and Jazz, 1900–1950*, 4 vols, New Rochelle, New York: Arlington House Publishers.
Kitanaka, Masakazu. (1993), 'Interview–The Boom: tabi-o tsuzuke, deai-o kasane-nagara ongaku-o' (Interview with The Boom: Performing music through keeping on travelling and repeating encounters), *Music Magazine*, September, 155–63. (In Japanese.)

Kitanaka, Masakazu. (2000), interview with Biji Kuroda, *Record Collectors*, September: 100–3, Tokyo: Music Magazine. (In Japanese.)
Kobayashi, Noriharu. (1995), *Asian Japanese*. Tokyo: Jōhō Center Shuppankyoku. (In Japanese.)
Kōbundō. (1991), *Taishū-bunka Jiten* (Encyclopedia of popular culture), Tokyo: Kōbundō. (In Japanese.)
Koizumi, Fumio. (1994), *Nihon-no Oto* (Sounds in Japan). Heibon-sha. (In Japanese.)
Kojima, Tomiko. (1970), 'Shin-min'yō undō-no ongakushi-teki igi' (Significance of the new-folksong movement in the history of music), *Engeki-gaku* (Theatrical Studies), Waseda University, 11: 1–29. (In Japanese.)
Kojima, Tomiko, Akira Higuchi, and Kiyoko Motegi, comps. (1991), *Nihon-no Ongaku* (Japanese music), *Bessatsu Taiyō*, no. 75, Tokyo: Heibon-sha. (In Japanese.)
Kokita, Kiyohito. (2002), 'Imjin-gawa no sūki-na unmei' (Ups and downs of River Imjin), *Aera*, 12–19 August: 18–20. (In Japanese.)
Komota, Nobuo, Yoshibumi Shimada, Tamotsu Yazawa and Chiaki Yokozawa. (1970), *Nippon Ryūkōka-shi* (History of Japanese popular songs), Tokyo: Shakai-shisō-sha. (In Japanese.)
Kosaka, Kazuya. (1990a), *Made in Occupied Japan*, Tokyo: Kawade-shobō-shinsha. (In Japanese.)
Kosaka, Kazuya. (1990b), liner notes to CD *Wagon Master 1954* (Nippon Columbia COCA 6715–6). (In Japanese.)
Kurata, Yoshihiro. (1979), *Nihon Record Bunka-shi* (Cultural history of records in Japan), Tokyo: Tokyo-shoseki. (In Japanese.)
Kurata, Yoshihiro. (2006), *Nihon Record Bunka-shi* (Cultural history of records in Japan), new edn, Tokyo: Iwanami-shoten. (In Japanese.)
Kurosawa, Susumu, ed. (1992), *Nippon Folk-ki* (Folk in Japan), Tokyo: Shinkō Music. (In Japanese.)
Kuwabara, Takeo, ed. (1966), *Nakae Chōmin-no Kenkyū* (Study of Chōmin Nakae), Tokyo: Iwanami-shoten. (In Japanese.)
Lloyd, A. L. (1982), 'Electric Folk Music in Britain', in William Ferris and Mary L. Hart (eds), *Folk Music and Modern Sound*, 14–18, Jackson, MS: University of Mississippi Press.
Lummis, Charles Douglas. (1993), 'Japan's radical constitution', in Setsuko Tsuneoka, et al. (eds), *Nihonkoku Kenpō-o Yomu* (Reading Japanese Constitution), 155–93, Tokyo: Kashiwa-shobō. (In Japanese.)
Machida, Kashō. (1970), '*Ryūkōka*-toshiteno zokkyoku, ha-uta, min'yō-nitsuite' (About zokkyoku, ha-uta and min'yō as *ryūkōka*), in Mutsu Takita (ed.), *Original-ban-niyoru Meiji-Taishō-Shōwa Nihon Ryūkōka-no Ayumi* (History of Japanese popular songs in the Meiji, Taishō and Shōwa eras through original discs), 28–30. A book accompanying a 10-LP set with the same title (ADM1001-1010), Tokyo: Nippon Columbia. (In Japanese.)

McClure, Steve. (1998), *Nipponpop*, Tokyo: Charles E. Tuttle.

McNeil, A. (1995), 'A mouse, a frog, the Hawaiian guitar and world music aesthetics—Vishwa Mohan Bhatt and Ry Cooder Meet by the River', *Perfect Beat*, 2 (3) July: 82–97.

Maeda, Yoshitake, and Kōji Hirahara, eds (1993), *60 Nendai: Folk-no Jidai* (1960s: the age of folk), Tokyo: Shinkō Music. (In Japanese.)

Manabe, Noriko. (2013), 'Representing Japan: "National" style among Japanese hip-hop DJs', *Popular Music*, 31 (1): 35–50.

Manabe, Noriko. (2015), *The Revolution Will Not Be Televised: Protest Music After Fukushima*, Oxford: Oxford University Press.

Manuel, Peter. (1988), *Popular Musics of the Non-Western World: An Introductory Survey*, New York and Oxford: Oxford University Press.

Masaoka, Iruru. (1968), *Nippon Rōkyoku-shi* (History of rōkyoku in Japan), Tokyo: Nanboku-sha. (In Japanese.)

Masui, Keiji. (1990), *Asakusa Opera Monogatari* (Story of Asakusa Opera), Tokyo: Geijutsugendai-sha. (In Japanese.)

Matsue, Jennifer Milioto. (2008), *Making Music in Japan's Underground: The Tokyo Hardcore Scene*, Abingdon: Routledge.

Matsumura, Hiroshi. (2015), *Nihon Tetsudō Kayō-shi* (History of Japanese songs about railways), 2 vols, Tokyo: Misuzu-shobō. (In Japanese.)

Mattfeld, Julian. (1971), *Variety Music Cavalcade: Musical-Historical Review 1620–1969*, New York: Prentice-Hall.

Mihara, Aya. (1998), 'Was it torture or tune? First Japanese music in the western theatre', in Tōru Mitsui (ed.), *Popular Music: Intercultural Interpretations*, 134–42, Kanazawa: Graduate Program in Music, Kanazawa University (the proceedings of the 9th Conference of IASPM (the International Association for the Study of Popular Music) organized by its Chair, Tōru Mitsui).

Mihara, Aya. (2000), 'Dai-ikkai kenbei-shisetsu-to America-no butai: Tateishi Onojirō-koto "Tommy"-o megutte' (The first Japanese mission to America and American theatres: About Onojirō Tateishi known as "Tommy"), *Eigo Seinen* (Rising Generation), 146 (5): 2–6. (In Japanese.)

Mihashi, Kazuo. (1975), 'Nippon folk nenpyō' (Chronology of folk in Japan), in Kōtarō Yamamoto, Kazuo Mihashi, et al. (eds), *Warera Folk Sedai* (We are the folk generation), 229–43, Tokyo: Arechi Shuppan. (In Japanese.)

Mihashi, Kazuo. (1979), *Folkutte Nanda* (What is folk?), Tokyo: Nippon Hōsō Kyōkai. (In Japanese.)

Miller, Mike. (1988–9), 'Old-time music in Japan—a small but fanatic following', *The Old-Time Herald*, 1 (6) (November–January): 11–12.

Minakami, Haruko. (1979), liner notes to Japan's *Adolescent Sex*, Victor VIP-6564. (In Japanese.)

Minami, Hiroshi, et al., eds (1981), *Unaru: Naniwabushi-no Sekai* (Groan: the world of naniwabushi), Tokyo: Hakusui-sha. (In Japanese.)

Mirai-eno Nostalgia (Nostalgia for the future). (1980), interview with Shōkichi Kina, Tokyo: Bronze-sha. (In Japanese.)

Mitsui, Tōru. (1963), 'Folksong and folk-singers: on the occasion of Pete Seeger's coming'. Fukuoka: Privately printed.

Mitsui, Tōru. (1965), 'Correspondence', *Sing Out!*, 15 (2): 97.

Mitsui, Tōru. ([1967] 1975), *Bluegrass Ongaku* (Bluegrass music), 2nd rev ed, Tokyo: Bronze-sha. 1st edn published in 1967. (In Japanese.)

Mitsui, Tōru. (1970), *Eikei America Minzoku-ongaku-no Gakki* (Instruments of Anglo-American folk music), Toyohashi: Traditional-Song Society. (In Japanese.)

Mitsui, Tōru. (1971), *Country Ongaku-no Rekishi* (History of country music), Tokyo: Ongakunotomo-sha. (In Japanese.)

Mitsui, Tōru. (1975), 'Reggae: Jamaica-no Soul' (Reggae: Soul in Jamaica), *FM fan*, 10 March, 38–9; 24 March, 38–9. Subsequently reprinted in Tōru Mitsui, *Rock-no Bigaku* (Aesthetics of rock), 238–49, Tokyo: Bronze-sha, 1976. (In Japanese.)

Mitsui, Tōru. (1991), 'Introduction' to Popular Music, 10 (3), October (Japanese Issue), 259–61.

Mitsui, Tōru. (1992), 'Awaya, Noriko' (134-5), 'Dark Ducks' (629), 'Inoue, Yōsui' (1230), 'Kasuga, Hachirō' (1344), 'Kitarō' (1388-9), 'Li, Kōlan' (1480), 'Matsuda, Seiko' (1641), 'Mattōya, Yumi' (1644), 'Mihashi, Michiya' (1687), 'Misora, Hibari' (1709), 'Minami, Haruo' (1702), 'Murata, Hideo' (1779-80), 'Nakajima, Miyuki' (1791), 'Sakamoto, Kyū' (2179), Sakamoto, Ryūichi (2179), 'Yamaguchi, Momoe' (2745), 'Yamash'ta, Stomu' (2745-6), in Colin Larkin (ed.), *The Guinness Encyclopedia of Popular Music*, four volumes, London: Guinness Publishing.

Mitsui, Tōru. (1993), 'The Reception of the Music of American Southern Whites in Japan', in Neil V. Rosenberg (ed.), *Transforming Tradition: Folk Music Revivals Examined*, 275–93, Urbana and Chicago, Illinois: University of Illinois Press.

Mitsui, Tōru. (1994), 'Copyright and Music in Japan: A Forced Grafting and its Consequences', in Simon Frith (ed.), *Music and Copyright*, 125–45, Edinburgh: University of Edinburgh Press.

Mitsui, Tōru. (1997), 'Interactions of Imported and Indigenous Musics in Japan: A Historical Overview of the Music Industry', in Alison J. Ewbank and Fouli T. Papageorgiou (eds), *Whose Master's Voice?: The Development of Popular Music in Thirteen Cultures*, 152–74, Westport, CT: Greenwood Press.

Mitsui, Tōru. (2001), 'Far Western in the Far East: The Historical Development of Country and Western in Post-war Japan', *Hybridity: Journal of Cultures, Texts and Identities*, 1 (2): 64–83.

Mitsui, Tōru. (2002), 'Twentieth-Century Popular Music in Japan', in Robert C. Provine, Yoshihiko Tokumaru, and J. Lawrence Witzleben (eds), *The Garland Encyclopedia of World Music*, vol. 7: East Asia: China, Japan, and Korea, 741–7, New York & London: Routledge.

Mitsui, Tōru. (2005a), 'Japan', in John Shepherd, David Horn and Dave Laing (eds), *Continuum Encyclopedia of Popular Music of the World*, vol. 5: Asia and Oceania, 132–56, London & New York: Continuum.

Mitsui, Tōru. (2005b), *Popular-ongaku-to Academism* (Popular music and academe), Tokyo: Ongakunotomo-sha. (A Festschrift in Japanese.)

Mitsui, Tōru. (2013), 'Music and protest in Japan: The rise of underground folk song in "1968"', in Beate Kutschke and Barley Norton (eds), *Music and Protest in 1968*, 81–96, Cambridge: Cambridge University Press.

Mitsui, Tōru, ed. (2014), *Made in Japan: Studies in Popular Music*, New York: Routledge.

Mitsui, Tōru. (2018), *Sengo Yōgaku-Popular-shi 1945–1975: Shiryō-ga Kataru Juyō-netsu* (Reception of Western popular music in postwar Japan, 1945–1975: enthusiasm described in primary sources), Tokyo: NTT Publishing. (In Japanese.)

Mitsui, Tōru, and Shūhei Hosokawa, eds (1998), *Karaoke Around the World: Global Technology, Local Singing*, London & New York: Routledge.

Mitsui, Tōru, and Junko Matsumoto. (2005), 'Union Jack-o matotta mikako: "Miya-san" to "Miya-sama"' (Mikado dressed in Union Jack: from "Miya-san" to "Miya-sama"), *Bulletin of the Faculty of Education, Kanazawa University*, 54: 15–31. (In Japanese.)

Miyazawa, Jūichi. (1990), 'Maegaki' (Foreword) to Keiji Masui, *Asakusa Opera Monogatari* (Story of Asakusa Opera), 1–3, Tokyo: Geijutsugendai-sha. (In Japanese.)

Mogi, Takeshi. (1989), 'Singing the Fishing', *Folk Roots*, 11 (1): 35 and 39.

Molasky, Michael. (2005), *Sengo Nihon-no Jazz Bunka* (Jazz culture in post-war Japan), Tokyo: Seido-sha. (In Japanese.)

Mori, Tatsuya. (2003), *Hōsō Kinshi Uta* (Banned songs on the air), Tokyo: Kōbun-sha. (In Japanese.)

Mōri, Yoshitaka. (2014), 'J-Pop Goes the World: A New Global Fandom in the Age of Digital Media', in Tōru Mitsui (ed.), *Made in Japan: Studies in Popular Music*, 211–23, New York: Routledge.

Morimoto, Keiko. (1981), 'Meiji-Taishō-no *enka*' (*Enka* in the Meiji and Taishō eras), *Ongaku Bunka* (Music Culture), 9: 5–33. (In Japanese.)

Morimoto, Toshikatsu. (1975), *Onban Kayō-shi* (History of popular songs on discs), Kyoto: Shirakawa-shoin. (In Japanese.)

Morimoto, Toshikatsu. (1997), *SP Record-no Artist* (Artists of SP records), Kobe: Rokkō-shuppan. (In Japanese.)

Morita, Minoru. (1984), 'International', in Kunihiko Shimanaka (ed.), *Heibonsha Daihyakka Jiten* (Heibonsha Encyclopedia), vol. 2, 50, Tokyo: Heibon-sha. (In Japanese.)

Moto-ori, Nagayo. (1910), 'Gendai-no hayari-ura (Current *hayari-uta*), *Ongaku* (Music), 1 (9): 8–14.

Murao, Tadahiro. (1985), 'Comprehensibility of the Weakly Closed Pattern in Triple Meter Music: An Aspect of the Process of How the Japanese Have Been Getting Used to a Triple Meter', *Bulletin: Council for Research in Music Education*, 85: 146–55.

Muro, Kenji. (1969), 'Document: Tokyo folk guerrilla', in Kenji Muro (ed.), *Jidai-wa Kawaru: Folk-to Guerrilla-no Shisō* (Times are changin': philosophy of folk and guerrilla), 7–61, Tokyo: Shakai-shimpō. (In Japanese.)

'Music among the Japanese'. (1861), *All the Year Round*, May 11, 149–52.

Music Life. (1958), Tokyo: Shinkō-gakufu, March. (In Japanese.)

Nagahara, Hiromu. (2017), *Tokyo Boogie-Woogie: Japan's Pop Era and Its Discontents*, Cambridge, MA: Harvard University Press.

Nagai, Hideo, comp. (1975), 'Nihon-ban bluegrass record ichiran' (Bluegrass records released in Japan: a listing), in Tōru Mitsui, *Bluegrass Ongaku* (Bluegrass music), 2nd rev ed, 196–222, Tokyo: Bronze-sha. (In Japanese.)

Nagai, Hideo, comp. (2000), *Country Music Record Nihonban List, 1927–2000* (List of country music records released in Japan, 1927–2000), Yokohama: Privately printed. (In Japanese.)

Nagira, Ken'ichi. (1995), *Nippon Folk Shiteki Taizen* (Personal recollections of folk in Japan), Tokyo: Chikuma-shobō. (In Japanese.)

Nakagawa, Gorō. (1969), 'Boku-nitotte uta-towa nanika' (What is song to me?), in Folk Camp (ed.), *Folk-wa Mirai-o Hiraku* (Folk opens the future), 184–99, Tokyo: Shakai-shimpō. (In Japanese.)

Nakagawa, Nobutoshi. (1999), 'Tenshin-kashō-no kindai: ryūkōka-no cross-gender performance-o kangaeru' (Modernity in gender-changing singing: thinking about cross-gendered performance in *ryūkōka*), in Junko Kitagawa (ed.), *Narihibiku Sei* (Resounding sexuality), 237–70, Tokyo: Keisō-shobō. (In Japanese.)

Nakamura, Kōsuke. (2003), *Kindai-nihon Yōgaku-shi Josetsu* (Introduction to the history of Western music in modern Japan), Tokyo: Nihon-shoseki. (In Japanese.)

Nakamura, Tōyō. (1979), 'Rock kakumei-no naka-no Europe-no kage' (The shadow of Europe in the rock revolution), *New Music Magazine*, November: 39–43. (In Japanese.)

Nakamura, Tōyō. (1980), 'Japan as No. 1: *Quite Life*-no ninatteiru imi' (Japan as No. 1: The meaning represented by *Quiet Life*), *Music Magazine*, February: 78–85. (In Japanese.)

Nakamura, Tōyō. (1981), 'Record-sangyō-o meguru shomondai ⑪: Yōsō-o ippenshita yōgaku-bumon (1)' (Issues concerning the record industry ⑪: Imported-music section taking on a new aspect (1)', *Music Magazine*, August: 98–101. (In Japanese.)

Nakamura, Tōyō. (1988), 'Rainichi-shita artist-tachi-no sokuseki' (Contributions of artists from abroad), in Tōyō Nakamura (ed), *Music Guide Book 88*, 454–6, Tokyo: Music Magazine. (In Japanese.)

Nakamura, Tōyō. (1991), 'Early Pop Song Writers and Their Backgrounds', *Popular Music*, 10 (3) (Japanese Issue), Simon Frith and Tōru Mitsui (eds), 263–83, Cambridge: Cambridge University Press.

Nettl, Bruno. (1985), *The Western Impact on World Music*, New York: Schirmer.

Nihon Kokugo Daijiten Henshū Iinkai, ed. (2000), *Nihon Kokugo Daijiten* (Dictionary of Japanese language), vol. 1, Tokyo: Shōgakkan. (In Japanese.)

Nihon Sengo Ongakushi Kenkyūkai, ed. (2007), *Nihon Sengo Ongakushi* (History of music in post-war Japan), vol. 1, Tokyo: Heibonsha. (In Japanese.)

Nippon Columbia. (1976), 'Disco Graphy' attached to *Nippon-no Jazz Song* (Jazz songs in Japan), 5-LP reissue set. (In Japanese.)

Nippon Victor. (1967), *Oto, Sono-ayumi, Sono-yume: Victor, Oto-no Kaihatsu-shi* (Sound, its steps, its dreams: history of the development of sound by Victor), Diamond-sha. (In Japanese.)

Nishimura, Hideto. (2005), 'Nihon-ni-okeru Latin Americna ongaku jūyō-shi' (Reception of Latin-American music in Japan), *Asia (Nihon/Neikkei) Latin America* (Asia Yūgaku No. 76), edited by the Asia Yūgaku editors, 63–74, Tokyo: Bensei-shuppan. (In Japanese.)

Nishimura, Hideto. (2012), 'Nihon-ni-okeru Argentine tango-no juyō' (Reception of Argentine tango in Japan), in Sachie Asaka (ed.), *Chikyū-jidai-no Soft Power* (Soft power in the global age), 209–27, Ōtsu: Kōro-sha. (In Japanese.)

Nishizawa, Sō. (1990a), *Nihon Kindai Kayō-shi* (History of songs in modern Japan), vol. 1. Tokyo: Ōfū-sha. (In Japanese.)

Nishizawa, Sō. (1990b), *Nippon Ryūkōka Taikei: Ryakushi* (Popular songs in Japan: a short history), Tokyo: Ōfū-sha. (In Japanese.)

Nishizawa, Sō. (1992), 'Saijō Yaso-to jidai-haikei' (Saijō Yaso and his historical background), liner-note booklet to *Saijō Yaso Zenshū* (Complete collection of Saijō Yaso) in 16 CDs, 22–38, Tokyo: Nippon Columbia. (In Japanese.)

Noguchi, Hisamitsui. (1976), 'Nippon-no jazz-popular-no ayumi' (Historical sketch of Japanese jazz and popular music), liner notes to *Nippon-no Jazz-song*, 5-LP set, SZ7011-5, 6–9, Tokyo: Nippon Columbia. (In Japanese.)

OC. (1980), 'Business in foreign records—now and the future', a collection of interviews with the persons responsible for foreign records in various Japanese record companies, *Original Confidence*, 14: 664 (14 January), 74–85. (In Japanese.) (The original title is unavailable in 2019.)

OC. (1982a), 'Spotlight on international music: case studies', *Original Confidence*, 16: 777 (15 March): 28–31. (In Japanese.) (The original title is unavailable in 2019.)

OC. (1982b), interview with Ichizō Taguchi, the president of Victor, *Original Confidence*, 16: 785 (10 May): 92–3. (In Japanese.)

OCAR. (1979), *Original Confidence Annual Report*. (In Japanese.)

OCAR. (1980), *Original Confidence Annual Report*. (In Japanese.)

OCAR. (1981), *Original Confidence Annual Report*. (In Japanese.)
Ogawa, Hiroshi, Satoshi Odawara, Yoshiji Awatani, Kyōko Koizumi, Hideko Haguchi and Satoshi Masuda. (2005), *Media-jidai-no Kōkoku-to Ongaku* (Advertisements and music in the age of media), Tokyo: Shin'yō-sha. (In Japanese.)
Okabayashi, Nobuyasu. (1969), 'Ore-to folk-song-no ayashii kankei-ni kansuru hōkoku' (Report on my questionable relation with folk), in Folk Camp (ed.), *Folk-wa Mirai-o Hiraku* (Folk opens the future), 109–60, Tokyo: Shakai-shimpō. (In Japanese.)
Okada, Maki. (1991), 'Musical characteristics of *enka*', *Popular Music*, 10 (3): 283–303.
Ōkawa, Haruo. (1972), 'Nihon jazz record-no shoki' (Early days of Japanese jazz records), *Jazz Hihyō* (Jazz Criticism), 12, 71–2. (In Japanese.)
Original Confidence, ed. (1997), *Oricon Chart Book*, Tokyo: Oricon. (In Japanese.)
Orita, Ikuzō. (1981), 'Record-gyōkai-o meguru shomondai ⑬: Naibu-kara mita yōgaku-no muzukashisa' (Issues concerning the record industry ⑬: Delicate situations of the imported-music seen from the inside), *Music Magazine*, October: 114–17. (In Japanese.)
Osada, Gyōji. (1968), *Nihon Gunka Daizenshū* (Complete collection of *gunka* in Japan), Tokyo: Zen-on-gakufu.
Ōsuga, Takeshi, and Asian Beats Club, eds (1993), *Asian Pop Music*, Tokyo: Shinjuku-shobō. (In Japanese.)
Ōtaka, Shun'ichi. (1979), Review of Japan's concert in Tokyo, *New Music Magazine*, April: 149. (In Japanese.)
Peace-for-Vietnam Committee, ed. (1974), *Shiryō: Veheiren Undō* (Documents: Veheiren movement), vol. 1, Tokyo: Kawadeshobō-shinsha. (In Japanese.)
Pop Asia. (1995), first published as a special issue of *Black Music Review* (Tokyo: Blues Interactions) in February, and then followed in July and October of the same year by second and third issues. (In Japanese.)
Pope, Edgar W. (2012), 'Ideology, Exoticism, and Minshingaku: The Decline and Transformation of Chinese Music in Late 19th and early 20th Century Japan', paper presented at the third Inter-Asia Popular Music Studies (IAPMS) Conference at National Taiwan Normal University, Taipei, Taiwan, in July.
Pope, Edgar W. (2014), 'Nihon-no popular-ongaku-ni arawareru "Chūgoku"' (China appearing in popular music in Japan), in Mamoru Tōya (ed.), *Popular-ongaku-kara Tou* (Enquiring from popular music), 10–46, Tokyo: Serika-shobō. (In Japanese.)
RIAJ. (1993), *Nippon Record Kyōkai 50-nen-shi* (50-year history of the Recording Industry Association of Japan), Tokyo: RIAJ (Recording Industry Association of Japan). (In Japanese.)
RIAJ. (1999), *A Brief Description of the Japanese Recording Industry*, Tokyo: RIAJ (Recording Industry Association of Japan).
Roberts, Martin. (2013), '"A new stereophonic sound spectacular": Shibuya-kei as transnational soundscape', *Popular Music*, 32 (1): 111–23.

Robertson, Jennifer. (1998), *Takarazuka: Sexual Politics and Popular Culture in Modern Japan*, Berkeley, CA: University of California Press.
Rosenberg, Neil V. (1983), liner notes to *Here Today*, Rounder 0169.
Rosenberg, Neil V. (1985), *Bluegrass: A History*, Urbana, Illinois: University of Illinois Press.
RYB. (1981), *The Rock Year Book 1981*, London: Virgin Books.
RYB. (1982), *The Rock Year Book 1982*, London: Virgin Books.
Sanseidō. (1991), *Sengoshi Daijiten 1945–1990* (Encyclopedia of post-war years), Tokyo: Sanseidō. (In Japanese.)
Satō, Yoshiaki. (2019), *Nippon-no Uta-wa Dō-kawattaka* (How Japanese songs changed), Tokyo: Heibon-sha. (In Japanese.)
Savigliano, Marta E. (1992), 'Tango in Japan and the World Economy of Passion', in Joseph J. Tobin (ed.), *Re-made in Japan: Everyday Life and Consumer Taste in a Changing Society*, 235–52, New Haven, CT: Yale University Press.
Savigliano, Marta E. (1995), 'Exotic Encounters', in Marta E. Savigliano, *Tango and the Political Economy of Passion*, 169–206, Boulder, CO: Westview Press.
Sawano, Hiroshi. (1994), *Tokyo Lovesick Blues*. Tokyo: Magazine House. An autobiographical fiction. (In Japanese.)
Segawa, Masahisa. (1976a), liner notes to *Nippon-no Jazz Songs* (Jazz songs in Japan), LP-reissue set, Nippon Columbia, compiled by Hisamitsui Noguchi. (In Japanese.)
Segawa, Masahisa. (1976b), liner notes to *Nippon-no Jazz-Popular-shi* (History of jazz and popular songs in Japan), LP-reissue set, Victor, compiled by Hisamitsu Noguchi and Masahisa Segawa. (In Japanese.)
Segawa, Masahisa. (1983), *Jazz-de Odotte: Hakurai Ongaku Geinō-shi* (Dancing to jazz: imported musical entertainment), Tokyo: Simul Press. (In Japanese.)
Seki, Mitsuro. (1976), 'Boku-to jazz song' (Jazz songs and I), a liner-note booklet to *Nippon-no Jazz Song (Senzen-hen)* (Japanese jazz songs [pre-war volume]), LP-reissue set, Victor, 30–9. (In Japanese.)
Senauke, Alan. (1990), 'Alan-kara-no message' (A message from Alan), *Moon Shiner*, 7 (4): 10–11. (In Japanese.)
Shamoon, Deborah. (2009), 'Misora Hibari and the Girl Star in Postwar Japanese Cinema', *Signs: Journal of Women in Culture and Society*, 35 (1), Autumn, 131–55.
Shibuya, Yōichi. (1978), liner notes to Japan's *Obscure Alternatives*, Victor VIP-6593. (In Japanese.)
Shiga, Nobuo. (1991), 'FEN' in *Sengoshi Daijiten 1945–1990* (Encyclopedia of post-war years), 792, Tokyo: Sanseidō. (In Japanese.)
Shimokawa, Yūji. (1995), *Asia-no-kaze-ni Mi-o-makase* (Giving myself up to Asian wind), Tokyo: Shufunotomo-sha. (In Japanese.)
Shinbo, Takashi. (1978), 'Country ongaku nenpu' (Country music chronology), *Country & Western*, 86 (March-April), 40–9. (In Japanese.)
Shinozaki, Tadashi. (1953), *Jazz: Hyakuman-nin-no Ongaku* (Jazz: music for the million), Tokyo: Kantō-sha. (In Japanese.)

Shōwakan, comp. (2002), *SP Record 60,000-kyoku Sōmokuroku* (Comprehensive list of 60,000 tracks of SP records), Tokyo: Atene-shobō. (In Japanese.)

Simpson, Claude M. (1966), *The British Broadside Ballad and Its Music*, New Brunswick, NJ: Rutgers University Press.

Soeda, Tomomichi. ([1933] 1982), *Ryūkōka Meiji-Taishō-shi* (History of the Meiji and Taishō eras through *ryūkōka*), Tokyo: Tōsui-shobō. Reprint of the original published by Shunjū-sha in 1933. (In Japanese.)

Soeda, Tomomichi. (1963), *Enka-no Meiji-Taishō-shi* (History of the Meiji and Taishō eras through *enka*), Tokyo: Iwanami-shoten. (In Japanese.)

Soejima, Teruhito. (2002), *Nihon Free Jazz-shi* (History of free jazz in Japan), Tokyo: Seido-sha. (In Japanese.)

Spottswood, Richard K. (1990), *Ethnic Music on Records*, vol. 5, Urbana, IL: University of Illinois Press.

Stambler, Irwin, and Grelun Landon. (1987), *The Encyclopedia of Folk, Country and Western Music*, New York: St. Martin's.

Sterling, Martin. (2010), *Babylon East: Performing Dancehall, Roots Reggae, and Rastafari in Japan*, Bloomington, Indiana: Indiana University Press.

Stevens, Carolyn S. (2008), *Japanese Popular Music: Culture, Authenticity, and Power*, London & New York: Routledge.

Stickland, Leonie R. (2008), *Gender Gymnastics: Performing and Consuming Japan's Takarazuka Revue*, Melbourne: Trans Pacific Press.

Sugaya, Kikuo. (1975), *Shi-teki Rhythm: Onsūritsu-ni-kansuru Note* (Rhythm of poetry: note on *onsūritsu*), Tokyo: Yamato-shobō. (In Japanese.)

Suzuki, Fumio. (1958), 'Mountain music-no hanashi' (Story of mountain music), *Music Life* (Tokyo), 8 (3): 30–1. (In Japanese.)

Suzuki, Katsuhiko. (1972), *A List of C&W 78 rpm Record* [sic] *in Early Japan*. Privately printed in Tokyo. (In Japanese.)

Sweeney, Philip. (1991), *The Virgin Directory of World Music*, London: Virgin Books.

Sylvian, David. (1981), interview in *Sounds*, translated in *Rockin' On*, September: 2–5. (In Japanese.)

Sylvian, David. (1982), interview in *Music Life*, January: 124–9. (In Japanese.)

Taishū Bunka. (1991), *Taishū Bunka Jiten* (Encyclopedia of popular culture), Tokyo: Kōbundō. (In Japanese.)

Takaishi, Tomoya. (1969), 'Uta-to minshū' (Songs and the people), in Folk Camp (ed.), *Folk-wa Mirai-o Hiraku* (Folk opens the future), 19–108, Tokyo: Shakai-shimpō. (In Japanese.)

Takayama, Hiroyuki. (1963), *Western Ongaku Nyūmon* (Introduction to Western music). Tokyo: Ongakunotomo-sha. (In Japanese.)

Takechi, Tetsuji, and Taeko Tomioka. (1988), *Dentō Geijutsu-towa Naninanoka?* (What is traditional art?), Tokyo: Gakugei-shoin. (In Japanese.)

Tamura, Katsuhiko. (1978), 'Japanese Country Album Collection', *Country & Western*, 86 (March–April), 50–5.

Tansman, Alan. (1996), 'Mournful Tears and Sake: The Postwar Myth of Misora Hibari', in John Twittier (ed.), *Contemporary Japan and Popular Culture*, Honolulu: University of Hawai'i Press, 103–33.

Torio, Atsutaka. (1989), *Akihito-heika-no Seishun-to-tomoni* (My youth spent with His Majesty Akihito), Tokyo: Tairyū-sha. (In Japanese.)

Tsurumi, Yoshiyuki. (2002), *Veheiren*, Tokyo: Misuzu-shobō. (In Japanese.)

Uchida, Kōichi. (1976), *Nihon-no Jazz-shi: Senzen, Sengo* (History of jazz in Japan: pre-war and post-war), Tokyo: Swing Journal-sha. (In Japanese.)

Ugaya, Hiromichi. (2005a), *J-pop-towa Nanika: Kyodaika-suru Ongaku-sangyō* (What is J-pop?: Music industry becoming gigantic), Tokyo: Iwanami-shoten. (In Japanese.)

Ugaya, Hiromichi. (2005b), *J-pop-no Shinshō-fūkei* (Mental pictures of J-pop), Tokyo: Bungei-shunjū. (In Japanese.)

Viva Rock. (1982), September. (In Japanese.)

Wada, Seiji. (1969), Liner notes to LP, *All Japan Western Jamboree: Western All Stars* (Toshiba EP-7715), an abridged issue of a double LP, *Tokyo Jamboree*, released in 1958–9.

Wajima, Yūsuke. (2019), *Creating Enka: The "Soul of Japan" in the Postwar Era* (translated into English by Katō David Hopkins), Nara, Japan: Public Bath Press.

Wee, C. J. W-L. (1996), 'Staging the new Asia: Singapore's Dick Lee, pop music, and a counter-modernity', *Public Culture*, 8 (3): 489–510.

Western Hyakkyoku-shū (One hundred Western songs). (1952), Tokyo: Kyōdō Ongaku Shuppan-sha. (In Japanese.)

Western-no Tomo. (1958), January, Tokyo: Shinkō-gakufu. (In Japanese.)

Western-no Tomo, No. 2. (1958), March, Tokyo: Shinkō-gakufu. (In Japanese.)

Wada, Seiji. (1969), liner notes to LP, *All Japan Western Jamboree: Western All Stars* (Toshiba EP-7715), an abridged reissue of a double LP, *Tokyo Jamboree*, released in 1958–9 as the first and last LP recording of Japanese C&W bands. (In Japanese.)

Whitburn, Joel, ed. (1986), *Pop Memories, 1890-1954*, Menomonee Falls, WI: Record Research.

White, John I. (1975), *Git Along, Little Dogies: Songs and Songmakers of the American West*, Urbana: University of Illinois Press.

Yamada, Takao. (2002), *American Popular Music on Japanese 78-rpm Records: 1927–1958*, Kawaguchi, Saitama: Takao Yamada (privately printed).

Yamaguchi, Kamenosuke. ([1940] 1972), 'Hōgaku-ban Kaikoroku' (Recollections of Japanese music discs), in *Chinpin Record* (Rare records), 171–99, Tokyo: Gramophile-sha. Reproduced by Record-sha in 1972. (In Japanese.)

Yano, Christine. (2002), *Tears of Longing: Nostalgia and the Nation in Japanese Popular Song*, Cambridge, Massachusetts: Harvard University Asia Center.

Yano, Christine, and Shūhei Hosokawa. (2008), 'Popular music in modern Japan', in Alison Tokita and David W. Hughes (eds), *The Ashgate Research Companion to Japanese Music*, 345–62, Aldershot, Hampshire: Ashgate.

Yasuda, Hiroshi. (1999), *Nikkan Shōka-no Genryū* (Source of *shōka* in Japan and Korea), Tokyo: Ongakunotomo-sha. (In Japanese.)

Yasui, Takayuki. (2001), 'Tennessee Waltz (1)', *Yomiuri Shimbun* (Tokyo), Sunday Edition, 13 May: 4–5. (In Japanese.)

Yasui, Takayuki. (2002), 'Arabia-no Uta', *Yomiuri Shimbun*, 20 October 2002: 4–5. (In Japanese.)

Zakō, Jun. (1983), *Itsumo Kayōkyoku-ga Atta: Hyakunen-no Nihonjin-no Uta* (There were always *kayōkyoku*: Songs of the Japanese in a hundred years), Tokyo: Shinchō-sha. (In Japanese.)

Zen-Nihon CM Kyōgi-kai, ed. (1978), *CM 25-nen-shi* (25-year history of CM), Tokyo: Kōdan-sha. (In Japanese.)

Index

A&R man 131, 139, 144
ABBA 135
accordion 37, 42, 91, 180
African-American 80, 105, 158, 162, 187
Agata, Morio 128
"Aikoku Kōshinkyoku" (Patriotic March) 8
"Akagi-no Komori-uta" (Lullaby of Akagi) 177
"Akirame-bushi" (Resignation Song) 118
Akiyoshi, Toshiko 81
"Alexander's Ragtime Band" 43, 79
"Alles neu macht der Mai" ("Greenville", "Go Tell Aunt Rhody") 10
Allied Forces 43, 79, 80, 91
Amano, Kikuyo 56, 57–8, 60, 63
"Ame-no Blues" (Rainy Blues) 78
Andean music 83
"Andorra" 117, 127
Anka, Paul 83–3
"Annie Laurie" 79
Anthology of American Folk Music 157
anti-war 110–1, 115, 117, 120, 127
Anzai, Aiko 10, 35, 38–9, 80
Aoe, Mina 145
"Aogeba Tōtoshi" (Our Revered Teachers) 31
"Aoi Sanmyaku" (Blue Mountain Range) 80
"Aozora" (Blue Heaven) 54, 56–7, 60–9, 71, 76
Appalachian dulcimer 150
Arabesque 135
"Arabia-no Uta" (Song of Araby) 54, 56–8, 60–8, 76
Arai, Yumi (Mattōya, Yumi) 169
Ariola Hansa 136–7, 140
Armstrong, Louis 82
Asakusa Opera 44, 50, 55–6, 60, 65–6, 76
"Asawa Dokokara" (Where Does the Morning Come From?) 79
Asian 9, 23, 173–84
Association of Record Companies 132–3
"Auld Lang Syne" 10
Austin, Gene 63–5

"Automatic" 187
avant-garde 109–10
Awaya, Noriko 77–8

Baez, Joan 111
Baker, Joséphine 82
"Bakudan San'yūshi" (Three Brave Bombers) 7
banjo 3–4, 57, 60, 70–1, 99, 113, 119, 127, 149–50, 156, 160, 162–4, 167, 180
"Bara-ga Saita" (Roses Are Out) 127, 176
"Battō-tai" (Corps with Drawn Swords) 6, 18
Bay City Rollers, the 136
Beatles, the 82, 109, 125, 162–3, 179
"Bells of Scotland, The" 10
Billboard 111, 131
Bizet's *Carmen* 44
black music 83, 187
"Blowin' in the Wind" 115–6, 126
blue-blooded 92
"Blue Château" 125
blue-collar 92, 153
Blue Comets' "Aoi Hitomi" (Blue Eyes) 125
"Blue Light Yokohama" 129
bluegrass 101, 149–51, 154–6, 158, 160–8
blues 78, 88–9, 158, 181
"Boku-wa Amateur Cameraman" (I'm an Amateur Cameraman) 106
Bonny Jacks 105
boogie-woogie 80, 83, 126
brass band 5–6, 53
bridge (or middle eight) 55, 62, 66, 88, 106
Brothers Four, the 126, 157, 176
Buddhist 112, 117, 185
"Buttons and Bows" 94

Camden, New Jersey 50–1
"Camptown Races" 3
Carol 126
CBS Sony 128, 132–3, 179, 182
"C'est Si Bon" 83

cha-cha 82
Chage & Aska's "Say Yes" 108
Chamberlain, Basil 4
Champloos 176–8
chanson 82–3, 88, 93
Charles, Ray 126
Cherryland Jazz Band 58
Chika Hiroba (Underground Square) 120–1
China 7, 117, 141, 174, 179, 185
China, Sadao 178
chindon-ya 190
Chino, Kaoru 25
Chuck Wagon Boys 89, 92–6, 100, 153
"Cindy" 150
cinematization 66
classical music 4, 29, 32, 50, 175, 183, 185–6
Clayderman, Richard 135
'college-folk' 110, 137
"Comin' Through the Rye" 10
commercial song (CM song) 106–8
Commodore Perry 3, 5, 13
Cooley, Spade 94
copyright 8
Country & Western (C&W) 81–3, 85, 91, 96, 101–3, 150–3, 158
country music 90–1, 101, 103–4, 152–5, 157, 160–1, 163, 165–6, 179
cowboy 86, 89–92, 94, 96, 100, 103, 149, 153–4

dance-band music 43–4
dance hall 43, 82
"Dardanella" 43, 58
Dark Ducks 105
"Debune" (Outgoing Ship) 49–51
"Debune-no Minato" (Sea Port of Outgoing Ships) 49–50, 52, 65, 67
"Democracy-bushi" (Democracy Song) 21
de-westernization 175
"Devil's Dream, The" 152
Dickens, Jimmy 91
DJs 112–3, 189
dodoitsu 77
Donaldson, Walter 63
doo-wop 112
Downtown Boogie-Woogie Band 126

democratic rights movement, the 13–8
ditty 23, 52, 77, 79, 99
"Dōki-no Sakura" (Cherry Blossoms in the Same Class) 9
"Doko Itoyasenu" (I Don't Give a Damn) 119
domestic exoticism 173
drum and fife band 5
Duke Aces 105
Dylan, Bob 113–4, 116, 123, 126–7, 157, 176
"Dynamite-bushi" (Dynamite Song) 17

Ei, Rokusuke 106
eiga ko-uta 76
"Ekibasha" (Stagecoach) 93
'eleki' boom 125
Endō, Minoru 145
enka 13, 17–20, 21–3
Enomoto, Ken'ichi 44
Epic Sony 133, 180, 182
Eri, Chiemi 83, 88, 94

Far East, the 10, 85
Far Western 85
FEN (Far East Network) 81, 152
fiddle 19, 49, 86, 92, 94, 96–7, 99, 149, 162–3
Fisher, Fred 58–9
Flatt and Scruggs 151, 155–6
Flower Travellin' Band 126
folk 17, 77, 107, 109–13, 120, 126–9, 130, 145, 169–70, 188
Folk Camp 113, 117–9
Folk Caravan 120
Folk Crusaders 111–4, 117, 127
'Folk Guerrilla' 111–20, 122
folk music 112, 126, 156–7, 159, 165, 175, 180
folk revival 126, 156–9, 161, 176
Folk School 116, 119
folk-singer 116, 169, 17
folksong 6, 7, 10, 22, 52, 56, 100, 105, 109, 113, 127, 158–9, 177–9, 189
Foster, Stephen 3, 79
"Fou-sō-ka" (Fusō Song) 6
free jazz 109
French Revolution, the 13, 15–6, 20, 137
Frizzell, Lefty 87

"Frühlings Ankunft" 10
Fuji, Keiko 145, 187
Fujisawa, Morihiko 20, 23
Fujisawa, Ranko 82
Fujiwara, Yoshie 44, 50–1, 67
Fujiyama, Ichirō 77
Fukuda, Ichirō 135–6
Fukuoka 100, 149–51, 157
Funamura, Tōru 145
"Furusato" (Hometown) 34–8, 41
Futamura, Teiichi 44, 55–60, 63, 65–6, 76

"Gaikotsu-no Uta" (Skull's Song) 119
Gardner, Benjamin 47–8
geisha singers 77
GIs 91, 95–6, 102, 157
Gilbert and Sullivan 6
"Ginza Kankan Musume" (Kankan Girl in Ginza) 80
Giraud, Yvette 82
Gluck's *Orfeo ed Euridice* 44
Gō, Hiromi 129
"Gōchin" (Sending Straight to the Bottom) 9
Godiego 126
Golden Gate Quartet 82
"Gondola-no Uta" (Gondola Song) 53, 62
Goodman, Benny 82
Grammy Awards 106, 145
Grand Ole Opry 97, 156
Great Kantō Earthquake 44, 48, 50, 65–6, 75
Groemer, Gerald 83
Grofé, Ferde 71
'group sounds' 110, 125–6, 130
gunka 5–9, 18, 21–2, 76, 78
"Gunkan Kōshinkyoku" or "Gunkan March" (Battleship March) 6, 8
Guthrie, Woody 114, 119, 123, 127, 155

"Hab' ich nur deine Liebe" 44
"Habu-no Minato" (Port of Habu) 50–2, 54, 67
"Hail Columbia" 5
Haida, Katsuhiko 82
Happy End 126
Harada, Makoto 95
hard-rock 126

Hars 90, 103
Hatano Orchestra 43, 61
Hattori, Raymond 90, 103
Hattori, Ryōichi 78, 80, 83
Hawaiian 82, 88, 91, 93, 95, 100, 105, 150, 179, 181–2
Hayama, Peggy 105
hayari-uta 18, 61, 75–6
Hayashi, Eitetsu 173, 180
"Heartbreak Hotel" 99
"High-collar-bushi" (Stylish Song) 19
hillbilly 86, 82, 89, 91, 97, 100, 103, 151–3, 162, 165
hip-hop 189
hōgaku 183, 185
"Hoko-o Osamete" (Laying Down Arms) 51–2
"Home on the Range" 79
Horiuchi, Keizō 5–6, 9, 38, 40, 47–8, 53, 55–60, 62–6, 69
"Honky Tonk Man" 88
Honshū Hayride 96, 152
Hori, Takeo 95, 99
"Hoshikage-no Waltz" (Starlight Waltz) 42
Hoshino, Tetsurō 146
hybrid 49, 52, 76–7, 87–8, 189
hybridization 4, 69, 181–2, 189
hybridized 50, 173, 189

"I Saw the Light" 88
Iba, Takashi 45
Ida, Ichirō 57–8, 63, 65–8
'idol-*kayō*' 129
Ihara, Takatada 91–8
"I'm So Lonesome I Could Cry" 88
'image song' 107–8
"Imjin-gawa" (River Imjin) 112–3, 122
Imperial Military Band 6
Imperial Navy Band 6
indigenous 4, 19, 52, 77, 88, 147, 159, 183, 185
Inoue, Yōsui 128, 170
"Internationale, The" 110, 122
Ishida, Ichimatsu 24
Ishikawa, Sayuri 145
Italy 164
Itō, Takio 167, 173, 182
"Itoshi-no Ellie" (Ellie, My Love) 126

Iwai, Hiroshi 119
Izumi, Taku 106–7

Japan (group) 131, 136–41
jazz 22, 25, 43–4, 54, 56–8, 62, 64, 67–8, 76–8, 80–2, 85, 88, 91, 93–5, 98, 105–7, 109–10, 146, 154, 180
jazz *kissa* 98
'jazz song' 54, 76–77, 88, 105
"Jieitai-ni Hairō" (Let's Join the Self-defence Forces) 110, 117–9, 122, 127
jinta 5, 53
"Jiyū-no Uta" (Song of Liberty) 13–5, 20
JOAK 56–7, 61, 64, 69
joint venture 48, 69, 132–5, 141
J-pop 186–9
"Jūgo-dayori" (Letter from the Home Front) 9
"Jūgo-no Tsuma" (Wife on the Home Front) 78
"Jukensei Blues" (Examinee Blues) 110, 113–6, 122, 127
J-WAVE 186–7

"Kaettekita Yopparai" (Drunkard Returned from Heaven) 110–4, 127
Kagetsuen 43, 60
"Kago-no Tori" (Caged Bird) 22–3, 25–9, 31–8, 40, 53
Kaminaga, Ryōgetsu 19, 22, 26, 28, 146
"Kanashiki Kuchibue" (Plaintive Whistle) 80
Kansai 109, 110, 112, 117, 123, 137, 160, 162, 182
Kansai folk-song movement 110–1, 114, 116, 120, 122–3, 127
karaoke 30, 41, 147
"Kare Susuki" (Withered Silver Grass) 22, 53–4, 60, 67
Karn, Mick 140
Kasagi, Shizuko 80
"Katyūsha-no Uta" (Katyusha Song) or "Fukkatsu Shōka" (Resurrections Song) 22, 52–3, 62, 76
Kawabata, Shigeru 61, 64, 131–2, 134, 143
Kawachi-ondo 182
Kawai 170
Kawakami, Otojirō 17

Kawaraban 114, 117
kayōkyoku 54, 61, 69, 73, 75–6, 79, 85, 101, 105–6, 125, 127, 129–30, 145, 147, 157, 169, 170–1, 179, 188
"Keiko-no Yume-wa Yoru-hiraku" (Keiko's Dream Unfolds at Night) 145
"Kentucky Waltz" 157
Kikuchi, Kan 68
"Kimi Koishi" (Yearning for You) 49, 65–9
Kina, Schōkichi 176–7
Kindaichi, Haruhiko 10, 35, 38–9
King, Pee Wee 94
Kingston Trio, the 126, 157, 176
Kipling, Rudyard 4
Kishida, Tatsuya 45
Kiss 131
Kitajima, Saburō 145
Kobe 44, 57, 100, 110, 114, 127, 162
Koga, Masao 42, 77, 99
Kōhaku Uta-gassen 190
Koizumi, Fumio 42
Kojima, Tomiko 32, 42, 72, 181
"Kōkō San'nensei" (Twelfth Grade) 129
"Kōkoku Kesshitai" (Imperial Ready-to-die Squad) 18
Korea 113
Korean War 95
Kosaka, Kazuya 86, 89–90, 94–9, 101, 143
Koshiji, Fubuki 83
ko-uta 77
Ko-uta, Katsutarō 77
Kreisler, Fritz 50
Krupa, Gene 82
Kurata, Yoshihiro 41, 48, 51–2, 54, 58, 61, 64–6, 68, 80, 132, 143
Kuroda, Biji 92–4, 97
"Kuroi Hanabiara" (Black Petals) 105
"Kuso Kurae-bushi" (Go-to-hell Song) 116, 119
Kyoto 52, 61, 95, 110–1, 116–7, 119, 123, 127

"Last Rose of Summer, The" 10
late 1920s, the 23, 47, 76, 158
late 1960s, the 107, 109
Latin American 180, 182
Leroux, Charles 6, 18

Loan, Paul Van 70–1
"Love Story-wa Totsuzen-ni" (Love Story Starts Abruptly) 108

Machida, Kashō 56, 73
mambo 82, 175
mandolin 82, 175
"Manshū Kōshinkyoku" (Manchurian March) 7
"Marching Through Georgia" 22
"Massa's in the Cold Ground" 3
Matsuda, Seiko 129
Matsui, Sumako 52
Mauriat, Paul 135
Meiji 5–6, 10, 14, 23, 26, 38, 49, 56, 61, 78, 119
metropolitan area, the 22, 91, 110, 155
"Miagete-goran Yoru-no Hoshi-o" (Look Up the Stars in the Sky) 106
Mihashi, Kazuo 111, 114, 116–7, 119
Mikado 6
Miki, Torirō 106–7
"Minato" (Port) 38–40, 49–52, 54
Ministry of Education, the 9, 35
"Minken Kazoe-uta" (Democratic Rights Counting Song) 15
minshingaku 11
minstrel show 3
Misora, Hibari 80, 145
Miyako, Harumi 145
miyako-bushi 53
"Miya-san" (Dear Prince) or "Ton'yare-bushi" (*Ton'yare* Song) 5
Mizuhara, Hiroshi 105
Mon Paris, "Mon Paris" 45, 61
Monroe, Bill 151, 155, 166
"Montana Moon" 90
Montoya, Carlos 82
Moon Shiner 156, 160–1, 167
Mori, Shin'ichi 145
"Mugi-to Heitai" (Wheats and Soldiers) 9
Murahachibu 126
music industry 47, 107–8, 110–1, 119, 125, 128, 145, 169, 174–5, 186–7
Music Life 100–1, 137–9
Music Magazine 139
"My Blue Heaven" 47, 54–5, 62–4, 70–2, 76, 79

Nagai, Frank 105
Nagasaki 5
Nagoya 61, 120
Nakae, Chōmin 15–16, 20
Nakagawa, Gorō 113
Nakajima, Miyuki 169, 170
Nakamura, Hachidai 81, 106
Nakamura, Tōyō 139
Nakashima Family Band 149, 151, 165–6
Nakatsugawa Folk Jamboree 128
Nakayama, Shinpei 22, 50–1, 62, 67, 72, 76
"Nakuna Kobato-yo" (Don't Cry, Little Dove) 80
Namiki, Michiko 79
"Nangoku-Tosa-o Atonishite" (Leaving Tosa, My Southern Home) 105
naniwabushi (or *rōkyoku*) 24. 145
'nanmyō-hōren-gēkyō' 41
Nēnēs 173, 178–80
Nettl, Bruno 164
New Leftist 109–10, 127
'new music' 107, 128, 130, 147, 169–71, 186, 188
'new folksong' (*shin min'yō*) 49–51
NHK (Nippon Hōso Kyōkai) 55–6, 61, 73, 166, 188, 190
Nicchiku 48–9, 52, 54, 57–61, 63–6
Nikkatsu 68
Nippon Columbia 26, 29, 47–9, 57, 65, 70, 79–80, 89–90, 97, 99, 132–4, 143, 156
Nippon Phonogram 132
Nippon Victor 7, 47–51, 54, 57, 64–6, 69, 132
Noguchi, Gorō 129
Noguchi, Ujō 50–1, 53
Nolans, the 136
"Nonki-bushi" (Happy-Go-Lucky Song) 21, 24, 119
"North Country Blues" 113

Oakland, California 51
OECD (Organization for Economic Co-operation and Development) 132
Oka, Haruo 79–80
Okabayashi, Nobuyasu 116, 119
Okamoto, Atsuo 80
"Oka-o Koete" (Going over the Hill) 77
Okinawa 115, 128, 166–7, 173, 176–181

Okuyama, Ai 90, 103
old-time music 101, 150–1, 162–5, 167–8
ondo 77, 180, 182–3
"Orange Blossom Special" 95
orchestral sound
Original-ban-niyoru Meiji-Taishō-Shōwa Ryūkōka-no Ayumi 26
Original Confidence 111, 113–4
Osaka 8, 45, 61, 100, 110, 113–5, 120, 123, 127–8, 151, 174
Ōtani, Eiichi 107
Otowa, Shigure 50–1, 65, 69
Ozawa, Seiji 164
Ozawa, Shōichi 29, 32–3

Pacific War 55, 78–9
Page, Patti 94
Peace-for-Vietnam Committee (Veheiren) 101, 115, 120–1, 123
pentatonic major 6, 10, 21, 23, 28, 61, 77, 106
pentatonic minor 21, 26, 28, 76, 78–80, 105
pentatonicism 49, 52–3, 61–2, 67, 88, 99
Peter, Paul and Mary 126, 157, 176
phonograph 19, 23, 43, 47–8, 52, 55, 60, 75, 143, 152, 157
Polydor 7, 48–9, 75, 128, 133, 142, 177–8
Polyester 133
"Pop Goes the Weasel" 1–3
Pope, Edgar W. 11, 70–2
'pop-folk' 110, 126, 157
post-war 7, 54–5, 68, 79–83, 85–6, 93, 103, 128, 152–3
Prado, Perez 82
Presley, Elvis 83, 86, 99
pre-war 30, 54, 70, 81, 83, 85, 93, 152, 175
producer 96, 109, 135, 142, 170, 188
protest 15, 18, 21, 109–11, 113–6, 118–9, 121–3, 127–8, 156

radio 7–8, 19, 23, 29, 36, 48, 55–7, 61–2, 69, 79, 81, 89, 91, 106–7, 112–3, 123, 137, 147, 152, 186
Rakhmaninov, Sergei 50
rap 17, 180, 182, 189
"Rappa-bushi" (Bugle Song) 18, 21

Ray, Johnny 82
RCA (Radio Corporation of America) 132–3
Record Awards 106, 145
recording industry (record industry) 7, 48–9, 53–4, 57–8, 61, 65, 69, 75, 88, 131–3, 135, 145, 170
Red & Blue Club Orchestra 57–8, 60
'Red Seal' artist 50–1
reel-to-reel 112
reggae 173, 178, 180–1, 184, 189
requinto guitar 105
Reynolds, Malvina 114, 117, 127
right-wing 9
"Ringo-no Uta" (Song of an Apple) 79–80
Rinken Band 173, 176, 178–9
Risshisha 15
rock 82, 107, 125–6, 129, 130, 136–7, 142, 145, 160, 166, 169, 178–81, 184
rockabilly 99, 105–6, 125, 150, 155
rock 'n' roll 83, 99, 101, 107, 126
"Roei-no Uta" (Encampment Song) 8
Rosenberg, Neil V. 150, 163
Rossi, Giovanni Vittorio 44
Rousseau, Jean-Jacques 13–4, 16
Royal Albert Hall 51
royalty 133–5, 142
Russian 105
Russo-Japanese War 6–7, 19, 21, 23
RVC 132–4
ryōka 30–1
ryūkōka 26, 56, 61, 65–70, 73, 75–9
ryūkō ko-uta 75

Sadistic Mika Band 126
Saijō, Hideki 129
Saijō, Yaso 67, 72, 76
St Joseph International School 92–3
Sakamoto, Kyū 106
Sakamoto, Ryūichi 141
"Sake-wa Namida-ka Tameiki-ka" (Is Wine Tears or a Sigh?) 77
sanshin 177–9
"San'ya Blues" (Doss-house Blues) 116
Sassa, Kōka 44, 65–6
Satō, Chiyako 50–1, 66–8, 72
Seeger, Pete 111, 114–5, 117, 123, 126–7, 156–7
"Seishun Cycling" (Youthful Cycling) 99

Self-Defence Army Band 6
Self-Defence Forces 110, 117–8, 123, 127
Self-Defence Navy Band 6
Sen, Masao 145
"Sendō Ko-uta" (Boatman's Ditty) 22–3, 26, 51, 67, 76, 145
"Senjō-no Komori-uta" (Lullaby on the Battlefield) 9
"Sen'ninbari" (Thousand-Stitch Belt) 78
"Sen'yū" (Comrade in Arms) 7
"Sen'yū-no Ikotsu-o Idaite" (Embracing the Ashes of My Comrade) 9
"Sen'yū-no Uta" (Song of Comrades) 9
serious music 4, 164, 189
Setoguchi, Tōkichi 6, 8
"Seto-no Hanayome" (Bride in Seto) 129
"Shakaitō Rappa-bushi" (Social Party Bugle Song) 18
shakuhachi 146, 177, 183
shamisen 24, 28, 77, 146, 150, 177, 179–80, 182–3
Shang-Shang Typhoon 173, 180–1
Shibuya-kei 186
Shimamura, Hōgetsu 23, 52
"Shin Ginza Kōshinkyoku" (New Ginza March) 76
"Shingun" (Marching) 7
"Shingun-no Uta" (Marching Song) 8, 78
Shirakata, Buckie 82, 93
"Shiretoko Ryojō" (Traveller's Melancholy in Shiretoko) 129
shogunate 2–3, 5–6, 13
Shōji, Tarō 78
shōka 6, 9–10, 21, 23, 35
shosei-bushi 19, 22, 26
Shōwa 26, 56, 63, 65
"Shūchō-no Musume" (Daughter of the Chief) 40
silent film 7, 23, 26, 43, 51, 60, 72
"Sing Me a Song of Araby" 47, 54–5, 58–9, 63, 70–1, 76
singer-songwriter 21–2, 25, 109, 116, 119, 122–3, 127, 128, 156, 169, 176
Sino-Japanese War 6–7, 18, 21
"Smoke Gets in Your Eyes" 81
Soeda, Azenbō 18, 21, 24, 118–9, 123
Soeda, Tomomichi 123
Sogabe, Hiroshi 93–4

Sōma, Gyofū 23
sōshi-bushi 17, 21
"Sora-no Shinpei" (Divine Soldier in the Sky) 9
South, the 100, 103, 149, 151, 153–60, 162–7
Southern All Stars 126
southern whites 150, 157, 160, 165
Soviet Union 110, 117
Spector, Phil 107
Spiders' "No No Boy" 125
"Star-Spangled Banner" 5
steel-guitar 86, 91, 93, 95–6, 99
Suizenji, Kiyoko 146
"Sukiyaki" 106
Suppé's *Boccaccio* 44
Suzuki, Sandii 181–2
Sylvian, David 139, 141
synergy 23, 88, 108

Taishō 19, 26, 43–5, 56, 61, 123
Taishō Democracy 23, 52
Takaishi, Tomoya 113–7, 119, 127
talkie 7, 68–9
Takada, Wataru 117–9, 127
Takarazuka Revue 45, 61
Takeda, Tetsuya 128
Tanaka, Hozumi 53
tango 82–3, 88, 93, 152, 175
tape-recorder 132, 143
Tatsumi, Kyōko 25–7
Taya, Rikizō 44
Teagarden, Jack 82
"Ten'nen-no Bi" (Natural Beauty) (known also as "Utsukushiki Ten'nen") 53, 59
"Teki-wa Ikuman" (Enemy Amounting to Tens of Thousands) 6
television 82, 102, 106–8, 116–8, 123, 129, 145, 170, 188
"Tennessee Waltz" 83, 88, 94, 97
"Tenshi-no Yūwaku" (Angel's Temptation) 129
Teramoto, Keiichi 97, 99, 103
tie-up 48, 108
Tin Pan Alley 54, 66, 79, 91, 93, 150, 154
Tokita, Jimmy 102

Tokyo 3, 5–6, 8, 17–19, 21–2, 43–4, 48, 50, 57–8, 61, 64, 66–8, 73, 76–80, 83, 92–4, 97–8, 101, 103, 105, 108–110, 113–17, 120–3, 125–7, 141–4, 151–2, 155, 157, 160, 162, 167, 179, 183, 186–7
"Tokyo Blues" 78
"Tokyo Boogie-woogie" 73, 80
Tokyo City Band 5
Tokyo College of Music 22, 43, 44
"Tokyo Gozen Sanji" (Tokyo, 3.00 a.m.) 105
"Tokyo Kōshinkyoku" (Tokyo March) 61, 66–8, 73, 76, 83
"Tokyo-no Hanauri Musume" (Flower Girl of Tokyo) 79
"Tokyo Ondo" 77
Tolstoi, Lev Nikolaevich 23, 52
"Tom Dooley" 126
Tomita, Isao 133
"Tomo-yo" (My Friends) 116–7, 121
Top Ten 100, 112, 135
Torio, Atsutaka 96, 142, 152
"Tōsei Ginza-bushi" (Up-to-date Ginza Song) 67, 72
Toshiba 102, 111–3, 132
Tottori, Shun'yō 22, 25–9, 31, 53
Toyama, Hiroshi 91
Toyama, Takehiko 91
Toyama Military School Band 7–8
traditional music 4, 32, 42, 68, 150, 165, 189
Trénet, Charles 82
trumpet 60, 70–1, 78
Tsurumi, Yoshiyuki 120–1
Tubb, Ernest 91
Turgenev, Ivan Sergeevich 53
"Turkey in the Straw" 149

"Ue-o Muite Arukō" (I Look Up When I Walk) 106
underground 67, 109–11, 116, 120–1, 123, 189
'un-gra' 111, 113, 116
URC (Underground Record Club) 119
Utada, Hikaru 187
Utagawa, Yaeko 26–7, 33

Ventures, the 125
Verdi's *Aida* 44
vernacular music 4, 176

Victor (Victor Musical Industries) 132–3, 136–7, 139–41
Victor Jazz Band 57, 65–6
Vietnam War, the 109, 111, 115–6, 128
Vincent, Gene 83, 99
violin 19, 22, 25–7, 29, 33, 49, 57, 60, 66, 70–1, 77, 95, 146, 164, 168

"Wagon Master" 85–90, 97–8, 103
Wagon Masters 89–90, 94–100, 103
"Wakare-no Blues" (Farewell Blues) 78
Warner Pioneer 132
Watanabe, Sadao 81
"Watashi Konogoro Yūutsu-yo" (I'm Feeling So Down These Days) 77
"We Shall Overcome" 114–5, 121–2
West Germany 131, 135
'Western' 92–103, 153
Western/cowboy film 86, 89–92
Western Melodians 91, 95
Western Ramblers 91, 93–5, 97, 102, 152
westernization 9, 183, 185
"Where Have All the Flowers Gone" 115
White, Lester H. 48
Whiting, George 63
Williams, Hank 88, 95, 102, 150, 155
Wills, Bob 94
'world music' 173, 175–8, 183
World War I 7, 43
World War II 9, 79–80, 82, 91, 104, 131, 151, 153, 183

Xavier Cugat Band 82

Yamaguchi, Momoe 129
Yamaha 163, 170
"Yankee Doodle" 5
Yellow Magic Orchestra 126, 141, 181
"Yoake-no Scat" (Scatting at Dawn) 129
Yokohama 3, 5, 18, 43, 92, 95, 97, 120, 129, 144
Yokota, Akira 136, 139, 144
Yoshida, Tadashi 145
Yoshida, Takurō 128, 169–70
"Yoshiya-bushi" (*Yoshiya* Song) 15
"Yūrakuchō-de Aimashō" (See You in Yūrakuchō) 105

Zunō Keisatsu 126

www.ingramcontent.com/pod-product-compliance
Lightning Source LLC
Chambersburg PA
CBHW072233290426
44111CB00012B/2079